D0788918

CRITICAL INSIGHTS

George Eliot

CRITICAL INSIGHTS

George Eliot

Editor
Katie R. Peel
University of North Carolina, Wilmington

SALEM PRESS
A Division of EBSCO Information Services, Inc.
Ipswich, Massachusetts

GREY HOUSE PUBLISHING

Publisher's Cataloging-In-Publication Data
(Prepared by The Donohue Group, Inc.)

Names: Peel, Katie R., editor.
Title: George Eliot / editor, Katie R. Peel, University of North Carolina, Wilmington.
Other Titles: Critical insights.
Description: [First edition]. | Ipswich, Massachusetts : Salem Press, a division of EBSCO Information Services, Inc. ; Amenia, NY : Grey House Publishing, [2016] | Critical insights | Includes bibliographical references and index.
Identifiers: ISBN 978-1-61925-838-9 (hardcover)
Subjects: LCSH: Eliot, George, 1819-1880--Criticism and interpretation. | English fiction--19th century--History and criticism.
Classification: LCC PR4688 .G467 2016 | DDC 823/.8--dc23

First Printing

PRINTED IN THE UNITED STATES OF AMERICA

Contents _____

Resources

Dedication

For Amy

The world waits
For help. Beloved, let us love so well,
Our work shall still be better for our love,
And still our love be sweeter for our work

Elizabeth Barrett Browning, *Aurora Leigh*

To my father, Mark, who introduced me to George Eliot many years ago. To Margaret Sönser Breen, who continues to offer sage advice. To my family and friends: thank you. Your support has meant so much.

About This Volume

Katie R. Peel

Given the scope and richness of George Eliot's work, compiling a collection of scholarship on her oeuvre is a task not unlike preparing the *Key to All Mythologies*. I am grateful to the scholars who have contributed essays to this project and shared in this labor. All of the essays here are new and offer various approaches to material both familiar and not. Most Eliot scholarship addresses her novels. In this collection, we include critical approaches to her poetry, journalism, and shorter fiction, as well as her novels. This volume also contains essays working in queer historiography, masculinity studies, adaptation studies, and pedagogy. The Critical Insights series is designed for readers new to the author, and we have been careful to note various theoretical approaches and starting places for further explorations.

Critical Insights: George Eliot is divided into four sections: an introductory section, a "Critical Contexts" section, a "Critical Readings" section, and a "Resources" section. The introduction uses an adaptation for children to consider what we value in Eliot's work and why we would want to share it with readers of all ages. Joanne Cordón's biography of Eliot traces both her personal and literary developments and offers context for her literature. Using Eliot's own words, Cordón writes that the exercise of writing Eliot's biography "ploughed up her heart." The "Resources" section at the end offers a basic chronology of Eliot's life, as well as a list of her major works. It also includes a bibliography of secondary sources for further reading and research.

The "Critical Contexts" section of the collection takes four approaches to Eliot's work. In "Edith Simcox on George Eliot: Autobiography of a Love," Constance M. Fulmer approaches Eliot via her contemporary, Edith Simcox, a woman who knew and loved Eliot. In her own writing Edith Simcox provides many biographical details about Eliot's life; Fulmer's discussion of her love for Eliot provides a queer dimension or introduces the presence of queerness. Incidentally, it was upon hearing Fulmer's paper on Edith Simcox at a British Women Writers Association conference that my friend, eighteenth-century scholar Karen L. Cajka, laughed at me for not knowing that George Eliot could have a mean streak. Katherine Montwieler and Mark Edelman Boren took on the task of wading through a century and a half of scholarship on Eliot and compiled their findings in their overview, "Critical Tipples: Or, A Nip into George Eliot Criticism, *Then and Now.*" Jeffrey E. Jackson's "Reaching the Limit: *Middlemarch*, George Eliot, and the 'Crisis' of the 'Old-Fashioned English Novel' in the 1870s" is a study in genre and considers the role of *Middlemarch* in the context of the English novel tradition. Lastly, Magdalena Nerio reads Eliot in light of her intellectual predecessors (and subjects of one of Eliot's own essays) Mary Wollstonecraft and Margaret Fuller.

The "Critical Readings" section consists of new essays from a variety of approaches. In "Life, Death, and Identity in *The Lifted Veil*: George Eliot's Experiments with First-Person Fiction," Heidi L. Pennington looks at Eliot's rare use of the first-person point of view in her discussion of The Lifted Veil and autothanatography, or the narration of one's own death. Janis Chakars explores Eliot's journalism in "Mary Ann Evans, Marian Evans, George Eliot, and Journalism," which has only been examined as such by a few scholars. Carroll Clayton Savant's "'Whistle While You Work': The Construction of the Myth of Englishness through the Working Soundscapes in George Eliot's *Adam Bede*" connects sound, class, and the production of nation. Wendy S. Williams, author of *George Eliot, Poetess*, examines Eliot's poetry in light of sympathy (which others in this volume argue she does in her various other genres) in "George Eliot: Unsung Poet of Sympathy."

Gareth Hadyk-DeLodder's essay, "'The world must be romanticized': Tracing George Eliot's German Influences," makes connections amongst the influences of Eliot's extensive German studies and her own writing. In "Doubt, Devotion, Duty: George Eliot, the Death of God, and the Quest to Combine Transcendence and Coherence," Shandi Stevenson examines religion in a number of Eliot's narratives. While many critics have worked with George Eliot's representations of women, masculinity has not been focused upon nearly as much. Danny Sexton's "'How was a Man to be Explained?': Masculinity, Manhood, and Mothering in *Silas Marner*" corrects this and contributes to not only Eliot studies but masculinity studies as well. Another essay on mothering, Emilia Halton-Hernandez's "Missing Mother: Eliot's Philosophy of Sympathy and the Effect of Loss in *The Lifted Veil*" looks at one of Eliot's shorter fictions. Erin A. Spampinato takes on *Middlemarch* and the role of mythology in the novel in "Casaubon's 'Highly Esteemed ... Fable of Cupid and Psyche'; Or, Can We Take Myth Seriously in *Middlemarch*?" Lastly, Abigail Burnham Bloom discusses pedagogical approaches in using a film version of Eliot's work in her classroom in "What Can Be Learned from an Adaptation of *The Mill on the Floss*."

One goal of this series is to introduce readers to the work of and scholarship on a particular author. When it comes to George Eliot and her work (remember, the subtitle to *Middlemarch* is "A Study of Provincial Life," and her body of work approximates a panorama of the human experience), it is impossible to be comprehensive. Reading these essays has helped me continue to come to a fuller understanding and appreciation of Eliot and her work. I hope that this collection not only offers useful resources and starting places, but inspires your own explorations with the work of George Eliot.

CAREER, LIFE, AND INFLUENCE

On George Eliot for Children: From "Loose Baggy Monsters" to "Terrific Fun!"[1]_____

Katie R. Peel

Faced with the task of writing an introduction to this collection of scholarship meant to introduce readers to George Eliot, I have been thinking of an introduction of another sort. For today's reader, George Eliot may seem inaccessible. Her writing is steeped in nineteenth-century intellectual, political, and cultural contexts and laden with the gravitas and pacing of the exploration of psychological complexities. And then there is the matter of size: her novels are massive. When I approached a trusted colleague and Eliot scholar to write an essay for this anthology, she thought about it and, with a sigh, said, "I would just have to reread *so much*." Eliot's work can seem difficult to the reader who has yet to be acquainted with her. How much moreso, one might say, to a child reader: the lengths of Eliot's work, the dearth of whimsy, the Victorian contexts, the gravitas of subject—Virginia Woolf, after all, did name *Middlemarch* "one of the few English novels written for grown-up people" ("George Eliot").

The story of this project begins with an artifact I found while browsing in the children's literature section of a used bookstore. I came across a version of George Eliot's *Daniel Deronda* remarkably less hefty than the 800-page tome with which I was familiar. What I had discovered was a 119-page children's edition of *Daniel Deronda*, adapted by Philip Zimmerman in 1961, and consisting solely of the "Jewish section" of Eliot's novel.

This piqued my interest, and I began to seek other children's adaptations of Victorian novels. A popular series right now called BabyLit ™ publishes board books including *Anna Karenina* and *Jane Eyre* (both notably light on plot, the former is subtitled "A Fashion Primer," and there is no mention of Bertha in the latter). As is evident by the frequency with which these board books appear at English department baby showers, they are much more for the adult reader in the baby's life than the baby itself. Some of my other favorites include tiny versions (two inches by two inches) of *David Copperfield* and *Oliver Twist*, two different versions of *Little Women* in which Beth lives (she gets better and hangs out on the couch), and a film version of *David Copperfield* played entirely by a cast of cats.[2] As a Victorianist, I was appalled. As a scholar of children's and young adult literature, I was intrigued. These two responses produce the areas of enquiry for this essay: what happens to a reader's experience with narrative when a text is adapted from a version intended for an adult to one for a child? Can an adaptation of a Victorian novel be anything but reductive?

The adaptation of adult literature for young readers is nothing new. From the Bowdler family's creation of a family Shakespeare minus the naughty bits, to children's versions of Bible stories and *Paradise Lost*, to today's baby board books, adaptations of adult narratives for younger readers have long made up a portion of the children's literature market. The Victorians themselves loved to adapt narratives; Dickens' own granddaughter, Mary Angela Dickens, adapted his works for children. Many Victorian novels adapted for children are *about* child characters, making them a seemingly appropriate source for interpretation into children's narrative. Many of Dickens' novels, for example, have been abridged so that the stories focusing on the childhood of a character exist as stand-alone children's narratives. What I find particularly curious, though, are the adapted novels that are *not* for the most part about children or childhood. Jane Austen's *Pride and Prejudice*, Emily Brontë's *Wuthering Heights*, Charlotte Brontë's *Jane Eyre*, and George Eliot's *Daniel Deronda* all exist in various forms for young readers. Even if the source text and adaptation are similar, though, their implied readers, or, in the words of children's literature scholar Perry Nodelman, the reader best equipped to understand the narrative based on the narrative's subject and style, are different (*Pleasures* 16).[3] This raises the question of what the narrative presumes about the young reader and how it changes both the narrative and narrative experience. These questions take on additional significance in the study of children's literature when we think about the presumptions that adults—the primary producers but not necessarily the target demographic of children's literature—have about children and childhood. Furthermore, what does this particular adaptation indicate about the continuing importance of George Eliot?

Adult Agenda and the Landscape of Adaptation

Adaptations are artifacts of the historical and cultural moment of *their* production. Furthermore, adaptations of adult narratives for younger readers raise questions that other adaptations—for example, that of a book into a film for the same-aged audience—do not. Adaptations shed light on adult agendas for young readers and lead us to consider what the adults' concepts of childhood are. These ideas regularly serve an adult's best interest, as Nodelman notes in his essay "The Other: Orientalism, Colonialism, and Children's Literature," in which he argues that the relationship between adult and child can be read as one between colonizer and colonized.

According to Linda Hutcheon, author of *A Theory of Adaptation*, we cannot assume that those who adapt aim to simply reproduce; nor are derivations necessarily derivative or bad: "an adaptation is a derivation that is not derivative—a work that is second without being secondary" (9). In thinking about this shift in genre from adult to children's literature, we also confront the obstacle familiar to those of us who work with children's literature: the assumption that children's literature itself is derivative. Elizabeth Thiel, scholar of nineteenth-century and children's literatures, has worked with contemporary adaptations of Charles Dickens' *Oliver Twist* and finds that, "While adaptations necessarily reflect, to some degree, contemporary ideologies of the child, such emphases can seemingly result in a *sanitization* that *significantly impoverishes* the source text and simultaneously undermines its value as a socio-historic artefact of relevance to a contemporary reader" (143, italics mine). See *Anna Karenina* as fashion primer, and *Jane Eyre* sans Bertha.

When considering the adaptations of Victorian novels focused on adult issues and concerns, we might ask why someone would want to adapt them for a young reader. Not only does this act privilege adult literature, but often canonical literature, and thus white, heteropatriarchal values. Certainly nostalgia plays a role. *Jane Eyre* has a near cult-like following, particularly amongst adult women who, having identified with the character Jane, want to pass this book and reading experience down to young girls in their lives. For academics, this feeling may be further underscored by their experiences encountering the landmark work in feminist literary criticism, Sandra Gilbert and Susan Gubar's *The Madwoman in the Attic*.

For publishers, there is not only the cultural cachet of these canonical texts, but the fact that they pose a relatively low financial risk, especially given that adults are the primary purchasers of children's books. Not only are the publishers thinking about the commercial appeal for adult consumers, though, but also the role that these kinds of adaptations can play in education and literacy. Indeed, publishers often cite "whetting the appetite" for such literature as a premise, and many readers have had these experiences. My wife distinctly remembers reading a dramatized *Weekly Reader* version of Richard Wright's *Native Son* in school and then walking to the library to check out and read the novel in full. In the wake of the most recent film adaptation of Victor Hugo's *Les Miserables*, I have talked to a number of adults who have realized that they recognize elements from neither the novel nor the Broadway production, but vignettes that had been presented to them as children.

The publishers for such adaptations of Victorian novels offer a few other goals, but they tend to underestimate young readers. The Readable Classics website states that, "Readable Classics gently edits the great works of literature, retaining their essence and spirit, and *making them more enjoyable and less frustrating to the modern reader*." The Usborne Publisher website insists that its classics are "*Clearly written in a modern, approachable style* to introduce young readers to much-loved classic stories." Such adaptations are designed based on the premise that the nineteenth-century language will prove too difficult for young readers, as well as the fact that such literature can be used in literacy training. Dalmatian Press writes that "This Great Classic for Children by Dalmatian Press has been carefully condensed and adapted from the original version (*which you really must read when you're ready for every detail)*." This, of course, takes for granted that young readers are not ready for the detail-heavy Victorian novels. It also suggests that using such adaptations as training wheels for the adapted text is good, but using them as a crutch in lieu of the adapted text is bad. This publisher's approach, then, actually supports Thiel's findings that adaptations are derivative and impoverished versions.

Adaptation Theory and Children's Literature: No Palimpsest, So Just Reduction?

Adaptation theory, while focusing mostly on the adaptations of written texts for stage and screen, celebrates the relationships and conversations created between source text and adaptation. Hutcheon writes that "we experience adaptations [...] as palimpsests through our memory of other works that resonate through repetition with variation" (8). This palimpsestuous relationship, however, requires a familiarity with and prior knowledge of the source text. Likewise, Julie Sanders, author of *Adaptation and Appropriation*, also emphasizes the hybridity of the adaptation. Drawing on the work of Gérard Genette, Sanders writes that appreciating an adaptation's hybridity entails, "celebrating its ongoing interaction with other texts and artistic productions" (18). Again the enjoyment of this relies on readers' familiarity with the source text (Sanders 17). Such hybridities are less likely to be recognized in the case of adaptations for young readers, particularly when publishers are intending these texts to be substitutes for the source texts, that is, to be read in lieu of, not in addition to, the source texts.

In the case of classic *children's* texts, for example *Alice in Wonderland* or *Winnie the Pooh*, this relationship amongst versions can be possible because of the existence of Lewis Carroll's and A. A. Milne's full-length novels (still read by and to children), the various film reincarnations, and a multimedia life including toys and games (though we can ask what happens when the characters become free-standing identities and not necessarily bound to Carroll's and Milne's narratives). Of course, children might be flipping television channels and come across any of the many film versions of *Jane*

Eyre, but this seems less likely than a young reader encountering another version of *Alice in Wonderland* or *Winnie the Pooh*.

When we talk about storytelling, especially in children's literature, we talk about repertoire, performance, repetition, imitation, and versions of stories. Many instructors begin children's literature courses with fairy tales, narratives for which we have no originals. We are used to talking about adaptation as part of children's narrative experience. We lose intertextuality, however, when we move from adult to children's narrative, and with this, we lose the potential pleasure derived from the combination of the familiar and the new. In his discussion of children's literature, Nodelman, drawing from the work of Roland Barthes, refers to this as *plaisir*, as opposed to *jouissance*, or the pleasure of the familiar, versus the pleasure of the strange (*Pleasure* 23–6). We see this today with online memes: we delight in the recognition of the familiar, as well as the novelty of the change to that which is familiar. This particular pleasure of adaptation is removed from the young readers' experiences, leaving the pleasure of encountering the narrative alone.

Adaptations for children function like palimpsests *only* for readers who have encountered other versions of the narrative. In this case, these readers are more likely to be the older or adult reader reading to or with the young readers, buying the book for the young reader and putting it into their hands. The interactive narrative relationship, then, happens for this more experienced reader and not for the young reader first encountering the narrative. Later, of course, when the young reader encounters the source text, this kind of interaction can happen, though in reverse, which raises other interesting questions. For example, what happens when the young reader finds out that (spoiler alert) Beth *does* die in *Little Women*?

So, with publishers abridging and children reading adaptations without a prior referent, what can be gained from a reading experience that differs so greatly from that offered by the adapted text? While many adapted texts might, indeed, be impoverished versions of their source texts (à la the Baby board books), what we tend to overlook as adults are the actual reading experiences of young readers.

There are regular disconnects between the intentions of authors, publishers, and adult consumers and the actual reading experiences of children. Children's literature scholar Margaret Meek writes, "What we need is an analysis of narrative discourse which does not say that children's stories are simpler forms of adult telling, but insists that they are the primary kinds and structures of later telling" (176). Thinking about children's narrative in this way can affect our understanding of the potential offered by adaptations. A narrative without an earlier referent does not necessarily have to result in an impoverished text. While, at first glance, such narratives might look reductive, particularly from a formalist standpoint and in terms of what it does to the author's art, we ought to leave some room for the potential that we as adults cannot even imagine about a child's reading experience. In applying the fundamentals of narrative theory to children's reading practices and literature, Margaret Higonnet and Margaret Meek both argue for a particular dimension to interactivity in children's reading experiences. Meek specifically argues that narrative gaps allow for children to ask their own questions and make their own sense of the material (as opposed to adults' directed, specific questions that cannot anticipate young readers' experiences). Gaps in children's literature, according to Meek, thus allow children to "create a tissue of collaborative understandings for each other in a way that no single question from an adult makes possible" (176). This inability to anticipate what a young person's reading experience will be like means that we as adults should not rush to be dismissive of all adaptations. Furthermore, there is always the chance that the new narrative has something to offer, content-wise, to the new reader.

The Case of *Daniel Deronda*

Which brings me back to where I began, with this children's edition of *Daniel Deronda*. This edition was published in New York by the Herzl Press in 1961, specifically for a Hebrew school demographic. What makes it so small is that it consists of only the "Jewish section" of the narrative. *Daniel Deronda* is a novel about Gwendolen Harleth, a young English woman and her relationship with Daniel Deronda, a young man who was raised as an English gentleman, but discovers late in the novel that he is, in fact, Jewish. Daniel meets Mordecai, a Jew living in London, who ultimately becomes his spiritual guide. Having discovered his vocation and a bride, Mirah, Daniel departs for the East in order to help his newfound people. One of the main critiques of the novel both at its time of publication in 1876 and still today is that it lacks cohesion. Readers tended to agree with F. R. Leavis' verdict that the novel was constructed of two distinct parts, the "Jewish section" and the "English section." Leavis went on to explicitly prefer the "English section," writing that, "As for the bad part of *Daniel Deronda*, there is nothing to do but cut it away" (122).

Eliot, however, was quite open about both her intentions and her frustration with readers who resisted: she writes that, "I meant everything in the book to be related to everything else there" (qtd. in Perkins 73). Her goals of encouraging compassion amongst the British Gentiles and the Jews and presenting the British readership with an "Other" in their midst is evident in her letter to Harriet Beecher Stowe on October 29, 1876:

> Precisely because I felt the usual attitude of Christians towards Jews is—I hardly know whether to say more impious or more stupid when viewed in the light of their professed principles, I therefore felt urged to treat Jews with such sympathy and understanding as my nature could attain to. Moreover, not only towards the Jews, but towards all oriental peoples with whom we English come into contact, a spirit of arrogance and contemptuous dictatorialness is observable which has become a national disgrace to us. *There is nothing I should care more to do, if it were possible, than to rouse the imagination of men and women to a vision of human claims in those races of their fellow-men who most differ from them in customs and beliefs.* (qtd. in Perkins 67, italics mine)

Here Eliot makes her project explicit: she aimed to counter ignorance and encourage compassion and the appreciation of difference. Both sections of the novel, integrated, contribute to these goals.

We can also apply Eliot's appreciation of art that represents responsibly to her aims for *Daniel Deronda*. In her essay "The Natural

History of German Life" (1856), Eliot outlines her commitment to representing people, particularly those of the working classes, as faithfully as possible:

> But our social novels profess to represent the people as they are, and the unreality of their representations is a grave evil. The greatest benefit we owe to the artist, whether painter, poet, or novelist, is the extension of our sympathies. [...] Art is the nearest thing to life; it is a mode of amplifying experience and extending our contact with our fellow-men beyond the bounds of our personal lot. All the more sacred is the task of the artist when he undertakes to paint the life of the People. Falsification here is far more pernicious than in the more artificial aspects of life. [...] It is serious that our sympathy with the perennial joys and struggles, the toil, the tragedy, and the humor in the life of our more heavily laden fellow-men, should be perverted, and turned toward a false object instead of the true one. (Eliot, "Natural History" 2–3)

In this essay, she is writing about middle-class readers and their perceptions of working-class people and peasants, but her argument can be extended to her project regarding middle-class, Gentile readers and their perceptions of Jews. People who do not identify as the offered subjects need the narrative in order to understand; people who do identify as the subjects need the narrative in order to live. Her work, then, aims not only to educate, but to validate.

When the "Jewish section" is removed and presented as a stand-alone novel, the narrative itself changes. In the adaptation, there of course are some changes in the plot and notable exclusions. What we have in this version is the coming-of-age story of a young man who finds his vocation in his spiritual calling. More time is spent on Daniel's youth in the adaptation, which is disproportionate to the amount of space it is given in the source text. Eliot's novel is a story about adults, with Daniel's childhood mentioned in passing retrospect. The connection in the adaptation is ostensibly to young readers seeking their vocations and finding spiritual callings.

When reducing the number of characters in the adaptation primarily to Jewish ones, the proportions of representations change.

In terms of presenting parental failings and the roles of adults, which tend to carry weight in books aimed at a young readership, the adaptation does offer an interesting discussion of Jewish parents. In the book, both parents who neglect their filial duty (Daniel's birthmother and Mirah's father) are Jewish. When reading Eliot's full novel, we see lots of other bad people and other good Jews. This adaptation places more weight on the characters of Daniel, Mirah, and Mordecai to offer a counter to these representations. That said, Daniel's birthmother, the Alcharisi, tells him "I want you to think of me as a tender mother" (Eliot/Zimmerman, *Daniel* 90), which is definitely a softening of the antimaternal feeling with which Eliot endows her. In Eliot's novel, not only does the Alcharisi plan on separating from Daniel and never having any further contact, but she tells him openly, "'I am not a loving woman'" (Eliot, *Daniel* 571). Evidently, this lack of maternal feeling is too monstrous for a children's book.

Other, darker issues that are usually the terrain of adult literature are softened in the children's version of *Daniel Deronda*. In terms of representations of Jewishness, in the adaptation, Daniel feels less revulsion, and his feelings are not nearly as complex as in the adapted novel. He is less conflicted in the new version. Similarly, the anti-Semitic sentiment is present, but gentler. When she first meets Daniel, Mirah asks, "'I am Jewish. You'll not think less of me because of it?" (Eliot/Zimmerman, *Daniel* 13), when in Eliot's text she asks "I am a Jewess. Do you despise me for it?'" (Eliot, *Daniel* 164). In terms of adult issues, Mirah's suicide attempt is also rendered obliquely (Eliot/Zimmerman, *Daniel* 12), as is the act that makes her flee Prague. Her father wants her to marry the count (Eliot/Zimmerman, *Daniel* 19), which is less sinister than Eliot's adapted text, in which exists the threat of her father selling her to the count in order to pay off some of his own gambling debts (Eliot, *Daniel* 186).

One of the most curious omissions is that of Herr Klesmer, the Jewish musician that Gwendolen meets at the Arrowpoints' estate. Now, it makes sense that we would lose him in the excision of the "English section" of the novel, but when we lose Klesmer, we lose not only a prominent man of culture but a significant voice of worldly understanding and tolerance. The narrative also loses his intermarriage with the heiress Catherine Arrowpoint. This leaves us with the Jews marrying Jews at the end of the novel, supporting a less assimilationist point of view, which works with the Herzl company's mission, but not necessarily Eliot's desire to demonstrate connection.

Implied Readers

Just as the "Jewish section" lies at the heart of Eliot's novel, the Hand and Banner Pub passage is the heart of the adaptation (Eliot/ Zimmerman, *Daniel* 49–64). This passage consists of Mordecai's discussion with his philosopher friends about the state of Jews in England and abroad and presents arguments for and against cultural assimilation. It is a conversation heavily philosophical and political. The conversation remains largely intact in the adaptation, which is telling about the implied reader, or, again, the reader presumed by the narrative itself. In this version intended for a Hebrew school readership, there is no condescension, omission, or sugar-coated material. The adaptation presumes that the young readers will be able to understand this conversation, and if they cannot, that it is still appropriate for them to read. It treats the child reader seriously.

The Hand and Banner Pub passage offers a moment in which the implied reader of the adaptation overlaps with the implied reader of the adapted text. The two implied readers are not exactly the same, but rather their texts presume that they can handle the same material. In adaptations of adult literature for young readers, the implied readers are, from the outset, different than the implied readers of the adapted text. In the Hand and Banner passage, however, these implied readers coincide. This could be accidental, of course; there are adaptations in which an adapter does little work to modify the narrative for a different readership. Because the other chapters of this version of *Daniel Deronda are* explicitly modified, though, the Herzl Press offers a curious case. In this particular adaptation, we have a moment in which the implied child reader is treated as the implied adult reader of the adapted text. This matters because, at the moment of the most philosophical and political arguments, young, twentieth-century readers are given the credit of adult, nineteenth-century readers.

Given the difference in lengths, we might be tempted to argue that this *Daniel Deronda* is a reductive adaptation. When considering the implied reader, however, this changes. Eliot's implied reader is an outsider, a nineteenth-century adult who probably knew little about Judaism. Herzl's implied reader is an insider, an American Hebrew school student in the early 1960s. These young readers, familiar with the Old Testament, might *get Daniel Deronda* in a way that nineteenth-century adult readers might not and certainly better than some adult and young readers today.

In her *Oliver Twist* adaptation study, Thiel writes that, "If a classic text is to endure in popularity, it must remain *relevant to subsequent generations*" (151, italics mine). In the case of this children's version of *Daniel Deronda*, this relevance exists. The young Jewish reader will have referents and cultural associations, a web of context ready to place this narrative into. For example, Daniel's relationship with Mordecai is still the primary one of the text. Mordecai quotes Book of Ruth: "Where thou goest Daniel I shall go" (Eliot/Zimmerman, *Daniel* 119). The story of Naomi and Ruth is commonly used in Hebrew school education, particularly during the time of Shavuot, the Feast of Weeks, in the late spring, celebrating the receiving of the Ten Commandments. Themes of loyalty, loving kindness (*hesed*), and redemption are celebrated, as are the creation of kin between women and acceptance of converts. The average, Gentile, Victorian adult reader, while likely recognizing the story from the Old Testament, most likely did not have this fuller context, which is one among many reasons why Eliot was writing this novel to begin with.

The adaptation responds to contemporary anxieties and concerns. Thomas Recchio makes this argument about a series of school editions of Elizabeth Gaskell's *Cranford*. Popular in the early decades of the twentieth century, *Cranford* was used, Recchio writes, in response to anxieties about nation and race in the face of an immigration surge. The Herzl Press has a similar project, and in this instance, we can see how adaptation, as Julie Sanders asserts, is a political act (97). The website for the Herzl Press reads: "Through its publications, which deal with Zionism, with Israel, and with Jewish subjects in general, the Herzl Press aims to strengthen the ties between Jews everywhere and in Israel. […] the Herzl Press encourages research that will enrich the understanding of the Jewish intellectual heritage and of the complex problems now confronting all Jews today" (*Herzl Press*). This adaptation of *Daniel Deronda* was published in 1961 and bears a Zionist message, and we can think of the role this might have played in an American Hebrew school lesson in the wake of the Holocaust.

For the nineteenth-century, Gentile, adult reader of *Daniel Deronda*, the "Jewish section" might be new. To the twentieth-century, Hebrew-school demographic, this is most likely not new. These young readers are familiar with this discourse, rhetoric, history, and culture. It is neither foreign nor threatening to them. Additionally, this adaptation of Eliot's story takes on a new weight in a post-Holocaust world. Jewish children growing up in the years shortly after the attempted destruction of their people, culture, and history and following the establishment of the nation of Israel will experience this narrative with new and urgent significance. The Herzl Press makes this part of their own mission:

> The transformation of the Jewish people in the past generation has been titanic. In wake of the Holocaust, in the wake of the establishment of the State of Israel and of the profound changes in Jewish communities in the Diaspora, it is vital to broaden understanding of the issues that govern the lives of Jews everywhere. (*Herzl Press*)

This one, shared, Hand-and-Banner-Pub passage in the adapted version serves the "insider" reader, just as it serves the "outsider" reader in the adapted text. For the nineteenth-century reader, the narrative is didactic in nature. For Jewish readers regardless of century, the narrative is one of validation. Indeed, Eliot herself noted the favorable reception of *Daniel Deronda* by various Jewish communities:

I have had a delightful letter from the Jewish Theological Seminary at Breslau written by an American Jew named Isaacs, who excuses himself for expressing his feelings of gratitude on reading Deronda, and assures me of his belief that it has even already had an elevating effect on the minds of some among his people—predicting that the effect will spread. (*Journals* 146)

J. Russell Perkins also comments on the role Eliot's novel played not only in validating the experience of Jewish readers, but offering them a new literary presence:

However, *Daniel Deronda* did satisfy its Jewish readers, whose reception of the work was conditioned not only by their experience of social disadvantages in English society, but also by literary history. The conventional depiction of Jews in English literature proceeds in an unbroken line from Chaucer and the romances through Marlowe and Shakespeare to Dickens and Thackeray. Thus Jewish readers evaluated Eliot's novel in relation to a tradition which saw Jews as either totally depraved or, less frequently, as noble sufferers like Scott's Rebecca or Dickens's Riah. (72–3)

When it came to assessing how her novel might have met her goals of encouraging compassion, Eliot looked to the letters of thanks that she received from her insider readers: "Words of gratitude have come from Jews and Jewesses, and there are certain signs that I may have contributed my mite [*sic*] to a good result" (*Journals* 146). Interestingly, chances are that the Jews who sang *Deronda*'s praises were actually reading a version of the novel much like this Herzl Press adaptation. When *Daniel Deronda* was first translated into Hebrew in the nineteenth century, the Gwendolen material was removed, leaving readers with a version quite similar to this one for young readers (Himmelfarb 139).

Although considerably different from its source narrative, this Herzl Press version does have something to offer its readership, and it is not a watered-down, plot-only version of a fuller text. It carries part of what pleased Eliot about the reader reception of her novel: the validation of contemporary Jewish experience.

Conclusion

Indeed, in lifting the "Jewish section" from Eliot's *Daniel Deronda*, a few things happen narratively. We lose larger contexts, and granted, these are larger contexts of the Gentile world, but it is George Eliot: many of the larger contexts have to do with more universal aspects of the human experience. While the narrative itself is not assimilated, which works with Mordecai's pre-Zionist message and vision, we lose the texture offered by the whole fabric.[4] In considering Daniel's search for vocation, we no longer have the connection to Gwendolen's plight when she has no vocation herself or the potential to develop sympathy for the woman character who, unlike Daniel, has been educated only to marry. Likewise, in the adaptation, Sir Hugo tells Daniel to "'Always keep an English outlook'" (Eliot/Zimmerman, *Daniel* 9–10). What does this mean when we are missing the "English section" of the novel? Some of Eliot's intentions of connection are thwarted by the new adapter's agenda, which focuses on validating the insider reader.

While we lose the explicit connections to Englishness in the adaptation, something more is offered to a specific readership: a historical community in the face of destruction and the solace of the phoenix. Because of the historical context of the Holocaust, this adaptation is particularly significant. While assimilation and connections to European life would also be significant, in the face of the destruction of their people, the presence of a Jewish community and a homeland can be especially culturally resonant for young Jewish readers.

Regarding a responsibly-executed, realistic representation, Eliot writes that, "[M]ore is done toward linking the higher classes with the lower, toward obliterating the vulgarity of exclusiveness, than by hundreds of sermons and philosophical dissertations" ("Natural History"). Eliot's full-length *Daniel Deronda* has the potential to educate outsider readers—actually decreasing the gap in understanding and feeling between different groups of people— as well as validate insider readers. As twenty-first century readers, we all have a position different than those of our nineteenth-century subjects; they will necessarily be "Others" to us. To an extent, we are all outsiders with this text: it is about a world that we do not identify as our own contemporary reality. Ours is a leap of faith, then, and we must trust the work of our authors. What better, then, than to know that one author has committed deeply to rendering a faithful representation of her subjects, specifically because she wants to encourage understanding and compassion?

Eliot explicitly builds connections for those not in the know and validates for those who are. Her commitment to exploring and valuing humanity, offering empathy and compassion, are not only timeless, but certainly needed today. In the case of *Daniel Deronda* specifically, not only is Eliot's a lesson of valuing others, but also valuing difference. It's the social action that much of our teaching is about; it is the basis of the humanities, as well as our latest call to work to enact social justice. Thus, George Eliot is supremely relevant to today's readers, as Thiel argues adaptations must be. And who better to put into the hands of readers today than someone who cares to understand human complexity, the good and the flaws, who strives to faithfully represent all people, particularly the marginalized, with nuance and compassion, in a time marked by doubt, anxiety, and incredible technological transformation? An adaptation, or interpretation, presumes that there is something of value to be shared with another audience. In this case, that which is shared with young readers is exactly why we ought to introduce readers of all ages to the work of George Eliot.[5]

Notes

1. Henry James' comment regarding the nineteenth-century novel and Kathryn Knight's "Foreword" in the *American Classics for Children*.
2. This film is not unlike the *Wishbone* television series, in which a small dog reenacts the classics.
3. Here Nodelman uses Wolfgang Iser's narratological work on the implied reader and makes it particular to issues in children's literature, which accommodates the idea that adults create and produce narratives for readers over whom they have various kinds of authority.
4. The novel predates the founding of Zionism by about two decades.

5. Parts of this essay were delivered as a presentation at the Modern Language Association conference in 2013. I am grateful for this opportunity and the audience discussion that ensued. Thank you also to Rachel Schmidt, Katherine Montwieler, and Michelle Scatton-Tessier for their contributed adaptations and Liz Thiel and Barbara Waxman for their scholarly generosity. Thank you, as always, to Amy Schlag, for her thoughtful assistance every step of the way.

Works Cited

Adams, Jennifer. *Anna Karenina: A BabyLit® Fashion Primer*. Layton, UT: Gibbs Smith, 2013.

_____. *Jane Eyre: A BabyLit® Counting Primer*. Layton, UT: Gibbs Smith, 2012.

Brontë, Charlotte. *Jane Eyre: The Graphic Novel*. Ed. Amy Corzine & John M. Burns. Litchborough, UK: Classical Comics, 2008.

"Classics Retold: *Jane Eyre*." *Usborne Children's Books*. Usborne Publishing, 2016. Web. 16 Oct. 2015. <http://www.usborne.com/catalogue/book/1~fc~fcc~1332/jane-eyre.aspx>.

Eliot, George. *Daniel Deronda*. Oxford, UK: Oxford UP, 1998.

_____. *Daniel Deronda*. Adapted by Philip Zimmerman. New York: Herzl Press, 1961.

_____. *The Journals of George Eliot*. Ed. Margaret Harris & Judith Johnston. Cambridge, UK: Cambridge UP, 1998.

_____. "The Natural History of German Life." University of St. Andrews, n.d. Web. 17 Oct. 2015. <http://www.st-andrews.ac.uk/~jfec/ge/eliot.html>.

Herzl Press. The Theodor Herzl Foundation, Inc, n.d. Web. 17 Oct. 2015. <http://www.midstreamthf.com/books.html>.

Higonnet, Margaret. "Narrative Fractures and Fragments." *Children's Literature* 15 (1987): 37–54.

Himmelfarb, Gertrude. *The Jewish Odyssey of George Eliot*. New York: Encounter Books, 2009.

Hutcheon, Linda. *A Theory of Adaptation*. 2nd ed. London: Routledge, 2013.

Iser, Wolfgang. *The Implied Reader*. Baltimore, MD: Johns Hopkins UP, 1978.

James, Henry. "Preface." *The Tragic Muse*. London: MacMillan & Co., 1921.

Knight, Kathryn. "Foreword." *American Classics for Children*. Franklin, TN: Dalmatian Press, 2003.

Leavis, F. R. *The Great Tradition: George Eliot, Henry James, Joseph Conrad*. New York: New York UP, 1963.

Meek, Margaret. "What Counts as Evidence in Theories of Children's Literature?" *Children's Literature: The Development of Criticism*. Ed. Peter Hunt. London: Routledge, 1990. 166–82.

Nodelman, Perry. *The Pleasures of Children's Literature*. Boston: Allyn & Bacon, 2003.

_____. "The Other: Orientalism, Colonialism, and Children's Literature." *Children's Literature Association Quarterly* 17.1 (1992): 29–35.

Perkin, J. Russell. *A Reception-History of George Eliot's Fiction*. Ann Arbor, MI: UMI Research Press, 1990.

Readable Classics. Wayne Josephson, n.d. Web. 16 Oct. 2015. <http://www.readableclassics.com>.

Recchio, Thomas. "'Charming and Sane': School Editions of *Cranford* in America, 1905–1914." *Victorian Studies* 45.4 (2003): 597–623.

Thiel, Elizabeth. "Downsizing Dickens: Adaptations of *Oliver Twist* for the Child Reader." *Adapting Canonical Texts in Children's Literature*. Ed. Anja Müller. London: Bloomsbury, 2013. 143–62.

Woolf, Virginia. "George Eliot." *The Times Literary Supplement* 20 Nov. 1919: n.p. Web. 6 Oct. 2015. <http://digital.library.upenn.edu/women/woolf/VW-Eliot.html>.

Biography of George Eliot_____

Joanne Cordón

Christened Mary Anne Evans, George Eliot was born November 22, 1819 to Robert and Christiana Evans (née Pearson) at South Farm in Arbury, a small village near Nuneaton, Warwickshire, in the English Midlands. She joined a family of five older siblings: her sister Christiana (called Chrissey) was born in 1814, and her brother Isaac in 1816. The children of Robert with his first wife, Harriet Poynton, were much older: Robert was born in 1802, Frances in 1805.

The family moved to Griff House, between Nuneaton and Coventry, when Eliot was only a few months old. Shortly after the move, the family was reordered. Eliot's eldest brother Robert returned to Arbury to work under his father, with Frances serving as his housekeeper. Each eventually married and stayed local.

Conservative, fair-minded, and plain-spoken, Eliot's father was a big presence in her life. A carpenter-turned-land-agent, Robert was locally famed for "strength, integrity, and creativity in building, surveying, agriculture, mining, management, forestry, and road-building" (Hardy 1). Eliot's mother is a more shadowy figure in her daughter's life.[1] She declined after her twin sons died in March 1821, only ten days after their birth. Eliot was closest to her brother Isaac, though their temperaments were very different.

When she was five, she attended school locally with Isaac, but a year later, she was sent away for her education, perhaps because of her mother's illness. Though the schools were within a few miles of Griff House, and she was at home for holidays, she suffered from night terrors. From six to sixteen, her formal education took place in a trio of local boarding schools: Miss Lathom's school in Attleborough (1825–7), Mrs. Wallington's School in Nuneaton (1828–32), and the Miss Franklins' School in Coventry (1832–5). She made her first friend, the governess Maria Lewis, at Miss Wallington's. When Edith Simcox interviewed her after Eliot's death, Lewis described the young Eliot as "very loveable, but unhappy, given to bursts of weeping; finding it impossible to care for childish games and occupations" (Simcox 223). Lewis shared her faith of Bible reading and good deeds with her pupil, a faith that "was mild and sentimental, emphasizing love and salvation, rather than hell fire" (Haight 18).

The young Miss Evans was a gifted student: "Mary Ann was an excellent pupil and seems always to have had an intense imaginative and intellectual life stimulated by widely various readings and the study of languages" (Henry 31). Eliot read widely in philosophy, theology, history, science, and literature, especially the romantic poets—her favorite was Wordsworth—and the novels of Sir Walter Scott. Skilled in math as well as music, she also learned French and later Latin, Italian, German, Spanish, Greek, and Hebrew.

Her character was complicated. Sensitive and eager, her temperament could be both warm and sharp; her critical and sympathetic faculties were of equal measure. She valued truth, and her thinking was sophisticated. Her attachments were as strong and varied as her interests; she was also forgiving and did not hold grudges. She pushed herself to excel, and she craved praise and affection. Dutiful and rebellious, she was aware of the value—and the cost—of both convention and heterodoxy.

She was not a conventional beauty. She was of average size, with a long face, a large nose, and a pale complexion. Her best features were her pale blue eyes and rich brown hair. D'Albert Durade's flattering oil painting (1849) in the National Portrait Gallery shows a woman of contrasts, for the simple black figure with a lacy neckpiece is posed on a red couch. As Henry James noted, "The great G. E. herself is both sweet and superior, and has a delightful expression in her large, long, pale equine face" (James 172). The animation in her rich, musical voice transformed her face.

Her time at the Miss Franklins' school saw her take religious devotion more seriously. The school encouraged piety, and Eliot added more overt observances to her spiritual life. "It is not clear if Mary Anne underwent a sharply defined crisis in her mid-teens, but it is certainly the case that she became more ponderously religious than ever before" (Hughes 24).

Returning home from school in December 1835, Eliot helped her sister Chrissey nurse their mother, who was dying of breast cancer, in 1836. When her sister married a doctor the next year, Mary Anne changed her name, too. Her shift affected only her first name and solely its spelling: Mary Ann. She ran her father's household for a dozen years, including "supervising the kitchen, making the mince pies, damson cheese, and currant jelly, as well as overseeing the dairy" (Haight 28).

After her father retired and her brother took over his position, Eliot moved with Robert to Bird Grove in Foleshill, near Coventry. The new milieu offered her more intellectual companionship than her earlier environment. Among her new circle of friends were Charles and Caroline Bray, Cara's sister Sara Hennell and brother Charles, whose *Inquiry Concerning the Origin of Christianity* wrestled with the same religious questions that interested Eliot.

In January of 1842, Eliot caused a breach with her father over church attendance. Retaining respect for the moral teachings of Christianity but not its dogma, she no longer wanted to go with Robert to church. Her father was upset by her decision, and their compromise took over four unpleasant, tumultuous months to iron out. Eventually she agreed to outward conformity, accompanying her father to services, but continued to think as she liked.

A voracious reader, Eliot developed her intellectual engagement with more speculative endeavors. At Hennell's suggestion, she translated David Strauss's *The Life of Jesus, Critically Examined*, a key work of Higher Criticism. In her understanding of theology, she was "in an avant-garde minority of English thinkers, an unusual position for a future Victorian novelist" (Dodd 88). At this same time, she received an offer of marriage from an unnamed artist; their courtship was brief, intense, and ended in her rejection of him.

After a gradual decline, Robert Evans died at the end of May 1849. After the funeral, Eliot traveled in Europe, at first with the Brays and later on her own. She inherited a small trust and cash, totaling £2,100, which gave her, at thirty, the financial ballast to move to London for a wider sphere of social and intellectual engagement. Her friends helped her find lodgings at 142 The Strand, the same building that served as office and home for John Chapman, publisher of the Strauss volume.

In London, she changed her name to Marian and began working. After Chapman bought the *Westminster Review* in 1851, she did all the work of the editor for two years, although she did not get paid, nor does her name appear in the work. Her association with this publication introduced her to some of the most important and innovative writers in England at the time, from Charles Dickens to Harriet Martineau. She continued to contribute articles to the publication long after her stint as editor concluded.

The *Westminster Review* was also a source of romantic attachments, including the owner Chapman and two key contributors: Herbert Spencer and George Henry Lewes. At the Strand, Chapman's attentions to Eliot fomented the jealousy of his wife and his mistress, who were also in residence; after some disruption, the writer and the publisher vowed a platonic friendship. An involvement with Herbert Spencer[2] did not work out, but the one with Lewes famously did.

Eliot's relationship with Lewes was complicated by a marital situation both scandalous and irregular.[3] Lewes's wife Agnes was involved with Thornton Hunt, his closest friend, and she had already given birth to two children fathered by Hunt. For the duration of their liaison, both Agnes and Hunt, who eventually had ten children with his own legal wife Sarah and four with Agnes, stayed married to their respective spouses. Lewes maintained frequent contact with the family, and he (and later Eliot) continued to support them; his name appears on the birth certificate of all of Agnes's children.

The "pivotal event" (McCormack 3) of her life is her decision to live publicly with George Henry Lewes in 1854. Risking social exile and perhaps worse—for the price of failure if their union unraveled would be much worse for her than for him, at least socially—she took the step after careful reflection. As she explained to John Chapman: "I have counted the cost of the step I have taken and am prepared to bear, without irritation or bitterness, renunciation by all my friends" (Eliot & Haight, *Letters* VIII: 124).

The first phase of their relationship took place as they traveled to Germany, where Lewes researched material for his biography of

Goethe. Living with Lewes, she flourished, traveling and writing, and "pursued an astonishing course of self-education in art, music, theatre, as well as philosophy, social theory and science" (Henry 92).

When they returned to England the following year, they eventually settled in London. They lived quietly, seeing little company, and happily. "Though far different in intellectual temper, they had vigorous, philosophical minds, lively sense of humor, and romantic sentiments stirred by the same thing" (Haight 145). Supporting both themselves and the Lewes family, the pair worked very hard, doing lots of writing for the *Westminster Review* and other periodical outlets.

Eliot's partnership made a huge difference in her finances as well as her emotional life. He encouraged her to write fiction. "His deep understanding of her contradictory emotional needs allowed him to provide exactly what she required to keep working in the face of self-distrust and despair" (Hughes 327). Despite critical raves and commercial successes,[4] Eliot suffered from headaches and depression, and she often timed a trip to the Continent to coincide with the end of a novel's gestation.

Her pivotal union with Lewes disrupted her relationships with family and friends, as some relationships cooled but resumed, while others ended. At the end of May 1857, she finally sent letters to her family, announcing her marriage by signing her letters as Marian Lewes, the name she had been using since she returned to London after their first trip abroad. Once her brother understood that her relationship was not legal, the family cut off communication. The one exception to this silence was a letter from a dying Chrissey early in 1859. Hearing of her sister's regret for the break in communication, Eliot revealed to her friend Sara: "It has ploughed up my heart" (Eliot & Haight, *Letters* III: 23).

In 1864, they bought the Priory, the house where her increasing fame also softened their social isolation. Their Sunday afternoon salons at the Priory attracted "a large and elite, if slightly Bohemian, international social circle" (McCormack 4).[5]

Their partnership lasted twenty-five years, until Lewes's death on the last day of November 1878. He was sixty-one. In May of 1880, she married for the first time, to John Cross, a man twenty years her junior. They were together only seven-and-a-half months, but her legal marriage inspired her brother Isaac to send his brief congratulations. George Eliot died on December 22, 1880. Denied a place in Westminster Abbey, she is buried in Highgate Cemetery near George Henry Lewes.[6]

Life's Work

Her forays in writing began slowly. Her first publication was a religious poem, appearing with only her initials in *The Christian Observer* in January 1840. Her translation of David Strauss's *The Life of Jesus, Critically Examined* appeared, again without her name, in 1846. Her first review, of J. A. Froude's *Nemesis of Faith*, a novel about a clergyman's questioning faith, appeared in the *Coventry Herald and Observer* in 1849.

In the 1850s, she continued to alternate critical reviews, articles, and translations. Her first article in the *Westminster Review*, a reading of Mackay's *The Progress of the Intellect*, ran in the January 1851 issue. Her translation of Feuerbach's *The Essence of Christianity* appeared in July of 1854, and though she completed a version of Spinoza's *Ethics* in 1856, the book was not published until 1981.

Her famous essay "Silly Novels by Women Novelists" appeared in the *Westminster Review* in 1856. Ten days after she finished her essay on the flaws of bad fiction, she turned her own hand to writing better fiction. "At last, as she turned thirty-seven, her unusual life bore its literary fruit" (Ashton 171). With Lewes serving as critic, cheerleader, and agent, her maturation as a novelist was swift and prodigious.

In January 1857, *Blackwood's Edinburgh Magazine* published anonymously the first part of "The Sad Fortunes of the Reverend Amos Barton," a story set in the Midlands of her girlhood. The pseudonym George Eliot appeared for the first time in correspondence between the author and John Blackwood. "Mr. Gilfil's Love Story" and "Janet's Repentance" ran later that same year.

The stories occasioned much attention, and press and publisher fielded numerous inquiries over the identity of George Eliot as well as the real-life models for numerous characters in the three stories. The three stories were collected, and in January 1858, a two-volume version was published as *Scenes of Clerical Life*. When the one-volume edition appeared, the credited author was George Eliot.

Turning to her first novel, Eliot wrote steadily between October 1857 and November 1858. *Adam Bede* was published in January of 1859 to glowing critical reviews, including *The Times*. Jane Carlyle thanked the author for her inscribed copy with the compliment that reading the novel was "as good as going into the country for one's health" (Eliot & Haight, *Letters* III: 23). The book was a commercial success, too. The three-volume edition had seven printings in its first year, and a two-volume edition sold 10,000 copies.

The true identity of the author of *Adam Bede* gradually became known. Hearing through the grapevine that her brother Isaac suspected her authorship, she finally told the Brays and Sara Hennell about her literary endeavors. The gossipy Chapman heard the news from Herbert Spencer. Eliot received a congratulatory letter from Elizabeth Gaskell, and during a visit from Anthony Trollope, she learned that Queen Victoria was a fan.

Eliot began to work seriously on her next novel in April of 1859. She finished the manuscript of *The Mill on the Floss* in March of 1860, racing through the final volume in eight weeks. Unlike *Adam Bede*, which needed good reviews as a spark to sales, Eliot's second novel sold well immediately; 6,000 in its first three weeks; however, its reviews were not as stellar.

In November of 1860, she began work on *Silas Marner*. She wrote the story rapidly and was finished by March of the next year. A one-volume edition of the work was published in April 1861, and its reviews were positive. The book also sold well, with 8,000 copies its first year.

Romola had a long preliminary phase. Eliot took her second trip to Italy in two years to work on the novel, but until late August of 1861, she could not see the shape of the narrative. After getting a huge offer from George Smith, she allowed the book to be published in monthly installments in *Cornhill Magazine*, beginning in July 1862 and running the course of a year, with each installment consisting of forty pages and two illustrations. In August, Robert Browning sent her a congratulatory note telling her how much he liked it. A three-volume edition was published in 1863, but sales were not robust.

The rest of the 1860s saw mixed results in George Eliot's literary output. *Felix Holt* was published by Blackwood in 1866. Though reviews were quite good, sales were less so; the first edition of 5,250 copies did not sell out. *The Spanish Gypsy*, a poem in blank verse, appeared in 1868. Blackwood sold 3,000 copies, and the United States edition added a further 8,000 copies, but reviews were tepid or worse.

Her masterpiece *Middlemarch* was begun in 1869, a terrible year in which Eliot and Lewes nursed his twenty-five-year-old son Thornie through the last six months of excruciating suffering with spinal tuberculosis. The novel appeared in eight installments at two-month intervals between December 1871 and December 1872. Its greatness was recognized immediately, and it was a commercial success in multiple platforms. The installment version of the novel sold 5,000 copies; as a four-volume work, sales hit 3,000 copies; however, as a one-volume edition, it sold 10,000 copies in 1875, and by 1879, 30,000 copies were sold.

Daniel Deronda was also published in eight monthly parts between February and September 1876. Approximately 7,500 copies of each installment were sold, though its critical reception was not ideal. "The history of *Daniel Deronda*'s reception has always been overshadowed by the objection of critics that the novel falls into two insufficiently integrated parts: Gwendolen's story and Daniel's story, the English half and the Jewish half" (Henry 215).[7] While she was irritated by the critical partitioning of her work, she appreciated the positive response from the contemporary Jewish community.

Notes

1. The author's mother is a shadowy figure. Katherine McCormack speculates on her alcoholism in *George Eliot and Intoxication*. Gay

Sibley has an essay that reads Christiana's history in the hidden addition of Rachel Poyser in *Adam Bede*, and Henry looks at the maternal figures in the fiction through the same lens (34–37).

2. As Henry notes, Spencer's biographer Mark Francis disagrees with the typical portrayal of the Eliot-Spencer relationship, with her as ardent party, rejected for her lack of beauty, and theorizes that she "was the love of Spencer's life" and "his own fear of intimacy" causes the failure of the pairing (68).

3. As Henry summarizes (98–101), many contemporary biographers follow Gordon S. Haight's in reading the impossibility of Lewes getting a divorce. In addition to being very expensive, a divorce would not have been possible because putting his name on Edmund's birth certificate, Agnes's first child with Hunt, was tantamount to condoning adultery. The real reason for Lewes' failure to get a divorce was that no one "wished to be dragged into the courts and into the public limelight, exposing sensitive and ambiguous questions of sexual conduct and paternity that would be embarrassing to all parties and harmful to the many children now involved" (Henry 101).

4. Rosemary Ashton compared the earnings of the couple in 1855 and 1862 (Ashton 257). While his income has an increase (from £430 in to £639), hers is exponential. In 1855, she earns just shy of £120; for *Romola*, she earns £583 per month. The same jump applied to the fiction: *Scenes of Clerical Life* brought in £443 in 1858; *Adam Bede* £1,705 in 1859; *The Mill on the Floss* £3,685 in 1860; *Silas Marner* £1,760 in 1861; *Romola* £7,000 in 1862–3; *Felix Hole* £5,000 in 1866; *Middlemarch* £9,000 in 1871–81; and *Daniel Deronda* £9,000 in 1876; A collected edition of the novels brought in an additional £4,330 in the 1870s (Sutherland 84–5).

5. For a list of specific visitors, see McCormack's *George Eliot in Society*.

6. Her widower, John Cross, wrote *The Life of George Eliot* (1885), a biography that sought to present a version of his wife most in line with Victorian norms.

7. F. R. Leavis reiterates this view in *The Great Tradition*. He even tried to fashion a version of the novel focusing on Gwendolen alone; he was unsuccessful.

Works Cited

Ashton, Rosemary. *George Eliot: A Life*. New York: Allen Lane-Penguin Press, 1996.

Dodd, Valerie A. *George Eliot: An Intellectual Life*. Basingstoke: Macmillan, 1990.

Eliot, George & Gordon S. Haight. *The George Eliot Letters*. Vols. III; VIII. New Haven: Yale UP, 1975; 1978.

Haight, Gordon S. *George Eliot: A Biography*. Oxford: Oxford UP, 1968.

Hardy, Barbara Nathan. G*eorge Eliot: A Critic's Biography*. London: Continuum, 2006. *EBSCOhost*. Web. 19 June 2015.

Henry, Nancy. *The Life of George Eliot: A Critical Biography*. Malden, MA: Wiley-Blackwell, 2012.

Hughes, Kathryn. *George Eliot: The Last Victorian*. New York: Farrar, Straus & Giroux, 1998.

James, Henry. *Letters of Henry James, 1875–1885*. Volume 2. Ed. Leon Edel. Cambridge, MA: Harvard UP, 1975.

McCormack, Kathleen. *George Eliot in Society: Travels Abroad and Sundays at the Priory*. Columbus: Ohio State UP, 2013. *Project MUSE*. Web. 12 Jun. 2015.

Simcox, Edith Jemima. *A Monument to the Memory of George Eliot: Edith J. Simcox's "Autobiography of a Shirtmaker."* Ed. Constance M. Fulmer & Margaret E. Barfield. London: Routledge, 1997.

Sutherland, John. "The Fiction Earning Patterns of Thackeray, Dickens, George Eliot, and Trollope." *Browning Institute Studies in Victorian Literary and Cultural History* 7 (1979): 71–92. *MLA International Bibliography*. Web. 15 Jul. 2015.

CRITICAL CONTEXTS

Edith Simcox on George Eliot: Autobiography of a Love

Constance M. Fulmer

Edith Jemima Simcox (1844–1901) was a remarkable Victorian scholar and reformer. However, she is not primarily known for her own achievements but for her passionate love for George Eliot, a fact she never shared with anyone—nor did she share her pain that Eliot did not return her love. She recorded the details of her secret in her personal diary, which she entitled the *Autobiography of a Shirtmaker* but said would more appropriately be called the *Autobiography of a Love* (May 26, 1878). Even though George Eliot, who was twenty-five years older than she, refused to acknowledge her love, Simcox dedicates all of her accomplishments to the memory of George Eliot (December 4, 1878). Margaret Barfield and I called our edition of the journal *A Monument to the Memory of George Eliot* because she wanted everything she accomplished to serve as a tribute to her.

Edith Simcox was a very intelligent and well-educated woman who accomplished quite a number of impressive things. She was a successful businesswoman, a leader in the trades union movement, an elected member of the London school board, a social activist who worked to improve every aspect of women's lives, a regular contributor to the leading periodicals, and the author of three remarkable books. In *Natural Law*, she defines her own ethical system, and in *Primitive Civilizations*, she outlines the ownership of property in ancient Assyria, Egypt, China, and Babylon. *Episodes in the Lives of Men, Women, and Lovers* (1882) is a series of twelve fictional vignettes, five of which were originally published in *Fraser's Magazine* in 1881.

However, Simcox was literally a shirtmaker. For eight years, she managed every aspect of the daily operation of Hamilton and Company, a cooperative shirt and collar manufacturing company in London's Soho. She described her experiences in an article that appeared in *Nineteenth Century* in 1884. She and her friend Mary Hamilton started the business specifically to employ women under decent working conditions. She made shirts for George Eliot and George Henry Lewes and mentions delivering cuffs (February 26, 1878) and silks (June 2, 1878) to them at home at the Priory. When Eliot and Lewes visited Hamilton and Company, Simcox met them outside, and they remained in their carriage. However, on February 13, 1879, she writes: "just before 3—a visitor was announced!—Came forward and lo! In the middle of the room was my goddess! I threw my arms round her—she had on a spotted net veil that could have grieved me but for the angelic way in which she took it off at my prayer."

Edith Simcox was a strong and resourceful person, who wisely uses the pages of her journal to record the many details of her private life—intermingled with the details of her public life—as she uses the journal entries to help her work through her negative emotions and to transform into positive energy her disappointments in not being loved by George Eliot. Throughout her *Autobiography*, Edith Simcox is perfectly aware that her affection and admiration for Eliot—which she sums up as loving her "lover-wise" (January 18, 1881) —are not reciprocated; however, Simcox makes it absolutely clear from her very first journal entries that she knows it is her mission to love rather than to be loved (August 30, 1878) and says that the history of her life can be summed up "in two words—love and pain—endless and intense" (July 16, 1878). She faces the facts and has the courage to comfort herself by pouring out her pain in the pages of her private diary and living out her love in public service. She turns from her expressions of self-pity to self-affirmation and positive goals, which she works untiringly to achieve; she repeatedly makes statements like: "only, for her sake, I should like to do somewhat she might be glad to have inspired" (August 11, 1878).

Edith Simcox had met George Eliot in 1872, shortly after she wrote a review of Eliot's most well-known novel, *Middlemarch*. For the next seven years, Edith attempted to become a part of George Eliot's personal life. She frequently was among the literary elite who gathered on Sunday afternoons at the home of George Eliot and her "husband" George Henry Lewes. In the journal entries, which give detailed accounts of these occasions, Simcox makes many comments that indicate she is also well aware of the ambiguity of her own relationship to Lewes, feels a camaraderie with him in his love for Eliot, and expresses appreciation for his sympathetic understanding of her pain at having her love rejected. Simcox frequently comments that Lewes was kinder to her than George Eliot was. On several occasions, the bond is obvious between these two loving servants of George Eliot. After George Henry Lewes is dead, Edith often visits his grave, plants and tends ivy, and on June 29, 1879, she wonders whether "he would have felt it to be natural that out of all the warm friendships of his life, only mine should follow him thus after the end."

And with the acute and painful insight that only a rival in love can experience, Edith all along senses something more than friendship between "the hateful Johnny" Cross and George Eliot. On numerous occasions while Lewes is present, Eliot rebukes Edith for her rudeness to John Cross, and Edith, who clearly recognizes her negative feelings toward him as "little jealous promptings" (April 13, 1879) is perhaps the only person who is not surprised when George Eliot and John Cross are married on May 6, 1880, only eighteen months after the death of Lewes. Ten days after the wedding, Edith comments that an appropriate quotation from George Eliot's "Brother-Sister Sonnets" occurs to her; it is: "I think with joy/ That I shall have my share, though he has more/ *Because he is the elder and a boy*" (May 16, 1880).

Neither Edith nor John Walter Cross had much time to share their love with George Eliot because she died seven months after their marriage. Edith never grew any closer to Cross, even though they saw each other occasionally to discuss the biography of Eliot that Cross wrote.

Ironically Edith Simcox's *Autobiography of a Shirtmaker* has contributed in many ways to the biographical facts that are known about George Eliot's personal life, the circumstances of her death, and the details of her funeral. In addition to Gordon S. Haight's tremendously valuable collection of Eliot's letters, his 1968 biography of George Eliot defined the portrait of George Eliot that has prevailed since his *George Eliot: A Biography* appeared. In writing the definitive biography, Haight used an amazing number of carefully selected details from Edith Simcox's *Autobiography of a Shirtmaker.* Haight acknowledges Edith's journal as a source, but his references to the *Autobiography of a Shirtmaker* are not specifically documented. And the last volume of *The George Eliot Letters*, which Haight published in 1978, is largely made up of long passages taken directly from Simcox's *Autobiography* (Volume IX); these selections are not complete in any sense and are obviously selected for their relevance to George Eliot rather than to Edith. There is no indication when or where sections are eliminated. And so in many ways that have never been acknowledged, it is Haight's perspective of Edith's Simcox's perspective of George Eliot's life that has defined the limits and limited the scope of George Eliot's biography.

Whenever I have read a paper that included details related to Edith Simcox's view of Eliot as expressed in her *Autobiography* and/or her *Episodes in the Lives of Men, Women, and Lovers*, someone in the audience has pointed out to me that this view is only Simcox's personal perspective. I totally agree that this is true. However, without a doubt, I know that Edith Simcox spent more time and effort studying George Eliot as a person than anyone else and that her perspective is significant. After George Eliot's death on December 22, 1880, Simcox made a sentimental journey to Nuneaton and Coventry to meet the women who were significant to George Eliot when she was Mary Ann Evans. Maria Lewis and Sara Hennell were among them. Simcox also deliberately cultivated meaningful personal relationships with the other women who had loved Eliot, such as Elma Stuart, Barbara Bodichon, and Maria Congreve. These women shared with Simcox letters they had received from Eliot. Simcox copied long passages from Eliot's letter into her journal. Yet she never confided in any of these women either her love or her pain, even though they discussed their love for Eliot with Simcox.

A very enlightening but unacknowledged aspect of Simcox's perspective of Eliot is expressed in the most curious and most specifically autobiographical of the three books that Simcox published during her lifetime: *Episodes in the Lives of Men, Women, and Lovers* (1882). All of the *Episodes* mirror Simcox's own life, personality, and opinions; one is actually called "Looking in the Glass" (167–82). In her diary entry of April 30, 1882, she "confesses" that the entire work was pure reminiscence. She says, "Barring the Introduction which amounts to little, every scrap is taken direct from my own experiences." Several of the episodes involving the lovers are transgendered accounts of her unrequited love for George Eliot. *Episodes in the Lives of Men, Women, and Lovers* is an obvious companion to and an extension of the *Autobiography of a Shirtmaker.*

In her *Autobiography*, on June 5, 1880, Simcox expresses her surprise that the reviewers found *Episodes* to be an admirable literary creation, and she was concerned that she might be recognized in the male characters; she was amazed that even her mother and brothers did not see her as Reuben the male character in "At Anchor" (123–38). The settings as well as the characters in the stories are equally personal and equally significant as self-reflections and self-assessments. The accuracy and depth of Edith Simcox's sad but humorously ironic analysis of her own role and of George Eliot's is definitely unique. The two stories from the episode entitled "Love and Friendship" (Simcox, *Episodes* 183–215) illustrate the fact that Edith Simcox knew that she was hopelessly pathetic and that she saw Eliot as being intentionally cruel in rejecting her love.

Simcox's conscious intentions as stated in the *Autobiography* make it clear that she hoped that George Eliot would detect the true implications of each episode. However, Eliot died unexpectedly in December of 1880 before she read any of the vignettes, and without the help of the *Autobiography,* the contemporary readers were totally unaware of any autobiographical significance. Now, with a copy of the *Autobiography of a Shirtmaker* at hand, it is possible to see that numerous comments Simcox makes throughout the journal serve as marginalia, which point to the fact that Edith Simcox and George Eliot are the men, women, and lovers who are featured in the *Episodes.*

Simcox often bemoaned the fact that she and Eliot were seldom alone and made the most of the opportunities she had. And there are indications that George Eliot encouraged Simcox in expressing her love. On November 12, 1878, she writes, "I dream of all sorts of new ways of wooing her!" Simcox delighted in kissing and being kissed by Eliot; in a journal entry written only two months before Eliot married John Walter Cross, Simcox says (March 9, 1880), "I kissed her again and playfully expressed the hope that she did not mind having holes kissed in her cheek. She said I gave her a very beautiful affection—and then again She called me a silly child … I asked her to kiss me—let a trembling lover tell of the intense consciousness of the first deliberate touch of the dear one's lips. I returned the kiss to the lips that gave it and started to go—she waved me a farewell."

From Edith Simcox's perspective, Eliot and Lewes definitely are both unnecessarily cruel in encouraging her in the attention she paid Eliot, yet refusing to give her any meaningful place in their lives. Eliot seems deliberately to give her false hope—not only by returning her kisses—but by telling her on several occasions that her love letters should be preserved for posterity.

For example, Simcox describes August 11, 1878, as her "one happy day." Lewes and Eliot were away from London at Witley, where they spent so much of their time. Lewes wrote a postcard inviting Edith to come for the day. Lewes sent a carriage to meet her at the train station; when she arrived at Witley, she says, "I flew across the drawing room into her arms," and "we sat in the drawing room 'til luncheon," then "walked in the garden." And "she told me about Browning and his wife's Portuguese sonnets, and she said once more that she wished my letters could be printed in the same veiled way—the Newest Heloise." Simcox sums up her feelings about that day by saying, "I am quite happy about her, contented to live, to strive,"… "for her sake, I should like to do somewhat that she might be glad to have inspired" (August 11, 1878). And on February 6, 1878, Simcox had written, "I did nothing but make reckless love to her," and adds, "I brought her two of my least spoiled Valentines, which she humanely forebore to read in my presence. She said it was a pity my letters could not be kept some 5 centuries to show a more sober posterity what hyperbole had once been possible."

However, Eliot and Lewes often totally ignore her letters and refuse to see her for weeks at a time, and even worse—they both—

but particularly Eliot—constantly rebuke Simcox for not being married (September 23, 1881) and often taunt her for not being "more charitable to men" (October 1, 1877). Of course, Simcox deeply resents this and frequently expresses her strong objections to their remarks. On one occasion, she says (June 13, 1880): "it is rather humiliating to me to be told again and again that the association called up by my name is always that of a woman who might find a husband if she would take a little more pains with her dress and drawing room conversation—and this in the mind of some one that I love." Simcox often defended herself with indignant comments such as: "I have never wished to be married in the abstract and I would decidedly much rather not be married to any concrete Dick or Tom" (October 17, 1887). After the death of Lewes in November 1878, Eliot refused to see Simcox for four months, and she only admitted her a few times before she married John Walter Cross.

In spite of her repeated rejections of Simcox's love, Eliot seems to have thoroughly enjoyed receiving so much attention and at times actually encouraged Simcox's expressions of affection. Five years after Eliot's death (February 25, 1885), Simcox writes: "it is folly not to allow myself to believe that my love was real to Her when She spoke of it more than once in words which She had before appropriated only to Her most loving husband."

Many such comments in the *Autobiography* are specifically corroborated by events, which she describes in her *Episodes in the Lives of Men, Women, and Lovers.* The saddest and most curious of the stories is the one she called "Love and Friendship" (Simcox, *Episodes* 183–215). The male narrator is in Brittany, visiting with two old married friends who strongly resemble George Eliot and George Henry Lewes. After dinner, the old couple sit in front of an open fire with the male narrator and his intended lover, both the admiral and his wife tell stories for the edification of the younger couple.

The first story is shared by the hostess who is very beautiful and, like George Eliot, has bright eyes. She tells the story of a faithful lover from the age of chivalry—the story of the Lady of Éza and her faithful serving-man. She begins the story by saying that long ago in a remote castle, a fair maiden was served by a silent, awkward youth who was a foundling, brought up in charity by the maiden's father. "And whatsoever the lady's wish might be, he ran to do her will, but for the most part with a stupid haste that brought him little thanks" (Simcox, *Episodes* 196). He served her faithfully, from the time she was a thoughtless child throughout her life—time and time again he "pressed forward in her needs, and each time she bade another do her will" (197). When she died, the old trooper who had served her for forty-nine years without any appreciation or recognition was asked by chance to bear a taper to her grave. He knelt at the feet of the dead lady and held the taper "like an uplifted banner in the battle's charge" (199). When the service ended, he still knelt when the other mourners left the chapel. When the lady's family came the next day to lay her in the vault, the faithful lover still knelt, "stiff and cold as a statue of stone within his armour" (199–200). "And five centuries afterwards, a skeleton in armour was found kneeling still" at the foot of her coffin, and so "the henchman had his reward" (200).

When she begins to write in the journal, Simcox has just received a "stern letter" in which Eliot referred to herself as "a wife with a wife's supreme and sufficing love" and strongly recommended that Simcox renounce her love and find herself a husband (May 13, 1880). As long as George Eliot was alive, Edith endured many other rebuffs and lived with the knowledge that their "lives are to be shaped apart and independently" (February 1, 1880). In the same entry, Simcox dramatically says that her own "life has flung itself" at George Eliot's feet—and "not been picked up"…only "told to rise and make a serviceable place elsewhere." Simcox also goes on to say that her "fierce worship" has been "choked off by a churlish fate" so that she was been "hurled back upon the one inexhaustible gospel of Renunciation." Even though Edith Simcox definitely lived a serviceable life elsewhere, as long as Eliot was alive, she continued to remain "always watchful and ready to her call" (in a letter following the entry of March 28, 1880).

When George Eliot herself died, only eight months after her marriage to Cross, Simcox's journal writing remains her primary means of catharsis, and she finds comfort in writing and being able to say: "The grief is bitter, but it is only mine—it hurts no one else" (February 5, 1881). Simcox was the last person, other than Eliot's husband, to see Eliot alive. On December 23, 1880, she writes, "This morning I hear from Johnny—she died at 10 last night!… One slender comfort is left me—that I saw and kissed her so near the end."

On several occasions throughout the journal, she mentions the possibility of sharing her grief and her pain at being rejected with one of her female friends but always decided against it. In one entry (September 6, 1880), she describes having "dim visions of confiding in Mary Cross," who was the sister of John Walter Cross and a friend of Edith's. She specifically states that she entertained these thoughts while she was lying in the hammock and scribbling the "giant with no heart in his body."

The second story from the *Episodes*, titled "Love and Friendship" (183–215) is told by the host, an old admiral who tells the tale of the giant with no heart in his body, but "the place where his heart had been was just a hollow cavity, quite healed and skinned over" (Simcox, *Episodes* 206). The story takes place in South America, in Patagonia, where some princesses skilled in magic have the art of charming the hearts of giants out of their bodies. The giant Eieiaio's heart was kept by a strange princess called the Doña Violante. She dwelt in a magic palace with a magic spell upon it, and she carried a little round white dog named Fluff, which she used in her enchantments. She kept Eieiaio's heart in an embroidered velvet bag identical to the one in which she kept Fluff's treats and sweetmeats. She often confused the two and allowed Fluff to play with the bag containing Eieiaio's heart. When Fluff trampled on the bag, Eieiaio turned pale and suffered pain, as if his life were ebbing away. After he had endured this cruel treatment for a long while, another giant offered his heart to the princess. While she conversed with the second giant, Eieiaio's heart is tucked under her sofa-cushion between a rosary and a French novel, and she leaned her elbows on the cushion as she talked. Eieiaio writhed "under the malicious digs she gave his heart as she moved languidly from one graceful pose to another"

(212). And so Eieiaio begged her to return his heart, but she refused, saying that she will never part with it. While speaking, she "smiled fiendishly, and opened the strings of the little bag and took his heart in her hand," and clenched it until he felt his life ebb away (213).

In this story, it seems clear that Eieiaio is Edith, the princess is George Eliot, the little fluffy dog is George Henry Lewes, and the second giant is the hateful Johnny Cross. Like Edith, the giant Eieiaio has no heart because the princess mishandled his heart in the mockingly cruel way George Eliot mishandled Simcox's heart; she tortured him with jealousy and even held his heart clenched in her hand as he died.

Isn't it curious that Edith Simcox loved George Eliot so much in spite of her pain? Isn't it curious that this remarkable woman, her reform efforts, and her brilliant articles and books—including *Episodes in the Lives of Men, Women, and Lovers*—are never taken seriously by George Eliot scholars? And isn't it curious that Eliot's biographers have created a portrait of George Eliot herself, which is so different from the one which emerges from the *Autobiography of a Shirtmaker* and *Episodes in the Lives of Men, Women, and Lovers*?

As the years passed and the journal entries became less frequent, Edith focused more and more on her relationship with her mother, Jemima Haslop Simcox (1816–1897). She always made her home with her mother, who was also her best friend and dearest love. Edith tirelessly cared for her mother during her mother's many years of growing weakness and sickness and did everything possible to keep her entertained and happy. Mrs. Simcox died only four years before Edith, and the two are buried together in the graveyard at Aspley Guise near Bedford. Only her mother's name is on the headstone.

Even though there is no epitaph on her headstone, Edith Simcox explained what she wanted her own epitaph to be. On June 4, 1882, she mentions taking flowers to George Eliot's grave in Highgate Cemetery and ponders as a possible epitaph: "Here lies E. J. S. whose heart's desire lives wherever the memory of George Eliot is beloved," and she adds, "My Darling. I have lived—to have loved you suffices me." The last of her *Episodes in the Lives of Men, Women, and Lovers* is entitled *"Sat est vixisse"* (Simcox, *Episodes* 269–304), which translates to "I have lived." In the very first entry in the journal on October 1, 1877, Edith says she has looked back at the entries in an earlier journal (which has not been located) and that she is "counting the days till I may hope to see her again.... I have written *finis* on my tombstone and in sanguine moments force myself to mutter "Sat est vixisse"—I *have* lived for a few seconds now and then." She had said in her journal entry of September 18, 1881, she was working on the final episode and explains that by saying "I have lived," she is still referring to her love for George Eliot and means: "The lasting blessedness was that She is so good and dear and I loved Her beyond words."..."I accept my life."

Works Cited

Haight, Gordon S., ed. *George Eliot Letters*. 9 vols. New Haven: Yale, 1954–74.

_____. *George Eliot: A Biography*. New York: Oxford UP, 1968.

Simcox, Edith J. "Eight Years of Cooperative Shirtmaking." *Nineteenth Century* 15 (June 1884): 1037–1054.

_____. *Episodes in the Lives of Men, Women, and Lovers*. London: Trübner & Co, 1882; Boston: J. R. Osgood & Co., 1882. First published in *Fraser's Magazine:* "Consolations," (June 1881): 771–782; "A Diptych," (July 1881): 42–56; "Midsummer Noon," (August 1881): 204–11; "Love and Friendship" (October 1881): 448–61; "At Anchor," (November 1881): 624–29.

_____. *A Monument to the Memory of George Eliot: Edith J. Simcox's Autobiography of a Shirtmaker*. Eds. Constance M. Fulmer & Margaret E. Barfield. New York: Garland, 1998. Bodleian manuscript (Eng. misc. d. 494).

_____. *Natural Law: An Essay in Ethics*. London: Trübner & Co, 1877.

_____. *Primitive Civilizations; Or, Outlines of the History of Ownership in Archaic Communities*. 2 vols. London: Swan Sonnenschein & Co, 1894.

_____. "Review of *Middlemarch*." *Academy* 4 (1 January 1873): 1–4.

Critical Tipples: Or, A Nip into George Eliot Criticism, *Then and Now*_____

Katherine Montwieler & Mark Edelman Boren

The body of George Eliot criticism is large. Vast, and as marvelously varied as the responses among critics and in the popular press, her reputation as a writer has risen and fallen and risen again in what can be described—in her own words—as "many a melting curve" (Eliot, "The Legend of Jubal" li 75). While in any given moment countervailing responses and assessments to what we'll proffer here can be certainly found and in some cases abound, we'll describe some of the general contours, the hills and valleys of prevailing trends, touching here and there upon important points of distinction among her admirers, advocates, and detractors. This survey makes no pretense at comprehensiveness, offering a necessarily brief peep into the wondrous world of Eliot studies, proffering but a taste of the richness of the work surrounding her oeuvre.[1] This essay reveals the invested concerns and attitudes of a long gathered throng looking and commenting upon Eliot's corpus, conveying the deep impact and lasting influence of Eliot's tremendous literary performance.

With the 1859 publication of her first novel, *Adam Bede*, Eliot garnered public attention and secured for herself vocal admirers who placed her as one of the best among living English novelists. In *The Times,* E. S. Dallas went so far as to claim the author was, "among the masters of the art," a sentiment echoed across the pond in reviews ranging from *Harper's New Monthly* to *The Atlantic.*[2] The high praise was due to her unique form of realism and an ability to render the details of everyday rural life, combined with moralism, humor, and sympathy—all things she'd experimented with but not fully developed in her *Scenes of Clerical Life*, published the previous year. With *Adam Bede*, though, she set off a public reaction that propelled her on her way to a literary stardom that, although at times contested, would nevertheless outlive her, lasting a quarter of a century before declining in orbit. *Adam Bede*, it was generally assumed, was authored by a man: a first-hand, moral observer of country life, perhaps even a member of the clergy, and the character of Mrs. Poyser had few contemporary rivals for fans. This was perhaps why the discovery that George Eliot was actually a woman cohabitating with a married George Lewes came as such a shock to her reading public, a scandal that both lost and gained her readership.

The year 1860 saw the publication of *The Mill on the Floss*, which critics both praised and condemned, but could not ignore. Eliot's realism served to bring public attention to issues of childhood and femininity, but the novel was also noted for "certain crudities" by the same *Times* critic (Dallas) who had so highly praised *Adam Bede*. Critics such as Dallas acknowledged the writer's genius, but they also began to point out flaws: "George Eliot is as great as ever. She has produced a second novel, equal to her first in power, although not in interest."[3] The knowledge that Eliot was a woman, "living with a man," gave her mostly male critics the excuse to find fault. Her realism now, especially her focus on the female body, was condemned; and her use of sympathy, although recognized by many as artistically aimed for a greater moral good was criticized by others as dangerous for focusing too much on the physical effects of feeling. And what had been praised as intellectual and philosophical considerations of doubt and faith in *Adam Bede*, now became issues of whether or not they were "appropriate contemplation" for a female author.[4] In short, this second novel was, like its predecessor, a novel of undeniable artistic achievement, but its author had extended her critics through her own life the means by which to voice their own ideological, often sexist stances. For better and worse, she was now compared to the other great English women novelists, raised and relegated to a feminine tradition (which included more "virtuous" authors). As for herself, Eliot remained a hot topic, and her impressive productivity—a novel a year—would keep tongues wagging.

With *Silas Marner* (1861), the recognition of Eliot's skill finally outstripped the clinging doubts about her moral character. This seemingly more "natural" novel was almost universally praised, with critics comparing its author once again to the best English novelists (male and female). Henry James, who liked to weigh in on every "notable" literary endeavor, though he waited a while on this one, in typically grudging fashion called it "nearly a masterpiece." The otherwise almost unreserved public praise lasted two years, that is, until she published again.

Although Eliot's reputation as one of the finest novelists was secure, her subsequent efforts met with alternating criticisms and compliments. *Romola* (1863) suffered from being thought "too intellectual" and straying too far afield of what she knew best. Although this view certainly reflected a reading public's taste, the fact that similar criticisms were leveled by her more literary critics revealed the continued, imbedded sexism that suggested women not ought to be writing about such things. *Felix Holt, the Radical* (1866) was applauded as a return to rural depiction, humor, morality, and humanity. Her dramatic poem, *The Spanish Gypsy* (1868), although meeting spotty praise, was again widely criticized for its "intellectualism."

In 1871, however, Eliot's public was exposed to something on an entirely different order: *Middlemarch*. The novel was immediately recognized as a supreme artistic achievement that wrestled with the psychological, the philosophical, and the human; it nevertheless materialized for its fans and critics (in comparison, say, to *Adam Bede* and *Silas Marner*) the polarized means by which all her work would, during her lifetime, be judged. Her subsequent novel, *Daniel Deronda* (1876), acknowledged as an important but lesser work than *Middlemarch*, continued to push boundaries and the reading public by forcing psychological and philosophical consideration of religious principles, reinforced by the public awareness of Eliot's own religious humanism. And finally, *Impressions of Theophrastus Such* (1879), her last novel, followed suit, garnering more ambivalent responses to the novel's intellectuality, psychological focus, and moral purpose. And yet by the sheer force of the achievement of her (depending on the taste of the critic, early or later) works, and indeed the span of all her work, critics universally agreed she was to be counted among the most important of England's writers. And this also enabled a public consideration (again both in support of or deriding) her ideas regarding femininity, her moral aims, religious questioning, and aesthetics.

Following Lewes's death, in 1880, Eliot married John Cross, a man twenty years her junior, and this, in concert with his infamous attempted suicide on their honeymoon, fueled more scandal about the author. Her own death due to an infection six months later kept her personal life a hot topic for public consumption. Following this one last shudder of Eliot muckraking, interest in her literary works began to wane. Although steadily decreasing since *Daniel Deronda*, modern critics mark the beginning of the serious decline of her status and readership with Cross's subsequent bizarrely sanitary biography, *Life of George Eliot* (1885), a three-volume tome based upon his heavy-handed expurgation of her letters, a work radically at odds with the public perception of the unconventional life of the author. With the nineteenth century drawing to a close and a new era on the rise, with a burgeoning interest in naturalism and a taste for a less Victorian literature, the public fervor for and critical interest in Eliot fizzled for a while.

Although her novels continued to sell to the reading public, for the first twenty years of the next century, critics turned to modernist and away from Victorian novels (by then typified by critics of Eliot's work).[5] They tended to dismiss her work as laborious, moralizing reading of the past. Paralleling the sexism of days gone by as well, critics acknowledged her abilities to render rural life while denigrating her intellectualism. Although Bellringer notes that while critics often cherry pick responses to Eliot's work that undercut a more subtle appraisal of the range of responses to her work, both supportive (Brownwell 1901; Stephen 1902) and deprecatory (most notoriously, Henley 1881), he does argue that by the end of the century, a number of the notably bad reviews had become rather extreme (such as George Saintsbury's characterization of much of her work as "dead" and *Daniel Deronda* as "a kind of nightmare").[6] Edmund Gosse's (1919) *London Mercury* summation of her literary achievements culminated with the declaration that "It was the fatal error of George Eliot, so admirable, so elevated, so disinterested, that for the last ten years of her brief literary life she did practically nothing but lay heavy loads on literature" (43). Countering Gosse's views in the same month, but to limited effect, Virginia Woolf argued in the *Times Literary Supplement* that Eliot's work must be considered separately from her life, calling for a reappraisal of *Middlemarch* as one of the few novels written "for grown-up people" (658). While these two stances allow us to make a point about general attitudes towards Eliot, they shouldn't oversimplify an unfolding critical narrative. There continued to be a steady stream of articles on Eliot's fiction, which can be grouped around those things critics discussed about her work from the beginning: rural life, her use of scenery (Olcott, Sharp), the role of women (Jones, Kawa, Lawrence), realist technique (Grabo), philosophical underpinnings (Wade), her construction of morality (Repplier), character development (Dawson), sympathy (Wright), humor (Meynell, Tomlinson), and so forth. These bread-and-butter subjects for Eliot critics were under discussion in print from 1860 on and have produced a giant body of their own; indeed, they continue to be discussed even today (though the terminology surrounding them has certainly changed).

The second half of the twentieth century, however, saw the kind of reappraisal of Eliot for which Woolf asked. F. R. Leavis began publishing articles on Eliot in 1945 and 1946 in *Scrutiny* and then in 1948 produced his (oft-cited by Eliot critics) *The Great Tradition: George Eliot, Henry James, Joseph Conrad*, which re-authenticated Eliot's work as a valid *and ripe* subject for new critical studies. A greater number of scholars began working on Eliot. Barbara Hardy's *The Novels of George Eliot* (1959) sought to centralize Eliot in the discussion of great British writers, contextualizing the author's narrative form in contrast to the works of Joyce and Faulkner, arguing she was as important an experimenter as they were. Hardy also compares Eliot's tragic characters, irony, and imagery to those in Shakespeare; in short, the critic analytically and convincingly situates Eliot's work in a Western tradition of serious literary, often experimental craft. Reinforced by a number of other scholars looking beyond recent, modernist works and employing what were largely formalist techniques of analysis, such studies opened the door for more scholars to enter the arena. Reflective of the widening approaches that would rapidly spread and develop across literary studies in general in the sixties and seventies, these landmark reappraisals of Eliot heralded what would be, for the next half century, a surfeit of different approaches to Eliot's work, from formalist to feminist to deconstructionist—approaches that, like her *Jubalian* flora, "rise and spread and bloom toward fuller fruit each year" (Eliot, "Legend" li 120).

Feminism, Women, Gender

The subject of women, their depiction and their roles in Eliot's work long has been the topic of discussion, from before Woolf's article (1919), to Maria Kawa's "The Women of George Eliot's Novels" (1922), to M. S. Jones's "Woman and Genius" (1926), to Margaret Lawrence's "George Eliot, Who Sat Like a Recording Angel and Wrote" (1936). But beginning in the mid-1960s, Eliot's work began to be regarded as explicitly engaging feminism in articles such as "George Eliot, Feminism, and Dorothea Brooke" (Fernando 1963). Much of the feminist discussion of George Eliot's work during the later sixties and throughout the next twenty-five years focused on whether or not her work was (or was not) feminist and if so, exactly how it was (or was not). Atkinson argues that critics such as Kate Millet (1970) suggested the scarcity of strong independent female characters was a problem and that Eliot's work reinforced masculinist ideologies and sexist traditions.

Zelda Austen in "Why Feminist Critics are Mad at George Eliot" explains this criticism is largely because the author didn't even grant her characters the independent existence that she herself led. According to Austen, disappointed feminists believe "George Eliot should have turned the mirror to reflect herself rather than the world out there" (549). Others, including Richard Conway (1973) in "The Difficulty of Being a Woman: The Study of George Eliot's Heroines" or Kathleen Blake (1976) in "*Middlemarch* and the Woman Question," underscore that instead of portraying how things should be, Eliot's power resides in her careful depiction of the realities of life for women, thereby drawing much needed attention to their plight. Ann Eliasberg (1975) argues Eliot's work was actually important because of its depiction of the "Victorian anti-heroine." Fueled by landmark texts, such as Patricia Spacks's *The Female Imagination* (1975), the feminist debate over Eliot raged and grew in complexity, but whether engaging with her corpus as a whole (Feeney; Hardwick; Kraft; and Milder) or, as increasingly was the case, discussing individual novels (and here the list is too large to do justice), the feminist appraisal of Eliot's work in the 1970s and 1980s radically changed the landscape of Eliot scholarship.

As the contours of literary criticism grew more varied, so did feminist approaches to Eliot. For example, Nancy Armstrong (1987) argued that Eliot reveals how empowerment for women is closely tied to class and that certain freedoms become available only as one rises in status and rank. In 1992, Katherine Bailey Linehan analyzed the interplay between the construction of gender and imperialism in Eliot's work, particularly her discussion of "Patriarchy, racialism, and nationalism" (323). Sophia Andres (1999) tackles gender, ambiguity, and power in "George Eliot's Challenge to Medusa's Gendered Disparities," and other critics, such as Deanna Kreisel (2002) and Ellen Moody (2004), extend the analysis of gender constructions through Eliot's work. Kathleen Slaugh-Sanford (2010) in her postcolonial gender analysis, "The Other Woman," studies the role and construction of the colonized woman in Eliot.

Marxism and Materialism

Not surprisingly, much of the work done on Eliot addresses issues of class. Raymond Williams (1969) argues that Eliot's work brings an increasing awareness of the representation of class in rural society. Terry Eagleton (1976) argues that Eliot's work conveys a nexus of competing, unresolved ideologies of individualism and community, romanticism and Victorianism, material wealth and the simplicities of rustic life. Many studies assess the construction of British bourgeois culture through her works, arguing Eliot promulgated ideologies of class and nationalism (Eagleton; Piece), while others argue that although class is naturalized in many of her works, in some, such as *Felix Holt*, "class consciousness is […] more visible" (Livesay 100).

More common than strict Marxist approaches though (mirroring a decline in Marxist criticism and a rise in works that explore bourgeois commodity culture) are studies that look at materiality and culture, particularly the depictions of artifacts that supplant or metaphorize human relations. Jeff Nunokawa (1993) studies Victorian sexuality and the exchange of physical objects. John Rignall (1996) in "George Eliot and the Furniture of the House of Fiction" looks at commodity culture metaphorically, and Natalie Houston's (1996) "George Eliot's Material History: Clothing and Realistic Narrative" examines clothing and fashion, highlighting the relevance of George Eliot during the rise of cultural studies.

Postcolonialism, Race, Ethnicity
For an author so famous for her focus on and careful depiction of English rural culture, Eliot's work has been the subject of myriad postcolonial readings, most of which begin with her inclusion of Jewish characters. Irving Howe (1979) undertakes an important analysis of *Daniel Deronda*, but the subject as an area of study doesn't take off until much later. Indeed while Bellringer's own (1993) study of *Daniel Deronda* discusses the role of Zionism in depth, his appraisal of Eliot's current critical context included in the same book doesn't remark on the subject as a separate area of study. Within a year, it would blossom and yield much. While some critics argued that Eliot's representation of Zionism speaks to a larger concern for Jewish community (and thus community in general), Atkinson notes that these early arguments are countered by critics such as Susan Meyer (1993) and Alicia Carroll (1999), who both explained that while drawing attention to issues of alienation, Eliot's work also promotes stereotypes of Otherness and exoticism and naturalizes colonial imperialism within the British middle class. Linehan's (1992) "Mixed Politics" places Judaism against a backdrop of social, sexual, and racial politics in Eliot's work. Pauline Nestor (2002) sees in Eliot's work a sophisticated drama of Otherness that elicits moral sentiment and challenges problematic cultural knowledge. This area of study continues to grow today, which is ironic, given that during her lifetime, Eliot's public often

voiced confusion and dissatisfaction with her interest in Jewish characters. A lone study between then and now stands out: Philipson dedicates a chapter to *Daniel Deronda* in *The Jew in English Fiction* (1911). Notably, Pam Hirsch argues in her book "Women and Jews in *Daniel Deronda*" that Eliot depicts "both groups as being exiles, homeless and powerless" (45). In 2003, Alicia Carroll came out with her *Dark Smiles: Race and Desire in George Eliot* (2003) and 2009 saw the publication of another book dedicated to Eliot, Gertrude Himmelfarb's *The Jewish Odyssey of George Eliot.*

Genre, Realism, Sympathy, Feeling

In the twentieth century, Eliot's work was often compared with that of Dickens and other male writers (witness Leavis), as it is now with the more "feminine" traditions. R. Montelle Bolstad addresses this in her (1972) "The Myth of Sensibility in George Eliot." A more recent study combining an interest in women's issues with other cultural historical methodology is Susan Rowland Tush's *George Eliot and the Conventions of Popular Women's Fiction: A Serious Literary Response to the "Silly Novels by Lady Novelists"* (1993). In an appraisal of the use of sympathy in Eliot, Melissa Raines undertakes in "Awakening the 'mere pulsation of desire' in *Silas Marner*" (2007) the connection between "the mind and the body that Eliot made a focal point in her writing" (24). Jim Endersby argues Eliot availed herself of Darwinian theory in her depiction of familial relationships in "The Sympathetic Science" (2009), but in 2010, Simon Calder argues that, on the contrary, a "conflict between 'sympathetic impulse' and 'the scientific point of view' exists at the heart of Eliot's art" (74). That Eliot uses sympathy (particularly for a moral purpose) has been acknowledged since the nineteenth century, but because her work is first and foremost considered realism and because her use of sympathy soon became suspect (due to her morality without religion and her intellectualism), her work hasn't received much specifically genre-based attention (other than reflecting the time and material culture of its production). In an unusual recent critical move, however, Royce Mahawatte's (2013) *George Eliot and the Gothic Novel: Genres, Gender, and Feeling* attempts to align Eliot's work with Mary Braddon, Wilkie Collins, and Edward Bulwer Lytton.

Historical and Cultural Criticism

Given the detail-specific nature of her work, her voracious intellect (she became proficient in eight languages in her lifetime so she could read works in their native tongues), and progressive ideas, it is not surprising that Eliot's novels have been a wellspring for scholars studying cultural manifestations of the era in which she wrote, hence all the commodity-oriented studies. In addition to these, however, there are many that deal with historical issues, ranging from childcare to eldercare. Jeffrey Franklin's "The Victorian Discourse of Gambling: Speculations on *Middlemarch* and the Duke's Children" (1994) is representative of specific types of studies undertaken in the last couple of decades.

Observations that started out suitably for *Notes and Queries* in the 1950s (such as Barbara Hardy's "The Image of the Opiate") were, by the twenty-first century, the focus of entire monographs. For example, Kathleen McCormack's (2000) book on drinking in Eliot's works argues that the author creates an "elaborate and comprehensive pattern of metaphorical figures and plot-level facts [...] related to the medicinal, recreational, linguistic, social, physical, political, and artistic causes and effects of nineteenth-century intoxication" (*George Eliot and Intoxication* i).

But of all the historico-cultural subjects studied, advancements in science and medicine head the list. As early as 1946, critics such as F. G. Halstead ("George Eliot: Medical Digressions in *Middlemarch*") were dedicating studies to these topics in Eliot's works. Gillian Beer's *Darwin's Plots* (1983) tracks how the language and concepts of evolution appear in Eliot's fiction. Lilian Furst (1993) follows the struggle for medical reform in *Middlemarch*, Christine Kreuger (1997) studies medicine and infanticide in *Adam Bede*, and Janis Caldwell (2004) studies a more general appearance and use of medicine at work in *Middlemarch*. George Levine's "Science and Victorian Literature" (2007) discusses Eliot's work as a prime example of how scientific discourse became a part of public discourse.

Other Themes, Odds and Ends

Other trends in Eliot criticism that sporadically appear include: morality (Carlisle 1974, Hornback 1972); tragedy (Friedberg 1972, Goldsberry 1972); narratology (Faville 1973); structuralism and deconstructionism (J. Hillis Miller 1968, revisited by K. M. Newton 2009); poststructuralism (J. Hillis Miller 1974); and music (Lynes 1970, Beer 1974, to mention just a couple). There is even sociolinguistic criticism, such as Lynda Mugglestone's (1995) "'Grammatical Fair Ones': Women, Men, and Attitudes to Language in the Novels of George Eliot"). As early as 1905, Alice Meynell placed Eliot in a tradition of English Women-Humorists, and in the seventies, when the comic in literature was being theorized more generally, there was a surge in analyses of Eliot's humor: Margaret Hall (1972), Robin Lee (1973), Patricia Shaw (1973), and Robert Martin (1975).

Although there are a few psychologically oriented studies— Robert McCullough's early (1946) essay; Diana Postlethwaite's "The Novelist as a Woman of Science: George Eliot and Contemporary Psychology" (1976); Philip Ranjini's "Maggie, Tom, and Oedipus" (1992); and Katrina Ruth's "The Imaginary Vision in *Adam Bede*" (1996)—one area of study visible for its relative invisibility in Eliot scholarship is psychoanalytic criticism, all the more conspicuous because of her novels' much talked about "psychological focus." While strictly psychoanalyst analyses of Eliot may be lacking, there have recently appeared some cognitive studies of her work.

With such detail and with so many pages comes a plethora of possible subjects for Eliot scholars to analyze. And with the proliferation of methodologies in the last twenty-five years, the list of subjects undertaken are too many to list here. Even the number of isolated studies that abound, which can't be grouped under major or even minor trends, is mind numbing, so we'll, at this point, beg off.

Biographies

With a life as productive and scandalous as Eliot's, it should come as no surprise that biographies of her abound. This has been especially true recently, and the last twenty years have seen as many biographies produced, most notably among them, Rosemary Ashton's *George Eliot: A Life* (1996), Kathryn Hughes's *George Eliot: The Last Victorian* (1998), Barbara Hardy's *George Eliot: A Critic's Biography* (2006), Brenda Maddox's *George Eliot: Novelist, Lover, Wife* (2009), Avrom Fleishman's *George Eliot's Intellectual Life* (2010), and Nancy Henry's *The Life of George Eliot* (2012). While not usually noted in a discussion of the critical reception of an author's work, because Eliot's life has been inextricably bound up with the discussion of her works, it seems appropriate to list some of the major recent biographies. And in the case of this particular author, it is also not surprising that the attention given her life recently has fueled a corresponding rise in the critical attention given her work.

Legacy

The critical appreciation for George Eliot is today stronger than ever. There are two scholarly journals dedicated to her work, and in preparation for this essay, the various bibliographic searches we conducted of her work in print and through databases produced upwards of four thousand entries. Indeed every year since the mid-nineties, there has been enough critical material produced for *GE-GHL* to annually support a survey article dedicated solely to the year's most notable Eliot criticism.[7] While the appraisal of her work since its production has, at times, been fickle, her readers never lost an appetite for her work, and Eliot seems more popular than ever in the popular press, fueled no doubt by numerous television and filmic adaptations of all of her novels. But the novels themselves have driven this interest, too. Martin Amis claimed in a 2010 interview, that Eliot was, "the greatest writer in the English language ever, [...] and the greatest novel, *Middlemarch*" (Long 4). David Brooks in *The Road to Character* (2015) devotes some thirty pages to a discussion of how Eliot's works shaped his own moral character and understanding of love, and Rebecca Mead's *My*

Life in "Middlemarch" (earlier excerpted in the *New Yorker*) made the *New York Times* bestseller list in 2014, showcasing yet another development in literary criticism: the rise of the memoir. Thus it seems in both critical circles and the popular press, and even at the same time, George Eliot's work has once again achieved stellar status.

Notes

1. This essay serves as an introduction to the critical field of Eliot studies. For more in-depth discussions of the intricacies of Eliot criticism, please see Barbara Hardy's *George Eliot: A Critic's Biography,* the three cited essays by Juliette Atkinson, George Levine's *An Annotated Critical Biography of George Eliot,* Alan Bellringer's *George Eliot*, Karen Pangallo's *The Critical Response to George Eliot*, and Donald Hawes's annual surveys of important published Eliot criticism for *GE-GHL Studies*—to all of which, this essay is indebted.

2. Cited in Atkinson, "Critical Responses to 1900." Atkinson's essays on the critical reception of Eliot comprise a critical narrative *tour de force* of concise synthesis and importantly includes significantly expanded charting of the development of feminist Eliot scholarship. Bellringer's work covers much the same ground (sans the focus on feminism), though he pays more attention to the early twentieth century response to Eliot by Henry James and his followers, and to the formalist, New Critical, and Marxist areas of scholarship, post Leavis. He also tends more towards more abstract discussions of discussed critical trends, whereas Atkinson relies more on specific examples to suggest trends.

3. Dallas's May 1860 review of *Mill on the Floss* is included in Pangallo (71).

4. See Kristin Brady for a discussion of George Eliot as a "Man-Woman Icon."

5. This study is also indebted to Marshall (1963) and Higdon (1978) for their early bibliographic surveys of Eliot criticism.

6. Cited in Bellringer 123.

7. For well over a decade, Donald Hawes gathered and assessed the year's Eliot criticism for *GE-GHL*.

Works Cited

Andres, Sophia. "George Eliot's Challenge to Medusa's Gendered Disparities." *Victorian Newsletter* 95 (1999): 27–33.

Anonymous. Review [*Adam Bede*]. *Atlantic Monthly* (4 Oct. 1859): 547–48.

_____. Review [*Adam Bede*]. *Harper's New Monthly Magazine* (18 Apr. 1859): 691.

Armstrong, Nancy. *Desire and Domestic Fiction: A Political History of the Novel.* Oxford, UK:Oxford UP, 1987.

Ashton, Rosemary. *George Eliot: A Life.* London: Hamish Hamilton, 1996.

Atkinson, Juliette. "Critical Responses to 1900." *George Eliot in Context.* Cambridge, UK:Cambridge UP, 2013. 65–73.

_____. "Critical Responses 1900–1970." *George Eliot in Context.* Cambridge, UK: Cambridge UP, 2013. 74–82.

_____. "Critical Responses 1970–present." *George Eliot in Context.* Cambridge, UK: Cambridge UP, 2013. 83–91.

Austen, Zelda. "Why Feminist Critics Are Angry at George Eliot." *College English* 37.6 (1976): 549–561.

Beer, Gillian. *Darwin's Plots: Evolutionary Narrative in Darwin, George Eliot and Nineteenth-Century Fiction.* Cambridge, UK: Cambridge UP, 2000.

Bellringer, Alan. *George Eliot.* New York: St. Martin's Press, 1993.

Blake, Kathleen. *Approaches to Teaching Eliot's Middlemarch.* New York: MLA, 1990.

_____. "*Middlemarch* and the Woman Question." *Nineteenth-Century Fiction* 31 (Winter 1976): 285–312.

Bolstad, Montelle. "The Myth of Sensibility in George Eliot." *Recovering Literature* 1.2 (1972): 26–39.

Brady, Kristin. *George Eliot.* New York: St. Martins, 1990.

Brooks, David. *The Road to Character.* New York: Random House, 2015.

Brownwell, W. C. *Victorian Prose Masters.* New York: Scribner's, 1901.

Calder, Simon. "The Art of Conduct and Mixed Science of Eliot's Ethics." *George Eliot Review* 41 (2010): 60–74.

Carlisle, Janice. "The Moral Imagination: Dickens, Thackeray, and George Eliot." *DAI* 34 (1974): 6630.

Carroll, Alicia. *Dark Smiles: Race and Desire in George Eliot*. Athens, OH: Ohio UP, 2003.

_____. "Arabian Nights: Make Believe, Exoticism, and Desire in *Daniel Deronda*." *Journal of English and Germanic Philosophy* 98 (1999): 219–38.

Conway, Richard. "The Difficulty of Being a Woman: A Study of George Eliot's Heroines." *DAI* 39 (1973): 722A.

Dallas, E.S. "*Adam Bede*." *The Times* (12 Apr. 1859): 5.

_____. "*The Mill on the Floss*." *The Times* (19 May 1860): 10.

Dawson, Thomas. "Character Development in *Romola*." *Four Years of Novel Reading*. Ed. Richard Moulton. Boston: 1895. 91–100.

Eagleton, Mary & David Pierce. "Aspects of Class in George Eliot's Fiction." *Attitudes to Class in the English Novel: From Walter Scott to David Storey*. London: Thames & Hudson: 1985.

Eagleton, Terry. *Criticism and Ideology: A Study of Marxist Literary Theory*. London: Verso, 1976.

Eliasberg, Ann. "The Victorian Anti-Heroine." *DAI* 36 (1975): 1495A.

Endersby, Jim. "Sympathetic Science." *Victorian Studies* 51.2 (2009): 299–320.

Fernando, Lloyd. "George Eliot, Feminism, and Dorothea Brooke." *Review of English Literature* IV (1963): 76–90.

Fleishman, Avrom. *George Eliot's Intellectual Life*. Cambridge, UK: Cambridge UP, 2010.

Franklin, Jeffrey. "The Victorian Discourse of Gambling: Speculations on Middlemarch and the Duke's Children." *English Literary History* 61 (1994): 899–921.

Friedberg, Joan. "Tragedy in George Eliot and Thomas Hardy." *DAI* 33 (1972): 1141A.

Furst, Lilian. "Struggling for Medical Reform in *Middlemarch*." *Nineteenth-Century Literature* 48 (1993): 341–46.

Goldsberry, Dennis. "George Eliot's Use of the Tragic Mode." *DAI* 34 (1973): 273A–74A.

Gosse, Edmund. "George Eliot." *London Mercury* (November 1919): 35–43.

Grabo, Carl. *The Technique of the Novel*. New York: Gordion, 1964.

Halstead, F. G. "George Eliot: Medical Digressions in *Middlemarch.*" *Bulletin of History of Medicine* XX (1946): 413–25.

Hardwick, Elizabeth. *Seduction and Betrayal: Women in Literature.* New York: Random House, 1974.

Hardy, Barbara. *George Eliot: A Critic's Biography.* London: Continuum, 2006.

_____. *The Novels of George Eliot.* 1959. London: Bloomsbury Academic, 2001.

_____. "The Image of the Opiate in George Eliot's Novels." *N&Q* IV (1957): 487–90.

Harris, Margaret, ed. *George Eliot in Context.* Cambridge, UK: Cambridge UP, 2013.

Hawes, Donald. "Articles on George Eliot in 2010." *George Eliot-George Henry Lewes Studies* 60–61 (2011): 147–155.

_____. "Articles on George Eliot in 2009: A Selective Survey." *George Eliot-George Henry Lewes Studies* 58–59 (2010): 111–117.

_____. "Articles on George Eliot in 2007: A Selective Survey." *George Eliot-George Henry Lewes Studies* 54–55 (2008): 148–154.

_____. "Articles on George Eliot in 2004: A Selective Survey." *George Eliot-George Henry Lewes Studies* 48–49 (2005): 110–118.

_____. "Articles on George Eliot in 2003: A Selective Survey." *George Eliot-George Henry Lewes Studies* 46–47 (2004): 91–96.

_____. "Articles on George Eliot in 2002: A Selective Survey." *George Eliot-George Henry Lewes Studies* 44–45 (2003): 97–105.

_____. "Articles on George Eliot in 2001: A Selective Survey." *George Eliot-George Henry Lewes Studies* 42–43 (2002): 100–108.

_____. "George Eliot and George Henry Lewes: Selected Articles, 2000." *George Eliot-George Henry Lewes Studies* 40–41 (2001): 68–75.

_____. "George Eliot and George Henry Lewes: Selected Articles, 1999." *George Eliot-George Henry Lewes Studies* 38–39 (2000): 85–89.

_____. "George Eliot and George Henry Lewes: Selected Articles, 1998." *George Eliot-George Henry Lewes Studies* 36–37 (1999): 85–90.

_____. "George Eliot and George Henry Lewes: Selected Articles, 1997." *George Eliot-George Henry Lewes Studies* 34–35 (1998): 83–88.

_____. "George Eliot and George Henry Lewes: Selected Articles, 1996." *George Eliot-George Henry Lewes Studies* 32–33 (1997): 74–78.

_____. "George Eliot and George Henry Lewes: Selected Articles, 1995." *George Eliot-George Henry Lewes Studies* 30–31 (1996): 63–70.

_____. "Articles on George Eliot in 1994." *George Eliot-George Henry Lewes Studies* 28–29 (1995): 74–79.

_____. "George Eliot Articles, 1993." *George Eliot-George Henry Lewes Studies* 26–27 (1994): 82–87.

_____. "Articles on George Eliot: 1992." *George Eliot-George Henry Lewes Studies* 22–23 (1993): 99–102.

_____. "George Eliot Studies in 1989." *The George Eliot-George Henry Lewes Newsletter* 16–17 (1990): 30–33.

Henley, W. E. *Views and Reviews.* London: Nutt, 1890.

Henry, Nancy. *The Life of George Eliot.* Oxford, UK: Wiley-Blackwell, 2012.

Higdon, David. "A Bibliography of George Eliot Criticism, 1971–1977." *Bulletin of Bibliography* 37.2 (1978): 90–103.

Himmelfarb, Gertrude. *The Jewish Odyssey of George Eliot.* New York: Encounter, 2009.

Hirsch, Pam. "Women and Jews in *Daniel Deronda.*" *George Eliot Review* 25 (1994): 45–50.

Homans, Margaret. "Dinah's Blush and Maggie's Arm: Class, Gender, and Sexuality in Eliot's Early Novels." *Victorian Studies* 36 (1993): 155–79.

Hornback, Bert. "The Moral Imagination of George Eliot." *Papers on Language and Literature* 8 (1972): 380–94.

Houston, Natalie. "George Eliot's Material History: Clothing and Realistic Narrative." *Studies in Literary Imagination* 29 (1996): 23–33.

Howe, Irving. "George Eliot and the Jews." *Partisan Review* 46.3 (1979): 359–75.

Hughes, Kathryn. *George Eliot: The Last Victorian.* London: Fourth Estate, 1998.

James, Henry. *"Scenes of Clerical Life."* *Atlantic Monthly* (May 1858): 890–92.

_____. "The Novels of George Eliot." *Atlantic Monthly* (Oct. 1866): 482.

Katz, Judith. "Rooms of Their Own." *DAI* 34 (1973): 1283A.

Kawa, Marie. "The Women of George Eliot's Novels." *English Studies* IV.5 (1922): 185–91; 217–23.

Kraft, Stephanie. "Women and Society in the Novels of George Eliot and Edith Wharton." 34 *DAI* (1973): 2632A.

Kreuger, Christine. "Literary Defenses and Medical Prosecutions." *Victorian Studies* 4 (1997): 271–94.

Lallier, Andrew. "'The Generations of Ants and Beavers': Classical Economics and Animals in *The Mill on the Floss.*" *George Eliot Review* 43 (2011): 47–55.

Lawrence, Margaret. "George Eliot, Who Sat Like the Recording Angel and Wrote." *The School of Femininity.* Port Washington, NY: Kennikat Press, 1936. 89–125.

Leavis, F. R. *The Great Tradition: George Eliot, Henry James, Joseph Conrad.* London: Chatto & Windus, 1948.

Lee, Robin. "Irony and Attitudes in George Eliot and D. H. Lawrence." *English Studies in Africa* 16 (1973): 15–21.

Levine, Caroline & Mark Turner. "Introduction: Gender, Genre, and George Eliot." *Women's Writing* 3.22 (1996): 95–6.

Levine, George. "Science and Victorian Literature." *Journal of Victorian Culture* 12 (2007): 86–96.

_____, ed. *The Cambridge Companion to George Eliot.* Cambridge, UK: Cambridge UP, 2001.

_____. *An Annotated Critical Biography of George Eliot.* New York: St Martin's Press, 1988.

Linehan, Katharine Bailey. "Mixed Poltics: The Critique of Imperialism in *Daniel Deronda.*" *Texas Studies in Literature and Language* 34 (1992): 323–46.

Livesay, Ruth. "Class." *George Eliot in Context.* Cambridge, UK: Cambridge UP, 2013: 95–103.

Long, Camilla. "Martin Amis and the Sex Wars." *The Times* (24 Jan. 2010): 4.

Lynes, Alice. "George Eliot and Music." *George Eliot Fellowship Review* 1 (1970): 2–3.

Maddox, Brenda. *George Eliot: Novelist, Lover, Wife.* London: Harper, 2009.

Mahawatte, Royce. *George Eliot and the Gothic Novel: Genres, Gender, and Feeling.* Cardiff, UK: U of Wales P, 2013.

Marshall, William H. "A Selective Bibliography of Writings about George Eliot to 1965." *Bulletin of Bibliography* 5.4 (1967): 88–94.

Martin, Robert. *The Triumph of Wit.* London: Oxford UP, 1975.

McCormack, Kathleen. *George Eliot and Intoxication.* New York: St Martin's Press, 2000.

Mead, Rebecca. *My Life in "Middlemarch."* New York: Crown, 2014.

_____. "*Middlemarch* and Me: What George Elliot Teaches Us." *The New Yorker* (14 & 21 Feb. 2011). 76–83.

Meyer, Susan. "Safely to Their Own Borders: Proto-Zionism, Feminism, and Nationalism in *Daniel Deronda.*" *English Literary History* 60 (1993): 733–58.

Meynell, Alice. "The English Women-Humorists." *North American Review* CLXXXI (December 1905): 859–62.

Milder, Gail. *Sublime Resignation: George Eliot and the Role of Women.* Cambridge, MA: Harvard UP, 1974.

Miller, J. Hillis. *The Form of Victorian Fiction.* London: U of Notre Dame P, 1968.

_____. "The Optic and the Semiotic in *Middlemarch.*" *The Worlds of Victorian Fiction.* Ed. Jerome Buckley Cambridge, MA: Harvard UP, 1975): 125–45.

Millet, Kate. *Sexual Politics.* New York: Doubleday, 1970.

Moody, Ellen. "Taking Sides." *Studies in the Novel* 36 (2004): 251–69.

Mugglestone, Lynda. "'Grammatical Fair Ones': Women, Men, and Attitudes to Language in the Novels of George Eliot." *The Review of English Studies* 46 (Feb. 1995): 11–25.

Nestor, Pauline. *George Eliot.* New York: Palgrave, 2002.

Newton, K. M. "George Eliot and Jacques Derrida: An Elective Affinity." *Textual Practice* 23 (2009): 1–26.

Nunokawa, Jeff. "The Miser's Two Bodies." *Victorian Studies* 36 (1993): 273–92.

Olcott, Charles. *George Eliot: Scenes and People in Her Novels.* New York: Thomas Crowell, 1910.

Pangallo, Karen, ed. *The Critical Response to George Eliot.* New York: Greenwood 1994.

Philipson, Rabbi David. "George Eliot's *Daniel Deronda.*" *The Jew in English Fiction.* Cincinnati: Robert Clarke Co, 1911. 126–60.

Postlethwaite, Diana. "The Novelist as a Woman of Science: George Eliot and Contemporary Psychology." *DAI* 37 (1975): 337–38A.

Raines, Melissa. "Awakening the 'mere pulsation of desire' in *Silas Marner.*" *George Eliot Review* 38 (2007): 24–31.

Ranjini, Philip. "Maggie, Tom, and Oedipus." *Victorian Newsletter* 82 (1993): 35–40.

Reinert, Linda. "Articles on George Eliot in 2011–2012: A Selective Survey." *George Eliot-George Henry Lewes Studies* 58–59 (2013): 90–98.

Repplier, Agnes. "Fiction in the Pulpit." *Atlantic Monthly* LXIV (Oct. 1889): 185–95.

Rignall, John. "George Eliot and the Furniture of the House of Fiction." *George Eliot Review* 27 (1996): 23–30.

Ruth, Katrina. "The Imaginary Vision in *Adam Bede.*" *George Eliot Review* 27 (1996): 49–55.

Sharp, Thomas. "The Country of George Eliot." *Literary Geography* (London 1907): 74–86.

Slaugh-Sanford, Kathleen. "The Other Woman: Lydia Glasher and the Disruption of English Racial Identity in George Eliot's *Daniel Deronda.*" *Studies in the Novel* 41 (2010): 407–17.

Spacks, Patricia. *The Female Imagination.* New York: Knopf, 1975.

Stephen, L. *George Eliot.* London: MacMillan, 1902.

Tomlinson, May. "The Humor of George Eliot." *Texas Review* V (April 1920): 243–48.

Tush, Susan R. *George Eliot and the Conventions of Popular Women's Fiction.* New York: Peter Lang, 1993.

Wade, Mabel. "George Eliot's Philosophy of Sin." *English Journal* XIV (Apr. 1925): 269–77.

Williams, Raymond. "The Knowable Community in George Eliot's Novel." *Novel* 2 (1969): 255–68.

Woolf, Virginia. "George Eliot." *The Times Literary Supplement* (20 Nov. 1919): 657–8.

Reaching the Limit: *Middlemarch*, George Eliot, and the "Crisis" of the "Old-Fashioned English Novel" in the 1870s

Jeffrey E. Jackson

> Every limit is a beginning as well as an ending.
> (George Eliot, *Middlemarch*)

In the history of the novel in English, *Middlemarch* still looms large. Written in the same generation as Charles Darwin's theories—and by a one-time intimate of evolutionary thinker Herbert Spencer—George Eliot's 1871–72 novel seems to mark the crown of creation, the fittest, most perfected example and telic endpoint of the species the development of which Ian Watt traced in *The Rise of the Novel* (1957)—what Daniel Defoe, Samuel Richardson, Henry Fielding, and (later) Jane Austen and Sir Walter Scott were striving toward. As a dense, multilayered reading experience—an absorbing, backward-glancing immersion in "Provincial Life"—its pleasures are what many of us look for in novels in general. As Hilda M. Hulme put it in passing, "[E]very novel would be *Middlemarch* if it could" (36). *Middlemarch*, I like to think, was the sort of thing D. H. Lawrence had in mind when he called the novel, as a genre, "the one bright book of life." It is a grandly capacious novel, its four volumes ranging across psychological introspection, historical sweep, an anthropologist's absorption in the minutiae and economies of rural life, and a philosopher's airy speculations about human nature—and all in narrative form. Indeed, *Middlemarch*'s all-encompassing ambitiousness may mark it as a successful essay at Casaubon's failed project: "The Key to All Mythologies." (In 1832, the epoch in which *Middlemarch* is set, the *Edinburgh Review* declares, "We have learnt … how greatly the sphere of the Novel may be extended, and how capable it is of becoming the vehicle almost of every species of popular knowledge": a declaration that anticipates George Eliot's masterwork [qtd. in Chittick 22].)

More to the point, *Middlemarch* remains an outlier within Victorian fiction: it is the Victorian novel for people who don't much like Victorian novels. In his seminal *The Great Tradition* (1948), F. R. Leavis saw in George Eliot's novel "the living representative of the great tradition" (13), an ushering-in of the modern fictional tradition of Joseph Conrad and Henry James. Leavis's study pushed back against the then-"present vogue of the Victorian age" among literary critics as it dismissed, en masse, "Trollope, Charlotte Yonge, Mrs. Gaskell, Wilkie Collins, Charles Reade, Charles and Henry Kingsley, [and] Marryat" (1); dispensed with Charles Dickens's "genius" as "that of a great entertainer" (19)—with the exception of *Hard Times* (1854), smuggled into the great tradition through the backdoor of an analytical postscript claiming it as the "only one of [Dickens's] books in which his distinctive creative genius is controlled throughout to a unifying and organizing significance" (19); and dealt with the Brontë sisters in a footnote, while maintaining the family produced only one unqualified genius, Emily, author of a single book. Indicatively, Leavis elevates George Eliot's novel "above the ruck of Gaskells and Trollopes and Merediths" (15). Some of such judgements are no doubt attributable to George Eliot herself: the agnostic free-thinker with the unorthodox private life seems more our peer than most of the other eminent Victorians, and as a learned, polylingual translator, editor, and critic, she was at a remove from the era's figures she famously appraised in "Silly Novels by Lady Novelists" (1856). A cursory glance at George Eliot's biographies yields such titles as Kathryn Hughes's *George Eliot: The Last Victorian* (1998). Indeed, Leavis traces "the proposition that 'George Eliot is the first modern novelist'" (a commonplace, for Leavis, in student essays and "examination papers") back to Lord David Cecil's *Early Victorian Novelists* (1934) (5). For Cecil, George Eliot's modernity meant she was "concerned, not to offer 'primarily an entertainment,' but to explore a significant theme—a theme significant in its bearing on the 'serious problems and preoccupations of modern life'" and did so by "break[ing] with 'those fundamental conventions both of form and matter within which the English novel up till then had been constructed'" (Leavis 5).

Within *Middlemarch*'s reception history, this verdict was most famously secured by Virginia Woolf's oft-quoted declaration that *Middlemarch* "is one of the few English novels written for grown-up people" ("George Eliot," 201). In *Middlemarch*, Woolf saw an important "first" in English fiction as well as an important precedent for the sort of work Woolf would champion in "Modern Fiction" (1919), with its conviction that "the proper stuff of fiction is a little other than custom would have us believe it" (106).

In this essay, I want to bring Woolf's assessment of *Middlemarch* into dialogue with the assessment of another formidable architect of "modern fiction." I am thinking here of Henry James's measured assertion that *Middlemarch* "sets a limit, we think, to the development of the old-fashioned English novel." If this is praise, it is curiously qualified praise—indeed, James elsewhere calls *Middlemarch* "a treasure-house of details, but it is an indifferent whole" (qtd. in Atkinson 69). The implication may be that, far from Woolf's important "first" in English fiction, *Middlemarch* is, instead, a bygone "last." I am reminded of an anecdote in which filmmaker and comic Mel Brooks was on a talk show and shown a clip of an upcoming film, to which Brooks replied, "Well, it's the sort of thing that has to be tried over and over again—until it's abandoned" (qtd. in Kael 465). George Eliot's novel stands as a tradition that must be abandoned. Her legion, fervent admirers can at least take solace in the thought that with *Middlemarch*, that "sort of thing" may have been, perhaps, perfected; authors following in George Eliot's stead would have to do something else, since she, as it were, got it right. After all, how does one follow up a "Key to All Mythologies"?

Indeed, to survey the status of British fiction in the 1870s, is to experience a sense of *traditions perfected* and *things abandoned*. I want to suggest that the 1870s mark a *crisis point* for what James called "the old-fashioned English novel." The first year of the decade saw the death of Charles Dickens (June 9, 1870), and indeed by the 1870s, a generation of canonical Victorian novelists had died, the Brontës by 1855, William Makepeace Thackeray in 1863, Elizabeth Gaskell in 1865. A sense persists, too, that the 1870s represented a last gasp for such sprawling multiplot novels as *Middlemarch* or

Anthony Trollope's capaciously titled *The Way We Live Now* of 1875, the sorts of works James affectionately dubbed "loose, baggy monsters": by the 1870s, a sense persists that we had reached the limit for the grand, Tolstoyan ambition of fitting the whole, wide world (and the way we live in it) between the covers of a book. I often tell my students that with *War and Peace* appearing right before 1870, *Anna Karenina* coming in 1878, and George Eliot's own *Daniel Deronda* published in 1876 (in addition to *Middlemarch* and Trollope's *The Way We Live Now*), it is tempting to think that by the 1870s, the novel had swollen, balloon-like, to the point of bursting. As Kelly J. Mays recounts, meanwhile, the 1870s in Britain began with the Education Act, which "vastly increased the size of the novel-reading public" and would undermine the hope that any one "Great Victorian Novel" could speak to everyone: "[T]he perceived increase in the size of the reading public was seen to entail an increase in diversity that rendered it impossible any longer to envision that public either as a culturally homogeneous group or as one that shared the same background and values as those seeking to reach it through the written word" (22).

More to the point, I want to place the liminal status of the novel in the 1870s in the context of a larger *crisis in representation* emerging in the same decade. The harbinger for this new mode was in April 1874, when the *Société Anonyme Coopérative des Artistes, Peintres, Sculpteurs, Graveurs*—a coalition of artists "frustrated with the continual exclusion of their works from the official Salons" (Dempsey 14)—held an exhibition of their art in the home of photographer Félix Nadar (14). Perhaps the most auspicious of their artworks exhibited at the so-called *Salon des Indépendants* (Watt 170) was Claude Monet's 1872 oil painting *Impression, Sunrise*, the name of which would become synonymous with a new artistic movement: impressionism. In Monet's depiction of a sunrise over a harbor, the foggy atmosphere of the maritime setting renders the scene's details as a fleeting, hazy impression of colors, shapes, and shadows. (John G. Peters notes that some would "identify sharp juxtapositions of colors, innovative use of light, and the use of 'empathetic and evocative brushwork' as [other] common techniques in impressionist painting") (15).

Impressionism proved controversial from the start—indeed, the very terms "impressionist" and "impressionists" as labels stem from critic Louis Leroy's dismissive review of the 1874 exhibition. As Ian Watt recounts,

> [O]ne of the most characteristic objections to Impressionist painting was that the artist's ostensive "subject" was obscured by the representation of the atmospheric conditions through which it was observed. Claude Monet, for instance, said of the critics who mocked him, "Poor blind idiots. They want to see everything clearly, even through the fog." For Monet, the fog in a painting … is not an accidental interference which stands between the public and a clear view of the artist's "real" subject. (170)

He goes on to note, "[T]he conditions under which the viewing is done are an essential part of what the … artist sees and therefore tries to convey" (Watt 170). More than a mere haze or distortion, impressionism sought to depict a limited and circumscribed viewpoint. As Watt notes, "In one way or another all the main Impressionists made it their aim to give a pictorial equivalent of the visual sensations of a particular individual at a particular time and place" (170). Similarly, E. H. Gombrich calls "the Impressionist movement a decisive role in the process of art's long transition from trying to portray what all men know to trying to portray what the individual actually sees" (qtd. in Watt 171).

Such ideas were given wider currency in literary and critical circles with the 1873 publication of Walter Pater's popular, scandalous *The Renaissance*. In a celebrated passage from that work's "Conclusion" (one worth quoting at length), Pater writes,

> At first sight experience seems to bury us under a flood of external objects, pressing upon us with a sharp and importunate reality, calling us out of ourselves in a thousand forms of action. But when reflexion begins to play upon those objects they are dissipated under its influence; the cohesive force seems suspended like some trick of

magic; each object is loosed into a group of *impressions*—colour, odour, texture—in the mind of the observer. And if we continue to dwell in thought on this world, not of objects in the solidity with which language invests them, but of *impressions*, unstable, flickering, inconsistent, which burn and are extinguished with our consciousness of them, it contracts still further: the whole scope of observation is dwarfed into the narrow chamber of the individual mind. Experience, *already reduced to a group of impressions*, is ringed round for each one of us by that thick wall of personality through which no real voice has ever pierced on its way to us, or from us to that which we can only conjecture to be without. (151, emphases added)

Through Pater, the notion of a tightly circumscribed point of view "became an important part of the cultural atmosphere" (Watt 172) of the 1870s.

"Literary" impressionists shared with their artistic forebears a conviction that the "epistemological process was an individual and not a universal phenomenon" (Peters 13). Peters is quick to note that literary impressionists "were a loosely knit group of artists who never produced a unifying artistic manifesto nor even a consistently similar product" (13). Nevertheless, they are united by the effort "to represent phenomena as they filter through a single human consciousness at a certain point in space and time" (Peters 34). We see such an objective in Joseph Conrad's 1899 novel *Heart of Darkness*. There is a distinctly impressionist quality to even the incidental imagery:

The sun set; the dusk fell on the stream and lights began to appear along the shore. The Chapman lighthouse, a three-legged thing erect on a mud-flat, shone strongly. Lights of ships moved in the fairway—a great stir of lights going up and going down. And farther west on the upper reaches the place of the monstrous town was still marked ominously on the sky, a brooding gloom in sunshine, a lurid glare under the stars. (Conrad, *Heart* 5)

Once in Africa, the character Marlow describes the scenery as a veritable impressionist painting:

[The African coastline] was almost featureless, as if still in the making, with an aspect of monotonous grimness. The edge of a colossal jungle, so dark-green as to be almost black, fringed with white surf, ran straight, like a ruled line, far, far away along a blue sea whose glitter was blurred by a creeping mist. The sun was fierce, the land seemed to glisten and drip with steam. Here and there grayish-whitish specks showed up clustered inside the white surf, with a flag flying above them perhaps. Settlements some centuries old, and still no bigger than pinheads on the untouched expanse of their background. (Conrad, *Heart* 13)

Later, he observes, "Nowhere did we stop long enough to get a particularized impression, but the general sense of vague and oppressive wonder grew upon me" (Conrad, *Heart* 14)—a sentiment he extends to the African workers pressed into slavery at the Belgian station: "They were not enemies, they were not criminals, they were nothing earthly now—nothing but black shadows of disease and starvation, lying confusedly in the green gloom" (17).

Conrad shared with Pater the sense that impressionism ultimately revealed the utter isolation—the limitations—of the thinking, viewing subject. Conrad's storytelling Marlow berates his listeners as follows:

"Do you see the story? Do you see anything? It seems to me that I am trying to tell you a dream—making a vain attempt, because no relation of a dream can convey the dream-sensation, that commingling of absurdity, surprise and bewilderment in a tremor of struggling revolt, that notion of being captured by the incredible which is of the very essence of dreams..."

He was silent for a while.

"...No, it is impossible to convey the life-sensation of any given epoch of one's existence—that which makes its truth, its meaning—its subtle and penetrating essence. It is impossible. We live as we dream—alone..." (Conrad, *Heart* 27)

As part of the 1870s' *Zeitgeist*, impressionism's mode of representation may very well have been bad news for *Middlemarch*. Pater's lonely, modern image of us all "ringed round by that thick wall of personality through which no real voice has ever pierced on its way to us" is a direct riposte to George Eliot's earnest conviction that "the greatest benefit we owe the artist"—literary or otherwise—"is the extension of our sympathies" (qtd. in Childers 411). *Middlemarch*'s formal qualities—its capacious length, its leisurely pace, its all-knowing omniscient narrator—can be seen as the corollary of its author's ethical-emotional commitment to ever-enlarging our sympathies. After impressionism, with its scrupulously maintained and delimited point of view, something like *Middlemarch*, with its "universal observer, divorced from space, time, and all other limiting factors" (Peters 21–22), could appear merely formless, justifying Henry James's good-natured description of traditional English novels as "great fluid puddings" (qtd. in Booth 28) or his judgment, above, of *Middlemarch* as "a treasure-house of details, but … an indifferent whole." Conrad famously said of fiction that "aspires, however humbly, to the condition of art" that it "should carry its justification in every line": "And in truth it must be, like painting, like music.… It must strenuously aspire to the plasticity of sculpture, to the colour of painting, and to the magic suggestiveness of music" ("Preface" xi–xiii). Such comments are tailor-made for the painstakingly formalist works that emerged out of the crisis in representation that, I suggest, arose in the 1870s. Moreover, such statements are at a far-remove from the sort of realistic, ethical mimesis George Eliot championed in her seminal essay "The Natural History of German Life" (1856), where a true and honest "picture of human life such as a great artist can give" is "a mode of amplifying experience and extending our contact with our fellow men beyond the bounds of our personal lot" (110). Was *Middlemarch*, then, moving toward quaintness and obsolescence even as it appeared, rather like one of Casaubon's heroic but doomed projects?

We may very well ask if such assessments are entirely fair, judging *Middlemarch* anachronistically, by the standards of later eras in fiction. I began this essay with a sense of *Middlemarch*'s perceived place in a developmental history of the novel, but Merritt Moseley, in her essay on *Middlemarch* entitled "A Fuller Sort of Companionship:

Defending Old-Fashioned Qualities," rightly attacks what she calls "a false teleology, according to which eighteenth- and nineteenth-century fiction is little more than well-intentioned floundering that stands in the same relation to William Faulkner, say, as the belief in the homunculus stands to modern embryology" (75–76). Adherents of this view, she notes, "are sometimes encouraged in this mistake by teachers who believe that the old-fashioned qualities of Eliot's fiction have been not just superseded but somehow proved wrong" (76). *Middlemarch*, for one, can be read as being as subversive of existing modes of literary representation as the fiction that succeeded visual impressionism. Even by the 1870s, the three-volume novel or "triple decker" was the paradigmatic format for new fiction.[1] With its neat, tripartite structure, the format privileged "well made" plots and overdetermined "happy endings": marriage, inheritance, the restoration of order. (Charlotte Brontë's *Jane Eyre* [1847], with Volume 3's triumphant "Reader, I married him" is perhaps the definitive example) (382). Released in eight half-volumes to comprise a four-volume whole, *Middlemarch* pushes against the boundaries of the triple decker in a manner recalling a famous declaration from *The Newcomes* (1853–55) by William Makepeace Thackeray, whose work George Eliot admired: "You gentlemen who write books … and stop at the third volume, know very well that the real story often begins afterwards" (Thackeray 286). Indeed, *Middlemarch*, it might be alleged *begins*, rather than *ends*, in marriage (i.e., Dorothea to Casaubon) and quickly moves on to the full disappointment that follows: the real story. As George Eliot writes in her "Finale," "Marriage which has been the bourne of so many narratives, is still a great beginning" (607–608).

Moreover, one can detect in *Middlemarch* intimations of an impressionist epistemology, as in chapter 27's celebrated "pier-glass" image:

Your pier-glass or extensive surface of polished steel made to be rubbed by a housemaid, will be minutely and multitudinously scratched in all directions; but place now against it a lighted candle as a centre of illumination, and lo! the scratches will seem to arrange themselves in a fine series of concentric circles round that little sun. It is demonstrable that the scratches are going everywhere impartially, and it is only your candle which produces the flattering illusion of a concentric arrangement, its light falling with an exclusive optical selection. (194–195).

Here, the limited, centralized perspective of the viewer's candle produces the fleeting, "flattering illusion of concentric arrangement," where all else is hazy chaos. The image is of a piece with Woolf's famous, impressionist dictum: "Life is not a series of gig lamps symmetrically arranged. Life is a luminous halo, a semi-transparent envelope surrounding us from the beginning of consciousness to the end" ("Modern Fiction" 106).

To return to James's verdict on *Middlemarch*, it is hard to shake off the sense that he was suggesting we abandon writing a certain kind of novel just as *a woman writer* had perfected it. Thus, Elaine Showalter has traced among male writers and critics in the years after impressionism an at-times "violent" dissent from "the matriarchal legacy of George Eliot" (76). Similarly, Sandra M. Gilbert and Susan Gubar have discussed how the literary modernism anticipated by James and Conrad was one "constructed" "as an integral part of a complex response to *female* precursors and contemporaries" (156). As many have pointed out, sexist language and binaries structure the postimpressionist and modernist disdain for the "loose and baggy" in fiction.[2]

Perhaps the final word on *Middlemarch* and limits should go to George Eliot herself, who had written (in the lines I provided as the epigraph to this essay), "Every limit is a beginning as well as an ending" (607). After all, its very title announces that *Middlemarch*'s focus will be neither beginning nor ending but *middle*: a site that can be either a fertile field of action or a *marshy* slough of despond. *Middlemarch* may ultimately be about making peace with being in the middle, even as Dorothea, of the "finely-touched spirit" (612), comes to see "[h]er full nature, like that river of which Cyrus broke the strength, spen[d] itself in channels which had no great name on the earth," content, perhaps, in knowing that "the growing good of the world is partly dependent on unhistoric acts" (613).

Jeanie Thomas has called George Eliot's novel "a guide to life in the 'middle distance,'" interpreting Woolf's praise of it as a novel for "grown-up people" as an acknowledgement of its capacity to teach acceptance of disappointment and mediocrity (162). Indeed, *the middle*—and its attendant senses of mediocrity; compromise; and, even, the *middle*brow—is the province of the novel as a genre, particularly the "old-fashioned English novel"—its lofty artistic or aesthetic aims threatened by a turn to middle-class realism, even as Saint Teresa (as we learn in *Middlemarch*'s "Preface") saw her epic aspirations turned back by "domestic reality" (3). For Woolf, the "old-fashioned" novel was the middle-of-the-road compromise for the nineteenth-century woman writers "excluded by their sex from certain kinds of experience" that could produce history, epic, philosophy, etc.: "Fiction was, as fiction still is, the easiest thing for a woman to write. Nor is it difficult to find the reason. A novel is the least concentrated form of art. A novel can be taken up or put down more easily than a play or a poem" ("Women and Fiction," 143). In its liminal status, somewhere between Woolf's "first" and James's "last," *Middlemarch* is a dream of better, more creative possibilities for women and fiction.

Notes

1. On the rise and dominance of the three-volume format, see, for example: Sutherland, J. A. *Victorian Novelists and Publishers*. Chicago: U of Chicago P, 1976.

2. See, for example: *The Gender of Modernism: A Critical Anthology*. Ed. Bonnie Kime Scott & Mary Lynn Broe. Bloomington: Indiana UP, 1990.

Works Cited

Atkinson, Juliette. "Critical Responses: To 1900." *George Eliot in Context*. Ed. Margaret Harris. Cambridge: Cambridge UP, 2013. 65–73.

Booth, Wayne C. *The Rhetoric of Fiction*. 1961. Chicago: U of Chicago P, 1968.

Brontë, Charlotte. *"Jane Eyre": An Authoritative Text, Contexts, Criticism.* Ed. Richard J. Dunn. 3rd ed. London & New York: W. W. Norton, 2001. Norton Critical Editions Ser.

Childers, Joseph W. "Victorian Theories of the Novel." *A Companion to the Victorian Novel.* Ed. Patrick Brantlinger & William B. Thesing. Malden, MA: Blackwell, 2002. 406–423. Blackwell Companions to Literature and Culture Ser.

Chittick, Kathryn. *Dickens in the 1830s.* Cambridge, UK: Cambridge UP, 1990.

Conrad, Joseph. *"Heart of Darkness": Authoritative Texts, Background and Contexts, Criticism.* Ed. Paul B. Armstrong. 4th ed. New York & London: W. W. Norton, 2006. Norton Critical Editions Ser.

_____. "Preface." *The Nigger of the "Narcissus."* 1897. New York: Doubleday, 1956. xi–xvi.

Dempsey, Amy. "Impressionism." *Styles, Schools, and Movements: The Essential Encyclopedic Guide to Modern Art.* London: Thames and Hudson, Ltd., 2002. 14–18. Web. 11 Jul. 2015.

Eliot, George. *Middlemarch.* 1871–72. Ed. Gordon S. Haight. Boston: Houghton Mifflin Co., 1956. Riverside Editions Ser.

_____. "The Natural History of German Life." 1856. *George Eliot: Selected Essays, Poems, and Other Writings.* Ed. A. S. Byatt & Nicholas Warren. London: Penguin Books, 1990. 107–139.

Leavis, F. R. *The Great Tradition: George Eliot, Henry James, Joseph Conrad.* 1948. New York: New York UP, 1967. Gotham Library Ser.

Hulme, Hilda M. "*Middlemarch* as Science Fiction: Notes on Language and Imagery." *Novel: A Forum on Fiction* 2.1 (Autumn 1968): 36–45.

Kael, Pauline. "The Actor and the Star." [Rev. of *The Gambler.*] *The New Yorker* (14 Oct. 1974): 174–181.

Mays, Kelly J. "The Publishing World." *A Companion to the Victorian Novel.* 11–30.

Moseley, Merritt. "A Fuller Sort of Companionship: Defending Old-Fashioned Qualities." *Approaches to Teaching Eliot's "Middlemarch."* Ed. Kathleen Blake. New York: Modern Language Association of America, 1990. 75–84. Approaches to Teaching World Literature Ser.

Pater, Walter. *The Renaissance.* 1873. Ed. Adam Phillips. Oxford & New York: Oxford UP, 1986. The World's Classics Ser.

Peters, John G. *Conrad and Impressionism*. Cambridge,UK: Cambridge UP, 2001.

Showalter, Elaine. *Sexual Anarchy: Gender and Culture at the Fin de Siècle*. New York: Viking Press, 1990.

Thackeray, William Makepeace. *The Newcomes: Memoirs of a Most Respectable Family*. 1853–55. Ed. Andrew Sanders. Oxford & New York: Oxford UP, 1995. World's Classics Ser.

Thomas, Jeanie. "A Novel 'Written for Grown-up People:' *Middlemarch* in the Undergraduate Classroom." *Approaches to Teaching Eliot's "Middlemarch."* 162–170.

Watt, Ian. *Conrad in the Nineteenth Century*. Berkeley & Los Angeles: U of California P, 1979.

Woolf, Virginia. "George Eliot." 1925. *Collected Essays*. Vol. 1. New York: Harcourt, Brace, & World, 1967. 1:196–204.

_____. "Modern Fiction." 1919. *Collected Essays*. Vol. 2. New York: Harcourt, Brace, & World, 1967. 103–110.

_____. "Women and Fiction." 1929. *Collected Essays*. Vol. 2. New York: Harcourt, Brace, & World, 1967. 141–148.

George Eliot, Margaret Fuller, and Mary Wollstonecraft_____

Magdalena Nerio

The younger generation's tendency to reject the predilections and perceived prejudices of the former—to spurn its greatest accomplishments in the search for something better—is well documented. We have only to look to Virginia Woolf for a classic and particularly strident repudiation of her feminist foremothers and literary predecessors among the Victorians. In a sharp critical dismissal of "Mrs. Gaskell," to take one memorably acerbic example, Woolf admitted with characteristically breezy understatement to "a kind of irritation with the methods of mid-Victorian novelists" (341). As the voice of the younger generation's spare, modernist aesthetic, Woolf disdains both Gaskell's narrative technique—citing its tendency towards "prettiness" over substance—and Gaskell's easy knack for storytelling rendered flat by a troubling lack of wit: "[w]hat we want to be there is the brain and the view of life; the autumnal woods, the history of the whale fishery, and the decline of stage coaching we omit entirely" (343). In Woolf's estimation, and in her efforts to theorize an aesthetically sound novel, Gaskell's talent for exposition is deemed tedious; superfluous; and, above all, illustrative of the narrative excesses and philosophical vacuity of the previous generation. Nearly fifty years earlier, in an anonymous 1856 *Westminster Review* article, "Silly Novels by Lady Novelists," Marian Evans mocked the formulaic and morally lax efforts of the bulk of women novelists writing at mid-century, classing them alongside the usual proliferation of "unwholesome commodities, from bad pickles to bad poetry" (Eliot, "Essays" 162). Where Woolf, her successor, calls for greater economy of style, Evans before her wanted the crop of amateur female novelists dominating the 1850s English literary marketplace to cease being uninspired amateurs and to hone instead their peculiarly feminine powers of "genuine observation, humour, and passion," all prerequisites for the morally serious fiction "George Eliot" would begin to make famous with the publication of *Adam Bede* in 1859 (Eliot, "Essays" 162). Needing to align her novels with ponderous philosophical and moral reflection meant that, at least early on in her novelist's career, Evans refused to compromise her literary vision, strictly adhering to a sobering realism that revealed ordinary people—clergymen, alcoholics, fallen women, and profligate aristocrats—at their worst, in their darkest and most desperate moments, their lack of religious faith and hypocrisy made visible by her keen powers of observation. With the rapid production first of *Scenes of Clerical Life* (1857) and *Adam Bede*, Evans bucked the popular trend for serialized fiction-light satirized in "Silly Novels," developing instead the unflinching realism so readily associated with George Eliot's mature style (Hughes 249–285). Responding to his reported early criticisms of "Janet's Repentance," she responded in a letter of June 11, 1857 to her always cautious publisher John Blackwood—a sympathetic reader almost too gentlemanly for his own good:

> When I remember what have been ... [my] successes in fiction even as republications from ... [*Blackwood's Edinburgh Magazine*] I can hardly believe that the public will regard my pictures as exceptionally coarse. But in any case there are too many prolific writers who devote themselves to the production of pleasing pictures, to the exclusion of all disagreeable truths for me to desire to add one to their number. (Eliot, "Letters" 174)

Once again signaling her distance from the implausible melodramas churned out in droves by the presumably leisured "Lady Novelists," Marian Evans lays claim to the rigors of her new vision for Victorian fiction—to the daring combination of scientific observation and moral complexity that quickly brought her lasting fame and an exalted place among the great nineteenth-century realists. Two important prototypes for the moral seriousness endorsed in George Eliot's mature novels are, perhaps surprisingly, the polemical writings of Mary Wollstonecraft and Margaret Fuller, two important and complex influences underemphasized in critical accounts portraying Eliot as a solidly mid-Victorian anti-feminist who, for all intents and purposes, eschewed the romantic political tendencies of her predecessors.[1] Marian Evans's less frequently discussed fascination with and attempt to weigh in—however cautiously—on the vexed literary legacy of Wollstonecraft and Fuller at midcentury deserves a prominent place among the stories we choose to tell about the novelist and reluctant commentator on the "Woman Question." As it so happened, and as this essay will demonstrate, Evans's eager and deliberate nod to Wollstonecraft and Fuller's philosophical nonfiction prose in her early journalism from the 1850s represents a decisive turning point in the construction of an authoritative critical voice to call her own.

What is the exact nature of Evans's relationship to her romantic predecessors Margaret Fuller and Mary Wollstonecraft? Is it as acrimonious as Woolf's view of the "mid-Victorian novelists," and why is this particular chapter of feminist literary history worth telling? Further, how should we begin to explain Marian Evans's fascination with the past achievements of celebrated literary women, as in evidence in her 1850s journalism? I argue that a reconsideration of Evans's 1850s journalism focuses attention on her dialogically-charged critical voice, cultivated in highly self-conscious imitation of her bolder romantic predecessors, as she worked to cultivate a literary persona captivating and authoritative enough to counter the pernicious influence of the "Lady Novelists" on the Victorian reading public, pointing to the moral dangers inherent in wildly improbable fictions. Moreover, Eliot's journalist's voice highlights as well her signature championing of women's innate moral benevolence, over and above the accommodation of their intellectual presence in the public sphere. Her early journalism thus warrants critical attention on its own terms, in light of its formal complexity, as illustrative of what Fionnuala Dillane calls the "fluency with which … [she] shapes her material to suit its context, and for the carefully constructed appeal of her public personae" (9). Finally, I contend that a reassessment of Eliot's analysis of her predecessors—and her analysis of historically situated women's roles and women's learning more broadly—provides a useful interpretive frame with which to reread attenuated female subjectivity as depicted in *Middlemarch*, with its famous redirecting of Dorothea Brooke's "noble" energies and public-spiritedness toward domestic duty as the wife of an MP (Eliot, *Middlemarch* 784).

Enamored of the "Lady Novelists," the Victorian reading public had, by the 1850s, long forgotten, or deliberately downplayed, the intellectual strain in English women's writing signaled retrospectively by the publication of Mary Wollstonecraft's *A Vindication of the Rights of Woman* (1792). Indeed, the Victorian periodical press's tendency to dismiss Wollstonecraft's philosophical arguments in defense of women's untapped intellectual capabilities as a coarse, indecorous quirk of intellectual history is a "vague prejudice" alluded to cautiously by Marian Evans in her 1855 *Leader* review of "Margaret Fuller and Mary Wollstonecraft." The publication history of *A Vindication of the Rights of Woman* (1792) alone suggests that it was not the instant and widely celebrated feminist classic revered by twentieth- and twenty-first-century readers. Originally produced in pamphlet form, the manifesto did not reach a wide readership from the outset nor was it reprinted for the benefit of a radical urban readership, as the works of Godwin, Paine, Byron, and Shelley had been from the 1820s through the 1840s. From the late-eighteenth through the nineteenth centuries *A Vindication* was easily subsumed by the dominant gender ideology of the period—its warnings against the subordination of women silenced by the heaps of conduct literature caricaturing female intellectuals as disheveled oddities (St. Clair 277–280).

Of course, the anti-Wollstonecraft tone of the romantic era conduct literature for women underscored by William St. Clair reminds us that Wollstonecraft's works had been swiftly marginalized and misconstrued by a reactionary British reading public—repudiating political radicalism, the excesses of the French Revolution and French culture more generally—in the early decades of the nineteenth century (Caine 53–54). Thus, Mrs. Sandford's 1830 *Woman in her Social and Domestic Character* features the unflattering portrait of the "disciple of Woolstonecraft [*sic*] ... [throwing] off her hat, and ... [calling] for a boot-jack; and ... [imagining] that by affecting the manners of the other sex, she should best assert her equality with them" (qtd. in St. Clair 279). Sandford's figure of the inelegant "female pedant" exploits the popular anti-radical backlash, reducing female intellectualism to an elaborate charade of dress-up and deception (qtd. in St. Clair 279).

Most damaging of all, the 1798 publication of Godwin's *Memoirs of the Author of a Vindication of the Rights of Woman* did little to rekindle public enthusiasm for Wollstonecraft's philosophy of women's rights, fixing critical attention instead on a prurient interest in Wollstonecraft's private calamities at the expense of her public writings. Revealing salacious details concerning her tempestuous affair with Gilbert Imlay and numerous failed suicide attempts, the *Memoirs* instantly ignited a maelstrom of public censure and professed outrage, thus ironically undermining Godwin's didactic intent to enshrine Wollstonecraft among "the illustrious dead" whose exemplary deeds and character "best deserve to be esteemed and loved" (43). A contemporary response to the *Memoirs* in the *New Annual Register for 1798* captures the emerging popular view of Wollstonecraft—not as the original mind given its due in Marian Evans's *Leader* review—as a bleak cautionary tale:

> ...[S]he was one who, ..., seems never to have had those good principles instilled into her mind, which would have enabled her to control and govern her passions; and who, under the influence of a warm constitution, and warm imagination, formed to herself notions of female delicacy, and the intercourse between the sexes, in direct variance with those generally adopted by the world, and incompatible, in the opinion of all old fashioned moralists, with the order and well-being of society. (Godwin 181–182)

Seen in this context, reading and reviewing Wollstonecraft admiringly, as Marian Evans did in the anonymous 1855 *Leader* article, is no insignificant or likely feat, and perhaps only possible under the guise of comfortable anonymity, before the fashioning— and eventual unmasking—of "George Eliot" would subject her to intense public scrutiny. Nevertheless, the *Leader* review elegantly courts and counters the mainstream vitriol directed at Wollstonecraft, while pointing to Evans's indirect attempt to align her early journalistic forays in literary criticism with the rationalism of her scandalous foremother, and the "vigorous and cultivated understanding" of the American romantic Margaret Fuller (Eliot, "Essays" 332). The cautious and contradictory notes sounded in Evans's journalism as a whole, and the conservative bent of her subsequent fiction notwithstanding, it is worth reconsidering the efforts of the Victorian writer to appropriate and temper the analytical strategies of her predecessors, without emulating Wollstonecraft's strident tone or Fuller's rhapsodic pronouncements and without appearing to endorse either's radical arguments in favor of sex equality.

As she published review after review anonymously in *The Westminster Review* and the *Leader* throughout the 1850s, Marian Evans endorsed certain historical models of flourishing female intellectual culture, as she began to sort out privately whether or not such a trajectory would even be possible for her. Margaret Fuller's tragically premature death by shipwreck in 1850 struck a nerve. As she remarked in a letter of March 27, 1852 to Mrs. Peter Taylor:

> It is a help to read such a life as Margaret Fuller's. How inexpressibly touching that passage from her journal—"I shall always reign through the intellect, but the life! the life! O my God! shall that never be sweet?" I am thankful, as if for myself, that it was sweet at last. (Eliot, "Letters" 92)

Why is Fuller's short life seen here as a cause for optimism and gratitude and not despair? In search of a critical and authoritative voice to drown out those of the anti-intellectual "Lady Novelists," Fuller's brilliant, though brief career suggests an immensely appealing critical voice for Evans to latch onto and refashion along more moderate lines, as she explored the state of the "Woman Question" at midcentury, from the strategic vantage point of the anonymous reviewer.

Anonymity also proved a productive position from which to advance controversial—somewhat tenuous—claims regarding the particular circumstances that enabled historically-situated women to thrive intellectually, as arbiters of taste and literary culture.

While living in Weimar in 1854 with the still-married George Henry Lewes, Evans wrote a piece for the *Westminster Review* purportedly reviewing a recent book on Madame de Sablé (Hughes 224). What she did instead is defend the gendering of literary production and the contributions of seventeenth-century French women above all in a remarkable essay titled "Woman in France: Madame de Sablé":

> Science has no sex: the mere knowing and reasoning faculties, if they act correctly, must go through the same process, and arrive at the same result. But in art and literature, which imply the action of the entire being, in which every fibre of nature is engaged, in which every peculiar modification of the individual makes itself felt, woman has something specific to contribute. (Eliot, "Essays" 8)

Evan's recent biographer, Kathryn Hughes, interprets the essay as evidence of an ambitious Evans resurfacing after a long hiatus in Germany, where she had been content to live for a short time in Lewes's celebrity shadow. Well-known in Continental Europe, he was regarded as a vulgar hack and carefree ladies' man by Evans's close friends and members of the Victorian literary establishment back home in England (Hughes 224). Most importantly, the essay reveals Evans's burgeoning interest in the work of her distinguished predecessors and may reflect an effort to tie the anomalous brilliance (in Evans's version of literary history) of Wollstonecraft and Fuller on the Anglo-American literary scene to the French influences that shaped their lively and prophetic output, both directly and indirectly. Fuller, as Gary Williams has shown, commented extensively on the influence of George Sand's novels on the formation of her own distinctive voice—a voice that captures, in Williams's words, "the perspective of both genders," thereby surpassing Sand's predominantly masculine commitment to intellectual rigor at the expense of feminine perspicacity (114).

How did Evans in turn negotiate these same tensions between masculine precision and refined feminine feeling? The Madame de Sablé essay furnishes a number of interesting clues to this literary riddle. Whether or not the essay in fact constitutes a meditation on her Anglo-American predecessors, and an attempt to work out the nature of her own nascent contribution to English literature in response to their legacy, can never be known for certain. What we do know is that anxiety as to the nature of her own vocation wrecked her health periodically during the spring of 1854 as she settled into exile on the Continent with Lewes. Explaining a sudden illness to Cara Bray in a letter of May 19, 1854, she writes: "My troubles are purely psychical—self-dissatisfaction and despair of achieving anything worth the doing" (Eliot, "Letters" 133). Thus, exploring the precise nature of the success of seventeenth-century French women in attaining literary celebrity would seem a logical place to start in the lifelong quest to define her gendered contribution to *belles lettres*, and, in so doing, cast her journalist's voice in dialogical relation to the coterie culture that produced and was, in turn, produced by women like Madame de Sablé, Madame de Sévigné, and Madame Roland, "great names, which ... soar like tall pines amidst a forest of less conspicuous, but not less fascinating, female writers" (Eliot, "Essays" 9). As Jenny Uglow maintains, the 1850s journalism positions Evans "sorting out precisely what it meant to be a woman in the mid-nineteenth century, and particularly what the implications were for a woman like herself, an intellectual, a professional writer, a potential novelist" (85–86).

The historical forces and ideology at work in Evans's own day, with their insistence on the virtue of gendered separate spheres, did not appear particularly auspicious for the flourishing of an authentic female literary culture. In the "Madame de Sablé" essay, Evans advances the far-fetched claim that the relatively "small brain and vivacious temperament" of French women help to explain their achievement in letters where "intense and rapid rather than comprehensive" powers of execution serve a writer better than a more philosophical and contemplative frame of mind, powers linked in the essay to "the larger brain and slower temperament of the English and the Germans" (Eliot, "Essays" 10). Evans's exhaustive survey of not only the physiological characteristics but also the peculiar socio-historical conditions that permitted Madame de Sévigné and Madame de Staël to become distinguished patrons of the arts are invoked in stark contrast to the rigid formality and exclusivity of the Victorian literary establishment, thus involving reader and critic in turn in an elaborate game of historical translation. The portrait of the coterie-salon world dominated by women reminds us that Evans the critic wielded her journalist's pen under a radically different set of conditions, in a less forgiving print culture dominated by male publishers, authors, and critics: Blackwood's world of the profit motive.

Though the "Madame de Sablé" essay should not be read as licensing extramarital liaisons of the Evans-Lewes variety—it upholds conventional morality in much the same way that George Eliot's mature novels do—it does highlight the advantages for intellectual women of a more permissive society, one not rigidly demarcated according to the Victorian ideology of gendered, separate spheres. Evans's momentous decision to court severe censure and gamble her future happiness on the oddball Lewes no doubt inspired the following passage from the "Madame de Sablé" essay:

> Heaven forbid that we should enter on a defence of French morals, most of all in relation to marriage! But it is undeniable, that unions formed in the maturity of thought and feeling, and grounded only on inherent fitness and mutual attraction, tended to bring women into more intelligent sympathy with men, and to heighten and complicate their share in the political drama. The quiescence and security of the conjugal relation, are doubtless favourable to the manifestation of the highest qualities by persons who have already attained a high standard of culture, but rarely foster a passion sufficient to rouse all the faculties to aid in winning or retaining its beloved object—to convert indolence into activity, indifference into ardent partisanship, dullness into perspicuity. (Eliot, "Essays" 11)

The mixed company of the literary salon involves women freely choosing intellectually stimulating male partners, Evans writes. Though stale and arranged domestic partnerships might not work against a fully-formed and mature female artist, conventional marriage is bound to stymie the female intellectual in search of a wider sphere of influence and inspiration, a woman like Evans before the appearance of "George Eliot." Evans's championing of the

French salon as a privileged moment in female intellectual history is invoked strategically, as if to say: "Look at the set of fruitful conditions I have NOT inherited! And what shall I do instead, under circumstances less conducive—if not downright hostile—to the cultivation of an authoritative feminine voice for English literature?"

The 1855 *Leader* review of "Margaret Fuller and Mary Wollstonecraft" is Evans's attempt to locate and endorse a compelling and intellectually rigorous feminine voice for English literature. The succinct format and analytical focus of the essay makes it more than a simple review, but rather a significant attempt to adapt the legacy of Fuller and Wollstonecraft for the Victorian reading public, while introducing a milder, though equally authoritative voice to the public: the voice of Evans, the morally-serious reader-critic. The essay begins by citing "the dearth of new books" as a fitting justification for a critical exploration of two carefully chosen older titles, Fuller's *Woman in the Nineteenth Century* (1845) and Wollstonecraft's *A Vindication of the Rights of Woman* (1792), effectively introducing a mini-canon in recent feminist philosophy (Eliot, "Essays" 331). Applauding the "strong understanding [that] is present in both," Evans makes a number of important distinctions between the two works:

> Margaret Fuller's mind was like some regions of her own American continent, where you are constantly stepping from sunny 'clearings' into the mysterious twilight of the tangled forest—she often passes in one breath from forcible reasoning to dreamy vagueness. ...her unusually varied culture gives her great command of illustration. Mary Wollstonecraft, ..., is nothing if not rational; she has no erudition, and her grave pages are lit up by no ray of fancy. In both writers we discern, under the brave bearing of a strong and truthful nature, the beating of a loving woman's heart, which teaches them not to undervalue the smallest offices of domestic kindness. (Eliot, "Essays" 333)

Here are the prophetic pronouncements of Fuller and the political railings of Wollstonecraft, translated and transmuted into domestic virtues for the benefit of Evans's Victorian readership. Making these women palatable for her readership entails softening their edges for an extended reflection on their words, over and above the various private disappointments that account in large measure for Wollstonecraft's vituperative, coarser tones, and, in the final analysis, help to explain Evans's retrospective assertion that Fuller's life could be "sweet" only as a result of her untimely death (Eliot, "Letters" 92). Attention to the words of her predecessors as they mingle with her own makes it clear that the feminine voice for a new era glimpsed here makes two (among many others) distinctive contributions to women's literary culture. First, Evans dispenses with Fuller's "dreamy vagueness" to make a series of critical judgments grounded in her extensive reading, thus supplying the "erudition" undermined by the inelegant stylistic tendencies of Fuller and Wollstonecraft. Second, the knowing reviewer suggests that the insights on women's social position, education, and a female literary tradition articulated in *Woman in the Nineteenth Century* and *A Vindication* should be resuscitated and brought to bear fruitfully on the present state of affairs, just as the reviewer begins to do here, in this short plea for greater "freedom and culture for women" (Eliot, "Essays" 337).

If the "Margaret Fuller and Mary Wollstonecraft" review, on the one hand, argues for an expanded role and a more authoritative presence for women in the cultural realm, then a novel like *Middlemarch*, on the other hand, appears to contradict this earlier public message, ending famously with the redirecting of Dorothea's philanthropic ambitions toward "not widely visible" domestic virtues (*Middlemarch* 785). Even if the journalism does not perfectly fit the contours of the novel, furnishing an easy key for decoding its multilayered moral valences, the 1850s essays pondering the historical shape of women's literary culture—and the frantic search for a dialogical-critical voice—resonate significantly with the fully-formed novelist's study of provincial life. Above all, *Middlemarch*'s commentary on gender shows us the extent to which Eliot had, by the 1870s, both internalized and parted ways definitively with the visionary feminist maxims of Wollstonecraft and Fuller. To this end, the novel alerts successive generations of readers to Evans's mature attitudes toward thwarted and distorted feminine personality types; to her implied contract with women readers as those most keenly interested in the limited, yet essential reach of an ordinary life; and to her implied assertion that women writers remain the chief purveyors of this kind of philosophical-domestic realism.

In a letter to Blackwood of July 24, 1871, Evans explains the ever-widening scope of *Middlemarch* as the only possible course of action under the circumstances:

> I don't see how I can leave anything out, because I hope there is nothing that will be seen to be irrelevant to my design, which is to show the gradual action of ordinary causes rather than exceptional, and to show this in some directions which have not been from time immemorial the beaten path—the Cremorne walks and shows of fiction. (Eliot, "Letters" 391)

Broadly, the novel's interest in the deformation of the feminine personality under the influence of determining historical forces and a particular sort of class-bound social conditioning takes as its focal point a less frequented garden walk: the private grievances and thwarted ambition of a set of provincial women, including Dorothea Brooke and her sister Celia, the future Lady Chettam, and the pretty Rosamund Vincy, who becomes the unhappily married "Mrs. Lydgate." The novelist's purported aim, to chart out new territory for literary realism, is enhanced immeasurably by her psychological treatment of a leprous feminine malaise, partly the result of an inadequate system of female education and partly owing to familial overindulgence, which amounts in the novel to a form of neglect, with infantilizing tendencies and dangerous social repercussions. The theme is not a new one, of course, though it may have seemed daring to Victorian readers, in much the same way that the Greek tragedy of Maggie Tulliver signaled a new victory for an emotionally-stirring brand of realism when *The Mill on the Floss* first appeared in serialized form in 1860. But the theme of women's lives tragically forestalled by the narrowness of their surroundings is taken straight from the pages of Wollstonecraft's bitter 1792 diatribe. By dramatizing the private fortunes and losses of the Brooke sisters and

Rosamund Vincy, "George Eliot" breathes imaginative life into the keynote of Wollstonecraft's *A Vindication*. Set against the backdrop of Wollstonecraft's complex legacy, *Middlemarch* explores the disastrous consequences of a superficial education, pettiness, and envy at the level of domestic tragedy (Rosamund Vincy and Dr. Lydgate) and also invites us to consider the unanticipated felicity of domestic retirement for a mature woman accustomed to suffering and experienced with loss (Dorothea Brooke by the end of the novel).

We also know that in 1871, while still immersed in the initial planning of "Miss Brooke," the novel that would become *Middlemarch*, the specter of Wollstonecraft's career began to preoccupy Evans, as her own failing health took a turn for the worse, curtailing her productivity and making her especially vulnerable to a series of dark moods. A letter of July 7, 1871, inquiring as to the health of the Rabbi Emanuel Deutsch, derives a hopeful lesson from one memorable incident in Wollstonecraft's life: her famous suicide attempt by drowning in the Thames after the final rupture with her American paramour Gilbert Imlay. Evans confides in the Rabbi Deutsch:

> Hopelessness has been to me, all through my life, but especially in the painful years of my youth, the chief source of wasted energy with all the consequent bitterness of regret. …it has happened to many to be glad they did not commit suicide, though they once ran for the final leap, or as Mary Wollstonecraft did, wetted their garments well in the rain hoping to sink the better when they plunged. She tells how it occurred to her as she was walking in this damp shroud, that she might live to be glad that she had not put an end to herself—and so it turned out. She lived to know some real joys, and death came in time to hinder the joys from being spoiled. (Eliot, "Letters" 389–390)

Interpreting Wollstonecraft's failed suicide attempt as a "parable," with serious implications for women writers and women readers, Evans resists the tendency among romantic and Victorian readers and critics to blacken Wollstonecraft's name (Eliot, "Letters" 389–390). This resolutely optimistic rereading of Wollstonecraft's career cloaks the second chapter in a short life in pointedly moral garb, layered in "real joys," a phrase readily suggestive of the fulfilling intellectual work, enduring friendships, and true intimacy that Evans cherished in her personal life, and conferred as rewards upon the more reflective and altruistic among her fictional characters.

That the construction of a cluster of oddly interdependent, stymied female characters in *Middlemarch*, and elsewhere in her fiction, constitutes Evans's attempt to recast the scandalous life of Mary Wollstonecraft and the lessons derived from her feminist philosophy in terms of the rhetoric of Victorian morality—as a parable for Victorian women writers and readers—suggests a fruitful interpretive frame for probing the novel's engagement with gender and women's literary history. The portrait of Rosamond Vincy is thus best seen as a revision on a Wollstonecraftian theme, a study in what it means for an intelligent and ambitious man (Dr. Lydgate) to marry a woman who is, in the main, "beautiful, innocent, and silly" (Wollstonecraft 95). The narrator of *Middlemarch* predicts Lydgate's demise at the hands of this elegant, attractive creature in terms that deliberately echo Wollstonecraft's earlier commentary on the social and domestic implications of women's education, "[f] or Rosamond never showed any unbecoming knowledge, and was always that combination of correct sentiments, music, dancing, drawing, elegant note-writing, private album for extracted verse, and perfect blond loveliness, which made the irresistible woman for the doomed man of that date" (Eliot, *Middlemarch* 252). The fact that lying comes easily to Rosamond is another disturbing facet of her character, underscored and ironically glossed over by the narrator as evidence of another one of her "elegant accomplishments, intended to please" (Eliot, *Middlemarch* 252).

The description of Rosamond Vincy as "a rare compound of beauty, cleverness, and amiability," and the suffering subsequently visited on her ambitious husband as he navigates the treacherous waters of the Victorian medical profession with little help or sympathy from his wife, is a domestic tragedy, which *A Vindication* predicts in no uncertain terms (Eliot, *Middlemarch* 252). Applying the logic of *A Vindication* to the Victorian novel, Rosamond Vincy, it becomes clear, exhibits the very same leprous frailty peculiar to all "civilized women… [systematically] weakened by false refinement," a moral blindness linked in *Middlemarch* to Lydgate's downfall (Wollstonecraft 65). Wollstonecraft's warnings about the complete warping of the feminine mind from birth as the result of routine exposure to sentimental culture of the most superficial variety acquires a haunting resonance when considered alongside Dr. Lydgate's unfortunate marriage:

> Novels, music, poetry, and gallantry all tend to make women the creatures of sensation, and their character is thus formed in the mold of folly during the time they are acquiring accomplishments, the only improvement they are excited, by their station in society, to acquire. This overstretched sensibility naturally relaxes the other powers of mind, and prevents intellect from attaining that sovereignty which it ought to attain to render a rational creature useful to others, and content with its own station: for the exercise of the understanding, …, is the only method pointed out by nature to calm the passions. (Wollstonecraft 66)

Throughout *A Vindication*, then, Wollstonecraft exposes and excoriates what amounts to little more than an educational ruse—a sham education in the "decorative" and pleasing arts—designed to overstimulate women's nerves at the expense of their intellects. Carefully repudiating Rousseau's controversial theories on women's education as put forth in *Émile* (1762), *A Vindication* constitutes a sustained and spirited assault on the fashionable eighteenth-century conceit that "beauty [above all] is woman's sceptre" (Wollstonecraft 48).

While *Middlemarch* continues Wollstonecraft's critique of an education in accomplishments that infantilizes and paralyzes women and who, as a consequence, become tyrants of the domestic sphere, in Margaret Fuller's *Woman in the Nineteenth Century* (1845), Evans must have found something akin to a spiritual meditation on the repercussions of a hastily-contrived marriage based on physical passion alone. *Middlemarch*, after all, employs the language of spiritual affliction to make Lydgate's suffering, following the unraveling of his marriage as a result of his mounting personal debts, pointedly analogous to the psychological torment to which the banker Bulstrode succumbs near the end of the novel, when Raffles threatens to expose his past nefarious connections. Thus, even once Lydgate's debts have been discharged fully, Dorothea is shocked by his gravely altered countenance, exhibiting by this point in the novel "not the change of emaciation, but that effect which even young faces will very soon show from the persistence of resentment and despondency" (Eliot, *Middlemarch* 716). Lydgate's tragic despondency—his premature aging and state of near-constant anxiety—reflects, in terms of the spiritual logic of Fuller's *Woman*, the failure of civilized "Man" (and "civilized Europe" more broadly) to regard marriage as a "meeting of souls" rather than a mere social contract "of convenience and utility" (41).

In *Woman*, Fuller reiterates Wollstonecraft's earlier vituperative pronouncements, while couching her predictions in an inclusive religious rhetoric that posits "Man" and "Woman" as twin souls whose union must, thus robustly reconsidered, involve "a religious recognition of equality," if there is to be any hope for the longevity and flourishing of the institution of marriage (42). Significantly, and for the purposes of the feminist genealogy considered briefly in this essay, it is Wollstonecraft and her biographer-husband, the philosopher William Godwin, who are singled out in a series of rhapsodic passages in *Woman* as memorably exemplifying Fuller's ideal of "a marriage of friendship" enlivened by "esteem" (Fuller 43). Indeed, with *Woman*, Fuller writes a prototype of feminist history, championing Wollstonecraft and her faithful husband in a glowing, undivided language that firmly places the radical couple on the right side of history, positioned here as the right kind of "outlaws"— outlaws brokering a daring "new interpretation of woman's rights" (44), while courting and even embracing the world's censure. And unlike Evans in the 1850s, moreover, Fuller cared not a fig for Victorian notions of propriety, reclaiming Godwin as the most unlikely—but all the more virtuous—of romantic heroes:

> This man [Godwin] had courage to love and honor this woman in the face of the world's sentence, and of all that was repulsive in her own

past history. He believed he saw of what soul she was, and that the impulses she had struggled to act out were noble, though the opinions to which they had led might not be thoroughly weighed. He loved her, and he defended her for the meaning and tendency of her inner life. (Fuller 44)

In cultivating the voice of the discerning female prophet, removed from the spiritual poverty that surrounds her, Fuller, in the earlier decades of the century, refined a humanistic rhetoric that would amply suit Evans's moral vision for the realist novel as it came magnificently to fruition by midcentury. In a letter of May 8, 1869 to Harriet Beecher Stowe that we would do well to link to Evans's theory of the novel, the nonbeliever Evans maintains that:

religion ... has to be modified ... [and made] more perfect than any yet prevalent, ... express[ing] less care for personal consolation, and a more deeply-awing sense of responsibility to man, springing from sympathy with that which of all things is most certainly known to us, the difficulty of the human lot. (Eliot, "Letters" 360)

The novel, in other words, and as commentators have long noted, is tasked in a secular age with disseminating a "practical religion" predicated on the knowledge of "what is good for mankind" and an innate aversion to "what is evil for mankind" (Eliot, "Letters" 361).

By the end of *Middlemarch*, it is Dorothea Brooke who exemplifies Wollstonecraft's ideal of "a rational creature useful to others, and content with ... [her] own station," her second and long-delayed marriage to the energetic Will Ladislaw roundly answering Wollstonecraft's call for a rationally-based partnership among equals to replace women's "train[ing] up to obedience" under the terms of conventional bourgeois marriage (Wollstonecraft 52). Dorothea's second marriage therefore corresponds—however imperfectly—to Fuller's notion of marriage as a "meeting of souls" predicated on the recognition of "Woman" as an equal endowed with "the rights of an immortal being" (Fuller 41). That Dorothea's quiet fate constitutes a breach with her romantic feminist predecessors, Wollstonecraft and Fuller, has less to do with their pervasive presence in her fiction than with Evans's own internal contradictions: her refusal to define in concrete and measurable terms a role for women in the public sphere that would adequately suit her expansive moral philosophy. And yet in the final passages of *Middlemarch*, as the narrator reflects at length on Dorothea's disappointingly ordinary trajectory, this meditation on the heroine's faults and misapprehensions makes her less of a paragon and—more appropriately for Evans, writing both for and against her foremothers—another version of Wollstonecraft and Fuller: ardent spirits radically determined by a habituation to loss and by the numerous personal tragedies that make up the fabric of a woman's life.

Notes

1. Margaret Anne Doody resists the tendency to construe the mature Eliot's fiction as the product of nineteenth-century influences alone, taking pains instead to document Eliot's indebtedness to the innovations of numerous popular and, by now somewhat obscure, eighteenth-century women novelists.

Works Cited

Caine, Barbara. *English Feminism 1780–1980*. Oxford, UK: Oxford UP, 1997.

Dillane, Fionnuala. *Before George Eliot: Marian Evans and the Periodical Press*. Cambridge, UK: Cambridge UP, 2013.

Doody, Margaret Anne. "George Eliot and the Eighteenth-Century Novel." *Nineteenth-Century Fiction* 35.3 (1980): 260–291.

Eliot, George. *Middlemarch*. Ed. David Carroll. Oxford, UK: Oxford UP, 1996.

_____. *Selected Essays, Poems and Other Writings*. Ed. A. S. Byatt & Nicholas Warren. London: Penguin, 1990.

_____. *Selections from George Eliot's Letters*. Ed. Gordon S. Haight. New Haven, CT & London: Yale UP, 1985.

Fuller, Margaret. *Woman in the Nineteenth Century*. Ed. Larry J. Reynolds. New York & London: Norton, 1998.

Godwin, William. *Memoirs of the Author of "A Vindication of the Rights of Woman."* Ed. Pamela Clemit & Gina Luria Walker. Toronto, Ontario: Broadview, 2001.

Hughes, Kathryn. *George Eliot: The Last Victorian.* London: Fourth Estate, 1998. St. Clair, William. *The Reading Nation in the Romantic Period.* Cambridge: Cambridge UP, 2004.

Uglow, Jenny. *George Eliot.* London: Virago Press, 1987.

Williams, Gary. "What Did Margaret Think of George?" *Toward A Female Genealogy of Transcendentalism.* Ed. Jana L. Argersinger & Phyllis Cole. Athens, GA & London: U of Georgia P, 2014. 105–127.

Wollstonecraft, Mary. *A Vindication of the Rights of Woman.* Ed. Deidre Shauna Lynch. New York & London: Norton, 2009.

Woolf, Virginia. "Mrs. Gaskell." *The Essays of Virginia Woolf.* Ed. Andrew McNeillie. Vol. 1. San Diego, New York, & London: Harcourt Brace Jovanovich, 1986. 340–344.

CRITICAL READINGS

Life, Death, and Identity in *The Lifted Veil*: George Eliot's Experiments with First-Person Fiction_____

Heidi L. Pennington

The Lifted Veil has frequently been considered George Eliot's oddest piece of published writing. Even her publisher, John Blackwood of *Blackwood's Edinburgh Magazine* (hereafter *Maga*), resisted appending her name to the tale when it was first published in July 1859. Although it was not common practice to name authors in *Maga*, Blackwood further claimed that this anonymity would prevent fatigue in readers (as Eliot had just made a splash with *Adam Bede* and was working on *The Mill on the Floss*)—he thought the name should be "kept fresh for the new novel" (qtd. in Haight 297). But letters between brothers John and William Blackwood suggest an additional reason for keeping Eliot's authorship anonymous. They seemed to fear that this curious little fiction might actually do damage to her reputation as a writer of sagely sympathetic literature (Haight 297).

Numerous critics have followed the lead set by the Blackwood brothers. *The Lifted Veil* is often read as an outlier in Eliot's oeuvre, not the least reason being its markedly unlikeable first-person narrator, Latimer. After all, Eliot's most popular novels feature third-person anonymous (if rhetorically distinctive) narrators. While so-called "omniscient" narration was indeed her dominant narrative mode, her catalog of experiments in first-person fiction includes not just *The Lifted Veil* (her only full-length first-person work), but also the first chapter of *The Mill on the Floss* and the frame of *Impressions of Theophrastus Such*. Just as Latimer does in *The Lifted Veil*, the first-person narrators in both *The Mill* and *Theophrastus Such* betray a marked hesitancy about the interpretive power that readers have over a writer's text. A preoccupation with these social acts of interpretation—and consequently with the narrator's ability to self-author—marks a unifying pattern among Eliot's works of first-person fiction.[1] Still, most scholars approach *The Lifted Veil* as an oddity, usually applying to it one (or a combination) of three interpretive lenses: (1) It is read as part of the gothic literary tradition, given its thematic focus on clairvoyance, the occult, and its plot similarities to Mary Shelley's *Frankenstein*[2]; (2) it is treated as early science fiction that explicitly engages with Victorian debates about various scientific fields and practices (including phrenology, mesmerism, blood transfusions, and revivification)[3]; and (or) (3) the story is read as a study in abnormal psychology and perniciously unreliable narration.[4]

But there's more to Latimer's account of psychic "foresight" and "insight" than any of the predominant interpretive models consider. *The Lifted Veil* is at once consonant with Eliot's broader commitment to exploring the complications of social understanding among individual humans (as in her more canonical novels, such as *The Mill on the Floss*) and also highly experimental in its form and in the relations it suggests might exist among those individuals. *The Lifted Veil* is an example of Victorian fictional autobiography, in which the main character is both protagonist of the story and the narrator of the discourse. The novella opens and closes with a highly unusual narrative event, in which this narrating protagonist actually tells the process of his death. In this way, *The Lifted Veil* is not only fictional autobiography, but a rather radical example of fictional *autothanatography*—or the narration of one's own death.

Scholarly discussions of autothanatography are most prominent in poststructuralist accounts of nonfictional texts of life-writing. Indeed, autothanatography has been discussed as both the dark sibling of autobiography and its necessary other. Drawing on the theory of Jacques Derrida, E. S. Burt suggests that autobiography must always attempt to construct the writing self by representing that which is different from the self—the other. In this way, "[s]uch writing would no longer exactly be autobiography, but rather *autothanatographical writing*: the writing of the death of the subject," because it is precisely the *absence* of the subject (or the self) that is revealed by its need for the other in order to exist (Burt 6). Most critics interpret autothanatography as a marginal form of nonfictional autobiography, in which the essential "absence" and "otherness" symbolized by death create, by contrast, an artistically unified identity for the writing self. Autothanatography thus challenges readers to rethink assumptions about the nature of self and other.

The present essay works from similar premises. I want to consider autothanatography in much more literal terms, however. Ironically, in order to find a literal example of autothanatography—the narration of a statement akin to "I am dead"—we must turn to a text of *fictional* autobiography. When taken in this sense, autothanatography is the act of narrating in writing one's own death: auto-thanato-graphy, or self-death-writing. With this stricter, less metaphorical definition, autothanatography begins to sound like an utter impossibility: how can one narrate, let alone transcribe, one's own death? After all, in order to tell all, one must be able to narrate a beginning, a middle, *and* an end. This obviously presents a problem. How can I tell and write anything after "I" am dead and cease to exist? By this account of autothanatography, it is unsurprising that we don't find many literal examples of this literary phenomenon in nonfictional autobiographies that claim to reference real events and real people.

Strictly speaking, then, autothanatography can only happen in fiction. For this reason, the narration of one's own death actually marks a text as explicitly fictional. A text of autothanatography forces readers to confront the blatant fictionality of the story, while at the same time operating through the conventions of a genre—autobiography and personal confession—that most often claims to be relating actual events and identities. As Ian Watt, author of *Rise of the Novel*, reminds us, traditional literary forms like the confession, the letter, and the diary seem to provide readers with "the most direct material evidence of the inner life of their writer" (191). The first-person fictional autobiography in the nineteenth century operates through similar literary conventions, and readers approach these texts (like *The Lifted Veil*) both with full knowledge of the tale's fictionality and with a simultaneous desire to discover some "inner life" of the overtly fictional writer (i.e., Latimer).

Eliot's experimental novella plays on precisely this tension between the actual and the imaginary, ultimately asking readers to question the (still-common) assumption that identity derives from some fixed, inward essence of self. *The Lifted Veil* proposes instead that the collaborative processes of fiction are how we come to create our sense of our Selves.

Because this is fictional autobiography as well as fictional autothanatography, Latimer-as-character and Latimer-as-narrator are distinct entities in this novella, each operating at a different level of the narrative. At the level of the telling, or the "discourse," Latimer is our narrator and selects what and how to tell the story of his life (just as in a traditional, nonfictional autobiography). At the level of the events within the fictional world, or the "story," Latimer is our protagonist who acts, thinks, and feels. In this way, all autobiographical texts feature a doubling of the narrating protagonist. Thinking of Latimer as both character and narrator immediately invites us to engage with questions of identity. Fictional autobiographies in particular often overtly foreground this doubling of identity between narrator and protagonist, and thus their very structure challenges the conception of personal identity as something unified, stable, and coherent. Instead of an essentialist conception of self,[5] fictional autobiographies instead tend to promote a vision of identity as something constructed through social narratives of self-making: these texts suggest that telling, revising, refusing, and accepting stories by and about ourselves and others creates our sense of "who we really are."

Latimer's Autothanatography: Narrative Structure, Sociability, and the Self

The Lifted Veil begins rather strangely for a text of (fictional) autobiography by predicting the narrating protagonist's death, rather than telling us anything specific about his life. "The time of my end approaches" the first line declares, sounding like a death-knell mourning the writer of the sentence before we even have a name for this first-person narrator (Eliot, *Lifted* 3). After suggesting his willingness, even his eagerness to quit the "wearisome burden of this earthly existence," the narrator declares "I foresee when I shall die, and everything that will happen in my last moments" (3). We soon come to learn how he is able to make such definite statements about his dire future: Latimer suffers from the curious capacity (what he calls his "abnormal sensibility") for "insight"—or the "obtrusion on [his] mind of the mental process going forward" in other people around him—and "foresight"—or the ability to "foresee" events, places, and people that he will encounter in the future (9, 11–14). It is precisely these dubious, "incessant" gifts that Latimer wishes to escape (3). After explicitly welcoming death, he narrates through foresight his "dying struggle," even transcribing the moments *after* he has entered "darkness."

In the following passage, note the transition from future tense ("it will happen") to present tense ("it happens") and the shift from concrete descriptors to more abstract language as Latimer's autothanatographical narration progresses:

> Just as I am watching a tongue of blue flame rising in the fire, and my lamp is burning low, the horrible contraction will begin at my chest. I shall only have time to reach the bell [to call the servants], and pull it violently, before the sense of suffocation will come. No one will answer my bell. [...] The sense of suffocation increases: my lamp goes out with a horrible stench: I make a great effort, and snatch at the bell again. I long for life, and there is no help. I thirsted for the unknown: the thirst is gone. O God, let me stay with the known, and be weary of it: I am content. Agony of pain and suffocation—and all the while the earth, the fields, the pebbly brook at the bottom of the rookery, the fresh scent after the rain, the light of the morning through my chamber-window, the warmth of the hearth after the frosty air— will darkness close over them forever?
>
> Darkness—darkness—no pain—nothing but darkness: but I am passing on and on through the darkness: my thought stays in the darkness, but always with a sense of moving onward.... (Eliot, Lifted 3)

The "movement" of this passage is from life to death, and beyond. In a novella like this one, which is preoccupied with epistemology and ways of knowing, it is worth specifying how we can validly claim that Latimer is really experiencing death in this passage. How do we know he actually dies as he predicts? On the one hand, as in any text of first-person fiction, achieving absolute knowledge of the "fictional facts" of the narrative world is impossible. On the other hand, however, Latimer's narration gives us some textual clues that he ceases to exist in the embodied way we associate with living. Namely, he moves from describing his specific, bodily sensations of "agony of pain and suffocation" to highly decontextualized declarations of "darkness—darkness—no pain—nothing but darkness." This transition from agony to painless nothingness seems to mark a transition from physical existence to a different form of being an "I." For this reason, I argue that this passage fulfills the requirements of a strict autothanatography: Latimer experiences death and—because of his "foresight"—is still able to write about the entire process, beginning, middle, and end.

The other remarkable feature of the above excerpt is that Latimer narrates his "foresight" of these posthumous moments in the present tense, *not* the future tense. This suggests that Latimer's knowledge of the future is more than mere knowledge received proleptically (or ahead of its chronological place in the linear unfolding of time). Instead, it suggests that he experiences his life in a nonlinear and multiple fashion. Latimer seems to live his life's events in the exact same way that readers experience narrative events: the narrative discourse (the text) can relate events to us in any sequence desired; the linear chronology of the events' occurrence in the story-world need not limit how and when those events are told to (and thus experienced by) the readers. Regardless of when the event actually takes place, Latimer has often already lived its full effects through his foresight. It is this narratively structured and markedly fictional quality Eliot gives to Latimer's lived experience that allows for the phenomenon of autothanatography in this text. Though he only tells us of his death once, Latimer also reports that he has been forced to live his demise "unnumbered times, when the scene of my dying struggle has opened upon me…" (Eliot, *Lifted* 43, ellipses original). This revelatory confirmation—that Latimer, unlike most mortals, has experienced death over and over again—comes in the final words of the novella. He tells us the present date, "the 20th of September 1850," which he predicts on the first page to be the day of his death. He recognizes the words as he writes them on the page, knowing that this is the moment in which his death throes begin. And his text stops.

The ellipses that both conclude and refuse to conclude the novella also ominously stand in for the *opening* scene of the book. After all, the novella features the end of Latimer's life and self at the very beginning of the discourse, on the very first page. Those ellipses, the final "marks" of Latimer's life, serve as a pointing arrow, directing us back to the beginning of the text to find out— or to remind ourselves of—what is happening in the portentous gap he leaves behind. In this way, *The Lifted Veil* is a circular text that accentuates the extent to which Latimer's life experience parallels the audience's *reading* experience: neither the reader nor Latimer encounter the story's events in their linear order; we are all experiencing Latimer's life in a highly narrative way. Helen Small argues that this framing of the narrative "[deprives] the reader, as Latimer himself has been deprived" by his unusual abilities "of the freedom not to know what will happen" (xiii). Small insists that Latimer's narration places us in an epistemological situation similar to his. And just as Latimer's forced knowledge of other people leads *not* to interpersonal understanding but rather to contempt and alienation, so too our excessive knowledge of Latimer makes him a difficult character to like.[6] In this way, Eliot's novella overtly questions the relationship between knowledge and sympathy. And the problems of knowledge don't stop there: knowing too much about Latimer and his death is not the only knowledge we are forced to receive. The very possibility of this act of autothanatography makes us highly aware of the fictionality of Latimer's tale, even as we read the text in an attempt to know "who he really is," per the genre conventions of the autobiography. This simultaneous desire for real knowledge and awareness of fictionality provokes in readers what Latimer elsewhere calls a "double consciousness."

The reader's feelings and experiences parallel Latimer's own significant doubleness. Returning to the above-quoted passage, we note the presence of two vastly different attitudes Latimer expresses towards his death: Latimer as writer welcomes it, but written Latimer (in this case, *future* Latimer) resists it and vehemently—heartbreakingly—wishes to live. The coexistence of Latimer's present weariness with life and the contradictory knowledge that he will long to go on living in the moment of his death is what he explains as "double consciousness" (Eliot, *Lifted* 21). While Latimer bemoans his double consciousness—that cognitive dissonance deriving from the confluence of conflicting present and future desires—his narrative instills in readers their own version of double consciousness. Readers seek the essence of Latimer's self while being fully aware of his self's nonexistence outside their own imaginations. Between its circular form and its evocation of a specific double consciousness, *The Lifted Veil* inscribes its own rereading, tempting readers back to the beginning of the fictional autobiography in order to complete our impression of Latimer's life and death and, perhaps, to encourage us to re-create him more sympathetically.

I linger on this point about the narrative structure and the double consciousness it creates because these two elements lead us to recognize Eliot's radical questioning of an essential identity.[7] In reconsidering who Latimer is, we are engaging in the same cognitive processes of gap-filling through which we create and experience identity in the real world. And Latimer's overt fictionality makes the imagined nature of his "self" easier for readers to perceive. Latimer needs us, the readers, in order to be. Without a readerly mind to interpret and to animate the flat, written symbols on the page, there is no Latimer. As Garrett Stewart points out, realist fiction operates through an active exchange between readers and the text.[8] *The Lifted Veil*, like other Victorian narratives, is "a tale for whose realistic manifestation as scene, if not for whose telling, you the obligated reader are always in part responsible—[the text's] coauthority and its conscript at once" (Stewart 4). Without our imaginations, which become narrative "coauthorities" along with the real-world author's words, to "manifest" his life, his death, and his identity, Latimer cannot exist. Even the original date of publication for *The*

Lifted Veil contributes to our sense of Latimer as a gap, an absence. Coming out in July 1859, nine years after the day Latimer gives for his own demise, the novella explicitly signals its fictional author's posthumous (that is, nonexistent) status, provoking a slippage between the imaginative and the actual. Latimer becomes a recalcitrant—even an unpleasant—riddle whose solution the reader must, in part, supply.

And yet, Latimer's very unlikability makes him *feel* real to us. He's no overly idealized hero; he's annoying, imperfect, difficult, and we must creatively grapple with his narration to understand him. Eliot's fictional autothanatography suggests through its very form that all real-feeling identities might derive from such collaborative acts of narrative imagination. Latimer further enacts this need of the self for the participation of the other by overtly petitioning the reader for her or his sympathy and understanding. Immediately following the curious commencement, he writes:

> I wish to use my last hours of ease and strength in telling the strange story of my experience. I have never fully unbosomed myself to any human being; I have never been encouraged to trust in the sympathy of my fellow-men. But we have all a chance of meeting with some pity, some tenderness, some charity, when we are dead: it is the living only who cannot be forgiven. (Eliot, *Lifted* 4)

Latimer's extreme alienation, brought about only in part because of his extraordinary abilities of insight and foresight, is underscored early in his tale by his failure to become a poet despite both his classically romantic "sensitive" nature and his "sensibility to Nature" (Eliot, *Lifted* 7). He accounts for his artistic failure by remarking that a poet must have faith in the mutual relationship of sympathy he cultivates with his readers; a poet "*believes* in the listening ear and answering soul" of his audience (7). Latimer, this explanation implies, credits neither. Why, then, does he rely on *us* to fulfill his lifelong yearning for reciprocal companionship and even to "revive" him in imagination after his death? Eliot's Latimer seeks sympathy from readers because they are his only hope for personal and narrative completion: "It is only the story of my life that will perhaps win a little more sympathy from strangers when I am dead, than I ever believed it would obtain from my friends while I was living" (4). Though this statement functions in a literal sense within his story-world, it also works metatextually: Latimer can only live when "the story of [his] life" is being read. Latimer's desire for interpersonal understanding both symbolizes and simultaneously evokes his need for interpersonal *creation*. After all, without us to read and to imagine Latimer into being, he won't just remain misunderstood, he won't exist at all.

These explicit petitions for sympathy operate in conjunction with the text's marked foregrounding of its fictional status. Through both Latimer's content and the novella's fictionally autobiographical (autothanatographical) form, we are reminded that Latimer is a gap for us to fill in and to animate with our narratively guided imaginings. Even Latimer's disastrous love story with Bertha Grant models how we "create" the identities of others: it is only Bertha's opacity to his power of "insight" that makes her so very appealing to him. She becomes, he declares, "my oasis of mystery in the dreary desert of knowledge" (Eliot, *Lifted* 18). Her inner self is, temporarily at least, a literal "blank" that he can imaginatively fill in with his own impressions and desires. Of course, when he finally gains insight into Bertha's inner self, he finds her inwardness to be "only a blank prosaic wall"—the rich "landscape" he had imagined there had been all his own creation (32). But this horrifying "blankness" of Bertha's interiority is only a slight variation on the earlier, productive kind of "blank" she presented for his imaginative filling-in. All that has changed, really, is that Latimer has confirmed for himself (and for us, his readers) that there was no profound self Bertha was hiding; she is no different from the other people he has been forced to "read." What devastates Latimer about this knowledge of Bertha's lack of a rich interiority is that it suggests all seemingly unified Selves are indeed fictional creations, constructed through imagined narratives of wholeness. What Latimer seems to fear is precisely what the structure of his own text implies and enacts: we are all creatively, if unconsciously, filling in the "blanks" of ourselves and others, imagining that we are discovering some pre-existing self while, in fact, we are busy creating those very Selves through the processes of fiction. All classical fictional autobiographies operate across this unstable, if complementary boundary of the real and the fictional. But Latimer's account of his death makes the haziness of that border all the more perceptible to readers by insisting on the confessional, personal nature of his tale as well as on the real-world impossibility of what he tells.

The readerly double consciousness that results from the novella's blurring of the line between actual and imaginary is foregrounded by Latimer himself. His early requests for our sympathy later become a more provocative kind of solicitation for our engagement with his life story and identity. Significantly, in his first description of double consciousness, he openly challenges the reader's capacity for what Rae Greiner calls "fellow feeling" (10). Upon describing his persistently passionate love for Bertha despite his knowledge of her future hatred for him, Latimer aims his rhetoric directly at the reader: "Are you unable to give me your sympathy—you who read this? Are you unable to imagine this double consciousness at work within me, flowing on like two parallel streams that never mingle their waters and blend into a common hue?" (Eliot, *Lifted* 21). Latimer taunts us for failing to understand his version of the same cognitive state (double consciousness) that we are experiencing in our encounter with his autothanatography. This overt antagonism of his readers further coexists with Latimer's ardent desire for the readers to understand and to share—and thus to validate—the experiences he describes. And while we may withhold our good feelings from Latimer, we nonetheless continue to read, and imaginatively to create, his life and self.

Eliot in the First-Person: The Realist Risks of the Fictional Self

Like all of Eliot's fictions, *The Lifted Veil* proves to be a realist text that is heartily invested in social modes of existence; and Latimer's *is* a markedly social form of being. We have seen how Latimer explicitly solicits (even as he seems to spurn) the active imaginative participation of the reader in his life story. The novella's narrative structure is itself "social," writing the reader into the discourse and relying on the reader to creatively animate the events and characters indicated by its words. Following Greiner's lead, if we take sympathy to be a mental process of imaginatively "going along with" another (15–16), then we understand how *The Lifted Veil* is invested in cultivating social connections among individuals. By choosing to "go along with" Latimer and read his story, we choose to share an "imagined mental companionship" with him. This choice becomes especially significant because we do not like him, pity him, or share any other merely "one-dimensional emotional identity" (Greiner 15) with him. The narrative processes in which we willingly engage when we select to read Latimer's story (and fictionally to animate his identity) are eminently social and invested in interpersonal understanding.

Eliot's creation of *The Lifted Veil* was underwritten by a similar desire to elicit the thoughtful consideration of others, if not their good feelings. Indeed, Eliot delayed her composition of *The Mill on the Floss*, often considered the most autobiographical of her novels, in order to compose this novella (Wilt 187). Her own troubles with identity and sympathy might explain the co-creation of these very different works. In 1857, Eliot first heard from an old friend that the "Warwickshire gossip" named a "Mr. Liggins" as the author of her *Scenes of Clerical Life*, and this "imposture" only increased in its vociferousness after the success of *Adam Bede* (Bodenheimer 130–131, 137). The "Liggins affair" dragged on in the press and in private gossip for nearly two years, eventually resulting in Eliot's forced coming out: Marian Evans Lewes had to identify herself with the pseudonym "George Eliot" in order to defend her authorial claim to her own literary works (Bodenheimer 130–134, 137–142). According to Rosemarie Bodenheimer, the protracted struggle against a reading public she was simultaneously wary of and dependent upon (thanks to her "hunger for approbation") resulted in Eliot's feeling "personally violated by the world *Adam Bede* had taken by storm" (132). *The Lifted Veil*, then, was composed at a time when Eliot was negotiating the risks of her own social identity as an author.

Eliot's struggle to be accepted, literally and figuratively, as "who she really was" by the reading public mirrors her personal history. For years, her brother Isaac refused all contact with her because of her relationship with George Henry Lewes. Bodenheimer suggests that one can read *The Lifted Veil* as dramatizing Eliot's struggles for interpersonal understanding and the right to a self-determined identity (134). Just as this novella's structure forces readers to experience a double consciousness that parallels Latimer's and encourages us to recognize the social nature of identity, so too does Latimer's recalcitrant narration and alienated life parallel (*in extremis*) Eliot's difficult experiences of public authorship and private relationships. Janice Carlisle even claims that Eliot wrote *The Lifted Veil* in the first-person as a way to exorcise the autobiographical instinct with which she began *The Mill on the Floss*. Carlisle declares, "that strange tale can be seen as an attempt to purge confessional impulses and to do so by treating through Latimer, an autobiographical narrator, material that is less strictly autobiographical than that treated in" *The Mill* (178). But is Latimer's motivation for writing his life story really that different from Eliot's as she navigates the narration of *The Mill on the Floss*? Latimer, much like Eliot, is never fully capable of trusting to the kindness of readers. In this way, the fears and desires expressed by the fictional autobiographer are markedly consonant with those of the actual author and her other first-person narrators, and they tellingly center on the risks (rather than the potential benefits) of the fictional and social nature of selfhood.

In all three of her first-person fictions, the discourses of Eliot's narrators evolve from self-consciously mediated and distanced (in *The Mill*); to resistant, yet needy (in *The Lifted Veil*); to crusty and utterly detached (in *Theophrastus Such*). Through each of these narrative strategies, which seem both self-expressive and dubious of external influence, we can detect a radical—and perhaps not altogether welcome—acknowledgement of the slippage of the boundaries between self and other, fiction and reality. While these first-person fictions challenge Eliot's commitment to narratorial "omniscience," they also participate in the profound ambivalence all of her novels evince about the prospect of productive social understanding among individuals. Eliot's texts of first-person fiction further interrogate the status of the individual by questioning whether we can reconcile our "double consciousness" into some unified whole. These texts question the value of others' creative influence on the self, even as they structurally and thematically recognize the individual's need for just such social input. Most strikingly, Eliot's experiments in first-person narration present us with the chance to rethink our own first-person existence. The fundamental nature of "I" as both a socially constructed fiction and an intimately personal lived reality remains an active paradox in Eliot's work. And that is radical indeed.

Notes

1. In the opening chapter of *The Mill on the Floss*, for example, the first-person narration both invites intimacy with and limits the reader's interpretive access to the fictional world of the novel through discursive layering. The apparent immediacy of the narrator's personal, present-tense discourse is revealed to be the illusion of memory, reverie, and narrative. Despite the seeming presence of the Tulliver family's mill, whose details the narrator lovingly lingers over, the refrain of "I remember" complicates the present-tense conjugations that describe the scene. The narrator's ultimate revelation that "I have been pressing my elbows on the arms of my chair and dreaming that I was standing on the bridge in front of Dorlcote Mill" reminds us further of the intensely mediated—if also intimately personal—nature of these opening passages in *The Mill* (11).

    The rhetorical estrangement of narrator and reader takes on new extremes in Eliot's final experiment with first-person fiction, *Impressions of Theophrastus Such*. For the fictional essayist Theophrastus, his audience must be imagined as a "far-off, hazy, multitudinous assemblage," as he "shudders" at the interpretive power of any "too corporeal auditor" (Eliot, *Impressions* "Looking Inward"). Miriam Bailin characterizes this intentional alienation of the narrator from the (imagined) readers as a "retreat" from "the compromise between individual perception and communal ways of being and knowing" (136).

2. Rosemarie Bodenheimer makes this observation (134), as do many others, including Judith Wilt. See also Royce Mahawatte's *George Eliot and the Gothic Novel: Genres, Gender, Feeling* (2013).

3. Beryl M. Gray's "Pseudoscience and George Eliot's *The Lifted Veil*" (1982) and Kate Flint's "Blood, Bodies, and *The Lifted Veil*" (1997) are influential studies of this kind. Flint's work also deals with the gothic overtones.

4. See Terry Eagleton's essay for an example of this kind of critical analysis framed by Marxist theory. Eagleton stresses the reader's inability—thanks to the fictionality of all "knowledge" in a fiction—to know for certain whether Latimer is "seeing the truth" or "inscribing himself in others" (60–61). See also Frederick Burwick's chapter for a synthesis of all three approaches that claims Eliot intended for readers to remain undecided about whether Latimer's visions are reality or hallucination (108).

5. In an essentialist account of human selfhood, each individual's true identity is defined by a permanent, inward essence. This essence of identity is unique to each person, and it pre-exists language and social context. An essential self cannot be changed, regardless of external conditions and individual experiences. This metaphysical model of identity builds on aspects of Platonic and Aristotelian philosophies.

6. Rachel Ablow notes Eliot's ambivalence about the connection between knowledge and sympathy, writing that for Latimer, "with understanding [comes] not pity, but revulsion" (285).

7. My claim that the form of *The Lifted Veil* resists the traditional ideal of innate selfhood intersects with a queer reading of the text and with queer theory's challenge to essentialist ideals of selfhood. Judith Butler in particular proposes that all identities are "performed" into being by the things we do, say, and desire. These "gestures" indeed "produce the effect of an internal core of substance, but produce this *on the surface of the body*, through the play of signifying absences that suggest, but never reveal, the organizing principle of identity as a cause" (2548, emphasis hers). In other words, this "stylized repetition of acts" (or embodied performances) in which humans engage creates the *illusion* of an essential self (Butler 2552). Both Butler's approach and my own seek to emphasize how identity is constructed and how it yet continues to seem innate.

8.   Wolfgang Iser proposes that all "acts of reading" consist of a "dynamic interaction *between* text and reader" (107, emphasis his), suggesting that all narratives—not just realist ones—operate in this way.

Works Cited

Ablow, Rachel. "Addressing the Reader: The Autobiographical Voice." *The Oxford History of the Novel in English*. Vol. 3. Ed. John Kucich & Jenny Bourne. Oxford, UK: Oxford UP, 2012.

Bailin, Miriam. *The Sickroom in Victorian Fiction: The Art of Being Ill*. Cambridge, UK: Cambridge UP, 1994 (2007).

Bodenheimer, Rosemarie. *The Real Life of Mary Ann Evans*. Ithaca, NY: Cornell UP, 1994.

Burwick, Frederick. "*The Lifted Veil*: George Eliot's Experiment with First-Person Narrative." *Women Constructing Men: Female Novelists and Their Male Characters, 1750–2000*. Ed. Sarah S. G. Frantz & Katherina Rennhak. Lanham, MD: Lexington Books, 2010.

Burt, E. S. *Regard for the Other: Autothanatography in Rousseau, DeQuincey, Baudelaire & Wilde*. New York: Fordham UP, 2009.

Butler, Judith. "Chapter 3: Subversive Bodily Acts." *Gender Trouble. The Norton Anthology of Theory and Criticism*. 2nd ed. Ed. Vincent B. Leitch. New York: Norton, 2011. 2542–2553.

Carlisle, Janice. "The Mirror in *The Mill on the Floss*: Towards a Reading of Autobiography as Discourse." *Studies in the Literary Imagination* 23.2 (1990): 177–1097.

Eagleton, Terry. "Power and Knowledge in *The Lifted Veil*." *Literature and History* 9 (1983): 52–61.

Eliot, George. *The Lifted Veil*. Ed. Helen Small. Oxford: Oxford UP, 1999.

_____. *Impressions of Theophrastus Such*. 2nd ed. London: William Blackwood & Sons, 1879. *Project Gutenberg*. Web. 30 Jun. 2015. <www.gutenberg.org/files/10762/10762-h/10762-h.htm>.

_____. *The Mill on the Floss*. Ed. A. S. Byatt. New York: Penguin Classics, 2003.

Greiner, Rae. *Sympathetic Realism in Nineteenth-Century British Fiction*. Baltimore, MD: Johns Hopkins UP, 2012.

Haight, Gordon. *George Eliot: A Biography*. Oxford: Oxford UP, 1968.

Iser, Wolfgang. *The Act of Reading: A Theory of Aesthetic Response*. Baltimore: Johns Hopkins UP, 1978.

Small, Helen. "Introduction." *The Lifted Veil*. Oxford: Oxford UP, 1999. ix–xxxviii.

Stewart, Garrett. *Dear Reader: The Conscripted Audience in Nineteenth-Century British Fiction*. Baltimore, MD: Johns Hopkins UP, 1996.

Watt, Ian. *The Rise of the Novel: Studies in Defoe, Richardson, and Fielding*. Oakland: U of California P, 2001.

Wilt, Judith. *Ghosts of the Gothic: Austen, Eliot, Lawrence*. Princeton: Princeton UP, 2013.

Mary Ann Evans, Marian Evans, George Eliot, and Journalism_____

Janis Chakars

What should we call her? She was Mary Ann Evans, Marian Evans (and further variations of this name), and, of course, George Eliot. Her tombstone carries both her famous pseudonym and the name Mary Ann Cross (Bodenheimer, "A Woman"). She was an editor, reviewer, essayist, novelist, and poet. We could call her a journalist, too. Her veteran advice, "examine your words well," is quoted in a textbook for students of journalism even today (Harcup). She began to render her name Marian Evans in 1850, just before her association with the *Westminster Review*, a time when she was most certainly a journalist. However, if we call her a journalist, then we also ought to explore a bit what that meant at the time. This essay seeks to synthesize scholarship on the writer and set such research on her life and work in the context of nineteenth-century journalism. Whereas able scholarship has shown what her journalism says about Eliot the novelist and, to a lesser extent, Evans the journalist, this essay seeks to use such research to explore what her experience indicates about nineteenth-century British journalism, and Marian Evans' place in the profession and print culture more broadly.

The Rise of Mass Media
Scholars have long argued that George Eliot's worldview as a novelist and a "progressive humanist," or exponent of "naturalism" and "realism," was forged during her time as Marian Evans, the journalist, but what was that world she was viewing and what was the place of the press in it (Fleishman 44–71; Hyde)? The nineteenth century was a time of tremendous social change, with shifts in technology and communication as far reaching in impact as our current digital age. Education spread and, with it, the reading public. While literacy rates are hard to pin down, economic diversification, school proliferation, and the desire for social mobility contributed to

the expansion of reading, especially in urban environments. Further, when people could not read, they were often read to by others (Williams 78–81). They had something to read because technological, economic, and policy changes—from postal services, to cylindrical printing presses, to excess manufacturing that necessitated advertising—made it easier to acquire the printed word. Trains ran and telegraph poles sprouted up alongside them, and eventually the telephone and radio—the wireless telegraph—reduced the time in which news travelled to just an instant. In England, taxes on the press were abolished. Some newspapers became as cheap as a penny. Industrialization caused overproduction. People then needed to be convinced to buy things they did not need or want in their own prior estimation. Publishers could exchange eye balls for advertising cash rather than rely on political patronage. Titles proliferated and circulations rose. Mass media were born (Starr; Wiener; Williams).

Media for the masses was a new thing, but it was not just behemoth titles like the *Daily Telegraph and Courier*, which reached a circulation of around 250,000 in the second half of the century, that marked the press landscape. The various *kinds* of titles expanded. Over 100 periodicals were launched during the 1820s in London, and the pace kept up across Britain in the nineteenth century (Dodd 159). For example, there were periodicals for women, by women, and for women's rights. Papers circulated for labor and even revolution. Religion kept an ever-strong presence (as did temperance and other religiously inspired subjects). Indeed, David Nord has argued that it was actually the missionaries of Bible and tract societies who invented the mass media, implementing the idea of putting the exact same words in ultimately everybody's hands (*Faith in Reading*). The idea of providing the exact same message to pretty much anyone and everyone was nearing reality. The possibility since then has sometimes terrified people (think the propaganda of Hitler or Stalin), but even then caused concern among the upper classes, who feared the masses, awakened to new ideas and organized through print communication, would not stay in their place.

Along with the profusion and diffusion of printed texts in the 1800s, social change raced with them. How people experienced community changed. This was an ever more expanding (think of the rise nationalism, for instance), but mediated—even imagined, as Benedict Anderson put it—experience. Anderson argued that the very idea of a nation was a social construction, enabled by the rise of what he called print capitalism (*Imagined Communities*). The press proved a marvelous tool of organization for myriad causes and, in the most generous assessment of its democratic potential, a marketplace of ideas. Certainly, it constituted a marketplace and with that was born a profession still recognizable today: journalism. Starting in London, people were paid to report news as a full-time occupation. So where do Mary Ann Evans, Marian Evans, or George Eliot fit in to this?

Evans, the journalist

There is an irony in discussing George Eliot as a journalist, for when she starting using that name and devoted herself to exclusively writing fiction, she actually renounced her journalism. She eventually cursed the periodical press and decried its artless, stunted intellectual culture and commercialism. Much of popular print made her cringe. "Avoid thee Satan!" she wrote to a friend. "Bad writing and good pay is not seductive to me" (Hadjiafxendi, "Profession"). Perhaps it is not surprising then that scholars have often seen her press work as a training ground or practice space, where Marian Evans studied to become George Eliot. "Without the journalism, the apprenticeship in the craft of writing … George Eliot the novelist might never have come into being," wrote Bel Mooney in 1983.

As an artist-perfectionist, Eliot and Evans before her could easily look back with a shudder at her past work. In 1839, she dismissed her first published item, a poem signed M.A.E. in the *Christian Observer* as "some doggerel lines" almost as soon as she wrote it (Ashton 29). She undoubtedly ended her life seeing herself as a novelist and poet striving for the highest levels of cultured creation.

While she may have been her own harshest critic regarding her participation in the popular press (and high and low culture swam together somewhat more closely at the start of her career than the end), she produced work that was then and ever after admired, and so scholars have also looked at her journalism as great work in itself as well as a practice space (Liddle 98–121). Interest in her journalism spiked quickly after her death. She had legions of fans and publishers could only turn to her essays to satisfy market demand. In a preface to an 1883 collection, Nathan Shepard claimed there was "much public curiosity" about her "contributions to periodical literature" and that a "leading newspaper" urged they be reprinted "because of the light they throw on the author's literary canons and predilections."[1] Serious consideration of her work as journalism, however, had to wait. Fionnuala Dillane, author of *Before George Eliot*, has done the most to liberate Marian Evans, the journalist, from being seen as simply an apprentice or whip-smart proto-novelist writing for the press. She sees her work for the press as critical to her entire literary oeuvre and has done more than any other to uncover Evans' experience as editor, essayist, reviewer, and fiction writer for periodicals.

George Eliot may not have looked back with admiration at her first writing career, but she *was* a journalist. That work constituted a significant part of her life, approximately a decade (essentially 1846–1857). In this essay, the focus is on what that meant, not to her next career as a novelist nor as a master craftsperson of periodical literature, but as a journalist, as a woman journalist in nineteenth-century Britain with a distinctive career in a wider milieu of journalism and print culture.

Now that we are calling Evans a journalist, let us explore some terms. Journalists report news, but news has always existed even without journalists. People have always shared reports of recent events, but news is what we most closely associate with journalism today. By the late seventeenth century, notice of such news was carried in newspapers. Such papers were produced by printers who also served as editors and often constituted the only paid writers. Such papers increased in popularity through the eighteenth century, although still mostly among the well-to-do. By the nineteenth century, there were paid staff reporters. The *Westminster Review* noted in 1829, that a morning newspaper typically employed between ten and fourteen staff reporters (King & Plunkett 342). They covered courts, crime, and by the 1850s even foreign wars. Evans was not one of these.

Journalism, however, is not just news reporting and newspapers. It was not then, and it is not now. In form, nineteenth-century journalism included daily papers, magazines, quarterly journals and variations in between. Today, the channels have proliferated even more. When we speak of journalism, we can speak of the entire nonfiction content of the press, exploring the current state of affairs, its antecedents and causes, its consequences, conflicts, and correlations. Such coverage seeks an understanding of reality, reader enjoyment, and edification be it through reporting, reviewing, analysis, illustration, or otherwise. The production of such material required, in Evans' time, not just writers, but editors, subeditors, copyeditors or "reading boys" (one would read copy aloud while a partner made corrections), compositors, printers, investors, advertisers, accountants, clerks, accountants, errand boys, postal workers, livery drivers, and salespeople: a whole industrial complex. Evans mainly worked in two wings of this complex, as an editor and as a contributing writer. Through her work, she came to know the ins and outs of the business-cum-profession well, ultimately leading to her rejection of it. We must also add that fiction and poetry were regular features of the popular press at this this time, and the matrix of print culture stretched far and wide in terms of publishing schedules, content, price, format, ideology, and audience.

Evans the journalist began as a contributing writer and first made her mark at the *Coventry Herald and Observer*, a paper acquired in 1846 by her friend Charles Bray, who used it to push the cause of liberalism (in opposition to the conservative *Coventry Standard*) and promptly invited Evans to contribute to it. In the end, she gave him six articles across the first two years of his proprietorship. She anonymously published commentary in the form of sketches of contemporary life under the heading "Poetry and Prose from the Notebook of an Eccentric." The eccentric was male and well-to-do, thus masking her own identity. The accounts were realistic description with biting commentary on social life, the authorship contained impersonation, and altogether the work illustrated the melding of genres possible in the nineteenth-century press, but might be most closely akin today to Op-Ed pieces. Her biographer, Rosemary Ashton, argued that one of them, "Notes on Snubbing," is particularly clever and suggestive of her later more acclaimed work (60–61). She also published reviews, something she would later be well known for and which constituted an important feature of the nineteenth-century press.[2]

This was a career-making gig for Evans. Through Bray, she did important networking and came to know John Chapman, who published her ground-breaking translation of David Strauss' *The Life of Jesus, Critically Examined*. This book, along with something of a break-out review of James Anthony Froude's *Nemesis of Faith*, which impressed both Froude and Chapman, precipitated her jump to the *Westminster Review*.

Evans wrote for numerous publications—*The Fortnightly Review, Fraser's Magazine, The Leader, Pall Mall Gazette*, and *Saturday Review* among others—however, her most consistent and significant journalistic contributions were with the *Westminster Review* (Ashton; Gray). This was a sophisticated publication with the highest pedigree, founded by none other than Jeremy Bentham in 1823. Bentham, of course, is still well known today and a standard figure in undergraduate philosophy, ethics, and other courses for his canonical contribution to intellectual history with his ideas about utilitarianism. Father and son, James and John Stuart Mill, prominent philosophers in league with Bentham, were also key contributors. Thus, people we now see as titans in the history of Western civilization and even at the time were highly prominent and influential put the *Westminster* on its pedestal. It was a place for the presentation and discussion of high ideas, paradigm-shifting thoughts, and progressive star power. The *Westminster*, for example, coined the term "Darwinism." It was a forum for elite radical thought, although the term 'radical' signified something perhaps more reserved than the word's contemporary associations. It was, in a word, highbrow.

In 1836, the journal merged with the *London Review* and, ten years later, the *Foreign Quarterly Review*, each time briefly sharing a title before reverting to just *Westminster Review* on the masthead. Between those mergers, William Hickson bought the paper from John Stuart Mill, but by 1851, he considered its sale and John Chapman offered to buy it. As he neared his acquisition, Chapman sought Evans' help. He wanted her to write for the *Westminster Review* and commissioned her to write a review of Robert William Mackay's *Progress of the Intellect* even before he officially owned the paper. He used her assistance to seal the sale, find supporters, and craft a persuasive prospectus. In May 1851, Chapman's purchase was complete, and he made Evans the unacknowledged editor. She kept this position until 1854, when she turned to original writing for the paper. She was involved with the *Review* from 1851 to 1857, when she began publishing fiction as George Eliot.

Evans at the *Westminster Review*

As an editor, she learned thoroughly the ins-and-outs of the journalism process. Her duties encompassed what are often today the multitude of tasks taken on by copyeditors, managing editors, and editors-in-chief. She solicited, assigned, and reviewed articles. She scrutinized their copy. She ensured cohesion of purpose and clear editorial policy. From the start, she was a forceful editor (Bodenheimer, *Real Life* 168–169). She not only criticized Chapman's punctuation but counselled him on his strategic communication (Gray 2000, 216). She guided him in his counsel of contributors. She chastised Chapman for "inexactness of expression," "mixed metaphors," and clichés. She even briefly convinced the less-than-talented writer Chapman to expel himself from the pages of his own journal.

Evans was a thoroughly confident and competent editor and acutely aware of market forces. The *Westminster Review* she inherited was prestigious and influential, but far smaller in readership than some of its rivals. Further, it had been dogged by mismanagement. Chapman promised no better on that front, and Evans set out to distinctively brand the publication, ensure its regular appearance, draw talented contributors, and increase its popularity.

As a quarterly, the pressure to fill the "news hole," so to speak, was not nearly as strong as it would have been at a daily, but that hole was still tremendous. Issues stacked hundreds of pages and competition was steep for the "men of high mental power" sought as contributors (prospectus qtd. in Dillane 37). Unlike popular newspapers, it did not have a wide staff to attend exclusively to the many tasks involved in putting out the publication. Subsequently, Evans involved herself in all phases of production and management.

Evans understood the need for financial backing from people like George Combe, whom she also convinced to write for free. She recognized the need for big-name writers, like James Martineau, whom she made sure was paid well. She also understood the limits of her ability to craft content in that she had to satisfy writers, readers, and finances. At the same time, she was bold in the stroke of her pen when it came to editing content and guiding authors.

The *Review* was a commodity for sale in a robust print market. Dillane argues that Evans' editorship appreciated this at all levels, not least of which included the design of the publication. For that she created a "blend of the magazine's approachability and the quarterly's authority." She guided readers with a clear system of table of contents, index, and articles tagged with headlines throughout for maximum readability. The resulting innovative layout earned the publication praise in daily press reviews. Moreover, the labeling of content by subject or title distinguished the article—as opposed to notes or reports—as a genre of writing of its own merit.

Lastly, her redesign of the book review section earned emulation and significantly pushed forward a mainstay of publishing. Rather than summaries and quick commentary of recent books, she encouraged long-form (twenty pages or more) literary criticism based on national literatures. In the process, she facilitated the quarterly's work in promoting European cultural nationalism through literary essays that encompassed far more than the assessment of a title. (Dillane 48). The measure of her talent as editor in the profession of journalism is attested to by the fact that she juggled so many tasks and indeed grew the publication in sales and influence. She was the consummate professional across all aspects of the trade, mastered its jargon as well as its professional politics and personalities, and it brought her much distress. By 1854, she was at unpaid wit's end, but the *Westminster Review* was on sure footing.

At this point, she donned a new journalistic hat and joined the ranks of her contributors as a paid writer. Across her whole journalism writing career, she penned around eighty articles, achieving the height of her production in 1855 and 1856. Her work was primarily as a review essayist and reviewer, a significant specialty at the time (Wilson). Her extended reviews encompassed social commentary far beyond short summaries with some kind of thumbs up or down, which was as common then as it is now. She did not invent such essays, but she had helped cultivate the genre as editor of the *Westmimster* and knew well its conventions. At the peak of her journalism career, she wrote for various places, but most consistently for Chapman's elite quarterly and George Henry Lewes' *Leader*. Whereas scholars have most frequently looked at her essays with a view toward understanding her work as great literature, Dillane usefully places such work in the constellation of journalism practice at the time.

Evans wrote brief articles and mammoth think-piece-type essays and varieties of reviews in between, all comprising standard features of the journalism of her day. Such work attests also to the pervasive nature of print in British culture at the time and the place of literature and social commentary embedded within that print culture. Her press contributions also testify to the economic and commercial sides of the periodical ecosystem and a glimpse at its business history as well as its literary conventions. Dillane notes Evans' keen understanding of the "trinity of genre-market-audience" (83). Commonly, journalists writing for more than one publication would often repurpose content and effectively double their money. Evans was no different and adapted work for *Westminster*'s elite audience and the *Leader's* more general public. She was supremely aware of journalistic conventions, why they existed, and how they varied.

The print culture of the nineteenth century not only brought new styles of composition to prominence, but also it made stars of writers like never before. It fostered the spread of ideas. It sped the sale of goods, and created new markets and professions. It also changed the nature of community, made it more a mediated experience, and shifted who could say what to whom as well as the circumstances of such intercourse and discourse. Evans was aware of these changes. Kyriaki Hadjiafxendi, elucidates some of this understanding through her explication of Evans' 1854 essay for the *Westminster Review*, "Woman in France: Madam de Sablé." In the essay, Evans describe the seventeenth-century salon of de Sablé as a convivial place in which ideas were shared on relatively equal footing among the assembled. Each in attendance contributed to the discourse of the day, providing her or his own influence and input as part of a dignified and cultured exchange. Madame de Sablé did not need to be an author to play a role in this social conversation. Evans addressed the trade-offs of the shift from the rarified salon days to her contemporary print-soaked age. She looked askance at the ever-widening public, which found its discourse in print rather than sociable creativity. The press set the agenda for conversation, not the other way around, and if one wanted a voice, it had to be in print, having first passed through the editorial gate. Further, living with the press meant living through the press, and social discourse was reduced to sharing texts like so many links posted to social media today: "Journalism tends to divert information from the channel of conversation into the channel of the Press," Evans wrote (qtd. in Pinney 80).

Evans' Experience as a Window on Nineteenth-Century British Journalism

Marian Evans joined the ranks of nineteenth-century journalists, in part, for the same reason as many others: she needed the money. Literary ambitions aside, this was a serious concern. Her father had died in 1849 and left her little (Karl 77). Particularly for women, the press offered more remunerative opportunities, provided greater personal independence, and demanded less physical expenditure than other options (Onslow 2000). Journalism was primarily a man's world (and word), and thus not easy for women, but as bylines were not yet standard, it was possible to hide the presumed inferiority of one's sex in mainstream media. There was also a burgeoning press explicitly by and for women attending to the political and social concerns of women (Tusan). Evans, therefore, was not a pioneer, except save perhaps in her editorship of such a prestigious quarterly as the *Westminster Review*. There were plenty of women working in the press, even if far fewer than men. As a woman journalist, was she not terribly radical in terms of gender politics. She did not publicly support suffrage, for instance. Although she wrote for "radical" (that is, liberal) publications and contributed to the elite *Westminster Review*, she stayed within recognized boundaries of debate ensconced in the conventional masculine world of the British press. Her presence in that world, as a woman, however, indicates one facet of that world underscored by her anonymity. As opposed to de Sablé's salon, this world was characterized primarily by the industrialized control of discourse by men. Evans appreciated the uphill climb women faced in this world and urged the necessity of woman to show exemplary skill in journalism (Easley 117–152). "Women have not to prove that they can be emotional, and rhapsodic, and spiritualistic; everyone believes that already. They have to prove they are capable of accurate thought, severe study, and continuous self-command," she said (qtd. in Onslow 75).

As a reviewer-essayist, Evans also found herself in company with many other women, who as a practical matter were attracted to this work because it could be done at home. As previously noted, this was a key corner of the journalism world, but Evans was "nauseated" by many of her contemporaries with their hack writing (Onslow 151, 206). As a woman editor, Evans was not only rare, but also followed a route contrary to the trends of the day, whereby fame as a novelist was more likely to lead to such a position than the other way around (Onlsow 106). Editorships were highly prestigious and generally well-rewarded. Here again, Evans bucked the wider trend by receiving no salary or recognition.

Evans' experience reveals much about the lived experience of journalism at the time. Her presence and dependence on men like Chapman highlight its male dominance, but she also participated in *all* of its mechanics. As noted above, her work extended from composition to copyediting. She processed manuscripts and page proofs. She assigned articles and edited them. She tackled layout and design. She worked with printers, authors, and financial backers. Through her work at *Westminster*, we get a view of the production of the press, industrial and intellectual, but in examining the principal places for which she wrote, we can also view some of its taxonomy.

Evans started her career in journalism with the *Coventry Herald and Observer*, a provincial weekly broadsheet newspaper, whose self-identification as liberal only serves to highlight the ideological stamp and political affiliation that was typical of papers at the time. Such newspapers existed in a world of competition over ideas. It was four pages. It carried advertisements and local news as well as a small literary section to which Evans contributed. It struggled to fill its columns and exhibited a mish-mash of fare courting a popular audience. The ads and the popular appeal underpinned the business imperatives and market competition of the time, and it made Evans sick of "cheap literature" (Dillane 79).

The *Westminster Review* was at the other end of the spectrum. It looked more like a hefty academic journal than a newspaper. It was published in London, came out only four times a year, and was aimed at an elite audience. It represented the higher journalism of the metropolis. This "higher" journalism had been the province of the well-heeled and highly educated and still was to a large degree. Its producers and consumers were at the upper rungs of society. However, Evans, with her modest background, stands as an example of the diversification of people writing for the press and the swelling influence of the middle and even working classes (Hampton; Williams). Indeed, word craft and publication were slipping from the strict control of the wealthy and powerful as the world of print and mass media exploded. Its intermittent financial difficulties and quest for financial backers rather than advertising set it apart from other journalism. It was not produced to be popular. It was meant to be cultured and refined, progressive, but not for all.

The *Leader* sat somewhere in between the *Westminster* and *Coventry Herald*. It was a twenty-four-page weekly. It was more ambitious than the latter, but more popular in tone than the former. Originally socialist in its political bent, it soon moved toward centrist politics. The run toward the center is the hallmark of mass media. Naturally, the quest for the greatest audience commands a publication cause offense to the fewest people possible. Widely-accepted positions generate the most readers. The *Leader*, however, was not on par with the largest papers of the day. By 1854, British newspaper circulation hit 122,000,000 (Lake 213). *The Daily Telegraph*, started in 1855, when Evans was in the thick of her journalism career, billed itself "The Largest, Best and Cheapest Newspaper in the World," and it was, for a time, the largest and cheapest. Indeed, the experience of Marian Evans hides a key trend of the era: the rise of hugely popular papers like *The Daily Telegraph* and *The Morning Post* to say nothing of quality papers like *The Times*. However, her exceptional experience reveals as much about the journalism of her age as her common. Her presence as a woman with name erased shows both the male dominance of the trade and its slow erosion. Her work on different kinds of publications reminds us of the immense variety in journalism of the time. At the same time, diverse publications faced similar pressures. They existed in competition with each other and adapted to standard conventions, while occasionally modifying them enough to carve a niche and stand out in a crowded marketplace. They faced similar challenges in terms of production and the acquisition of content. They could employ bombastic rhetoric and knew they needed to arrest and guide reader attention like never before. Even the *Westminster*, as elitist as it was, endeavored to create a space for wide ranging ideas, something like "balance" in today's journalistic parlance. As with every paper, the ones at which Evans worked made claims of fidelity to facts. Further, the realistic tenor of her work was an expression of intellectual impulses that grew into precepts of objectivity and expressed faith in rational discernment based on dispassionate observation, particularly at places like Reuters and the BBC (Hampton). Doug Underwood addressed how such trends in both fact and fiction mixed together at the time, and these grew into hallmarks of journalists in their own grandest self-perception as the scaffolding of democracy. Evans was not buying it. In a rare late-career essay signed George Eliot for the *Fortnightly Review*, a publication founded to furnish "responsible journalism," she questioned our capacity for reason and inasmuch notions of rationalism that underpinned emerging notions of the press as the fourth estate at the time (Pinney 397). While that article was a book review and not a treatise on journalism, in general, she came to see the debasement of thought and expression in the ever-expanding press. She concluded, "Art is the nearest thing to life," and turned to fiction. Finding fantastic celebrity as George Eliot, she then became an object of journalism rather than its producer (Bodenheimer, *Real Life* 119–160; Mangum).

Notes

1. Her authorized collection, *Essays and Leaves from a Note-Book* was published in 1884.

2. Frederick Karl called her an assistant to Bray as well (77).

Works Cited

Anderson, Benedict. *Imagined Communities*. London: Verso, 1983.

Ashton, Rosemary. *George Eliot: A Life*. New York: Penguin, 1996.

Bodenheimer, Rosemarie. *The Real Life of Mary Ann Evans: George Eliot, Her Letters and Fiction*. Ithaca, NY: Cornell UP, 1994.

_____. "A Woman of Many Names." *The Cambridge Companion to George Eliot*. Ed. George Levine. Cambridge, UK: Cambridge UP, 2001. 20–37.

Dillane, Fionnuala. *Before George Eliot: Marian Evans and the Periodical Press*. Cambridge, UK: Cambridge UP, 2013.

Dodd, Valerie A. *George Eliot: An Intellectual Life*. London: Macmillan, 1990.

Easley, Alexis. *First-Person Anonymous: Women Writers and Victorian Print Media, 1830–70*. Aldershot, UK: Ashgate, 2004.

Fleishman, Avrom. *George Eliot's Intellectual Life*. Cambridge, UK: Cambridge UP, 2010.

Gray, Beryl. "George Eliot and the 'Westminster Review.'" *Victorian Periodicals Review*. 33.3 (Fall 2000): 212–224.

Gray, Donald. "George Eliot and Her Publishers." *The Cambridge Companion to George Eliot*. Ed. George Levine. Cambridge, UK: Cambridge UP, 2001. 181–201.

Hampton, Mark. "Defining Journalists in Late 19th Century Britain." *Critical Studies in Media Communication.* 22.2 (June 2005): 138–155.

_____. "The 'Objectivity' Ideal and its Limitations in 20th century British Journalism." *Journalism Studies* 9.4 (2008): 477–493.

Harcup, Tony. *Journalism: Principles and Practice*. 3rd ed. Thousand Oaks, CA: Sage, 2015.

Hadjiafxendi, Kyriaki. "Profession, Vocation, Trade: Marian Evans and the Making of the Woman Professional Writer." *Nineteenth-Century Gender Studies* 5.2 (Summer 2009): 1–15.

Hyde, William. "George Eliot and the Climate of Realism." *PMLA: Publications of the Modern Language Association.* 72.1 (March 1957): 147–164.

Karl, Frederick R. *George Eliot: Voice of a Century*. New York: W.W. Norton, 1995.

King, Andrew & John Plunkett. *Victorian Print Media: A Reader*. Oxford, UK: Oxford UP, 2005.

Lake, Brian. *The British Newspaper: A History and Guide for Collectors.* London: Sheppard Press, 1984.

Liddle, Dallas. *The Dynamics of Genre: Journalism and the Practice of Literature in Mid-Victorian Britain.* Charlottesville, VA: U of Virginia P, 2009.

Mangum, Teresa. "George Eliot and the Journalists: Making the Mistress Moral." *Victorian Scandals: Representations of Gender and Class.* Ed. Kristine Ottesen Garrigan. Athens, OH: Ohio UP, 1992. 159–179.

Mooney, Bel. "George Eliot the Journalist." The *George Eliot* Fellowship Review. 14 (1983): 74–84.

Nord, David Paul. *Faith in Reading*. New York: Oxford UP, 2004.

Onslow, Barbara. *Women of the Press in Nineteenth-Century Britain.* New York: St. Martin's Press, 2000.

Pinney, Thomas, ed. *Essays of George Eliot.* London: Routledge & Kegan Paul, 1963.

Sheppard, Nathan, ed. *The Essays of "George Eliot." Complete, Collected and Arranged with an Introduction on Her "Analysis of Motives"* New York: Funk & Wagnalls, 1883.

Starr, Paul. *The Creation of the Media: The Political Origins of Mass Communications*. New York: Basic Books, 2004.

Tusan, Michelle Elizabeth. *Women Making News: Gender and Journalism in Modern Britain*. Urbana: U of Illinois P, 2005.

Underwood, Doug. *Journalism and the Novel: Truth and Fiction, 1700–2000*. Cambridge, UK: Cambridge UP, 2008.

Wiener, Joel H. *The Americanization of the British Press, 1930s–1914: Speed in the Age of Transatlantic Journalism.* New York: Palgrave Macmillan, 2011.

Williams, Kevin. *Read All About It! A History of the British Newspaper.* London: Routledge, 2010.

Wilson, Cheryl A. "Placing the Margins: Literary Reviews, Pedagogical Practices, and the Canon of Victorian Women's Writing." *Tulsa Studies in Women's Literature.* 28.1 (Spring 2009): 57–74.

"Whistle While You Work": The Construction of the Myth of Englishness through the Working Soundscapes in George Eliot's *Adam Bede*___

Carroll Clayton Savant

> Look at Adam through the rest of the day, as he stands on the scaffolding with the two-feet ruler in his hand, whistling low while he considers how a difficulty about a floor-joist or a window-frame is to be overcome; or as he pushes one of the younger workmen aside, and takes his place in upheaving [*sic*] a weight of timber.... (Eliot, *Adam Bede* 211)

Set in the provincial countryside village of Hayslope in the historical moment of the 1799 Regency period, *Adam Bede* looks, literally, at the construction of the myth of Englishness. George Eliot's Hayslope is filled with carpenters and laborers of all classes; peopling the village with these pre-industrial manual laborers allows her to represent the construction of provincial Englishness through the metaphor of the historical carpenter building and renovating the English countryside. Eliot combines this imagery of the Hayslope carpenter with the sonic representations of the sounds and music that permeate construction and provinciality, effectively creating a sonic landscape[1] that envelopes the lived experience of British provinciality. This all-encompassing sound/image of provincial life creates a mythic pastoral ethos that allows Eliot's novel to transcend the nature of history and investigate the significance of historical acculturation and transmission. Though writing on a different novel, Avrom Fleishman argues that *The Mill on the Floss* (and, one could further contend, this historical representation of the English "everyman" in *Adam Bede*) is "...a mythic novel, in which its vision of England derives from a founding myth" (101). Similarly, studying George Eliot's fascination/relationship with music in her own life, Percy Young makes a brief note on the social/mythic function of music in *Adam Bede*. He writes that "[t]he yeomen of England had no great respect for music outside their convention, but there were melodies consecrated by tradition which did hold meaning for them. The Harvest Home in 'Adam Bede' preserves the vestiges of nature-worship and enshrines native *mysticism in song*" (97, emphasis added). This reliance on the music of tradition, or of the people, is what is particularly interesting in relation to the development of the myth of Englishness by the use of musical representations of the provincial countryside. The goal of this project is to investigate this sonic-image landscape that permeates *Adam Bede* as a way of representing the founding myth of Englishness. By looking at the mythic representations of music and the British laborer, I intend to show that *Adam Bede* offers a unique opportunity for Eliot to build the provincial village of Hayslope around the musical sounds of the pre-industrial laborer, effectively creating an all-encompassing representation of the creation of English mythic identity.

While studies investigating the function of music in George Eliot's novels are almost ubiquitous, the vast majority of scholarship is concerned with the representation of music as an emotional marker or a metaphor for fictional character development. In a survey on the function of music in Eliot's novels, Alison Byerly writes that "[m]usic was considered the one art capable of mirroring human emotions—in Hegel's words, 'the language of the soul.' Eliot appropriated this view of music in order to establish within her novels a system of representation that would permit the impossible: the 'true' portrayal of a person's inner self" (2). Though Byerly attempts to mark the intellectual and social potential music serves in Eliot's fiction, by focusing on fictional characters, her study is lacking in that she does not take into account the bigger, "organic" picture that Eliot creates with the use of music in her novels. On the other hand, studies about *Adam Bede* predominately investigate the function of the representation of the English laborer. In a tone invocative of Dickens scholarship, Josephine McDonagh marks the social function of the representation of the worker. She writes that the:

...social view that working people are like animals, who struggle to accede to higher forms of consciousness and take their place in 'human' society, is one that is often found in George Eliot's work... Those particular characters [Adam, Felix Holt, and Silas Marner] are marked out from the generality by their superior physical strength, their moral virtues, their intelligence... (McDonagh 45)

The goal of this study is to find a middle ground between musicological and sociological scholarship in order to investigate their functions in Eliot's novel. What I wish to point out is that the function of music in this essay is multivalent: in most Eliot scholarship, the conversations on music tend to rely purely on Western European high-art music. What I wish to accomplish by looking at various representations of music in this essay is to show that Eliot provides a musical treatment of the sounds of the provincial laborer in order to raise the hierarchical status of the noble laborer. While I will be looking at various representations of music, in the Western European tradition, in this essay, I will be showing how Eliot fuses this representation of high art music with the noble representation of the pre-industrial manual laborer and the music of the provincial countryside in order to enhance (and even legitimize) the myth of provincial Englishness. My intention in studying the function of music in *Adam Bede* is as a symbolic representation of the development of the identity of Englishness. By blending soundscape/musicological scholarship with studies on the noble British laborer, I plan to show that Eliot's novel contributes to the myth of provincial Englishness. By looking at the larger mythic texts, of which Eliot was familiar—Carlyle, Strauss, Feuerbach, and Spencer—I will show that Eliot is building on the concept of myth-making by invoking all forms of mythic construction: imagery, identity, (human) experience, and sound in order to create an organic English provincial myth.

By the time she turned to writing the narrative of *Adam Bede*, George Eliot was well versed in the construction of the mythic. She began her comprehensive, and one might say "epic," translation of David Friedrich Strauss' seminal work of Higher Criticism, *The Life of Jesus, Critically Examined* in 1844. Fleishman writes that Eliot began her translation of Strauss' text almost immediately after her work on Spinoza's *Tractatus,* which initially altered her religious and theological sensibilities; and one could understand how Strauss' "mythological"/historical worldview could affect a burgeoning humanist thinker. Fleishman writes that "[t]he project [of translating Strauss' text] occupied more than two years of Eliot's life—beginning in January, 1844, and ending in April 1846..." (35). These all-consuming efforts, according to Fleishman, altered the author's outlook on life. According to Fleishman, Strauss' text was essential in shaping Eliot's worldview, particularly in relation to the concept of the "mythic." He writes that "[i]n translating *The Life of Jesus,* George Eliot experienced her earliest exposure to the idea, not merely of the unity and sanctity of mankind, but religion's symbolic expression of that unity and sanctity—or as Strauss might put it, of their *mythological embodiment* in the figure of Christ" (40, emphasis added). Though Fleishman is concerned with Strauss' theological influence on Eliot, the evolving humanist, what is interesting in studying Eliot's translation of Strauss is the skeptic's influence on Eliot, the burgeoning mythologist.

As Strauss introduces the purpose and the function of his study, he writes that "[t]he imaginary lights of *mythological tradition* must be put out, that the eye may *distinguish the false from the true* in the twilight of the Biblical origins of our religion" (vi, emphasis added). What is interesting in Strauss' call for a "truthful" (and one may posit, Truthful) read of biblical events, is that he demands a separation of the biblical text from the biblical legends/myths. One might argue that this is exactly what Eliot asks of her reader throughout all of her novels—the willingness to suspend all preconceived myths of Englishness as she constructs them in the historical and aesthetic imagination. As he studies the construction of the mythological narratives of the Bible, it is clear that for Strauss—and one can see, for Eliot—the creation of the mythic is rooted in the human use of language and the need for explanation. Strauss argues that "...the gospel narratives are mythical rather than legendary.... According to George, *mythus* is the creation of a fact out of an idea: *legend* the seeing of an idea in a fact, or arising out of it" (62, emphasis original). According to Strauss, the creation of myth is tied to the human need for causal explanation and historical tradition/ritual.[2] Strauss writes that "...the mythical element can be wanting only when religion either falls short of, or goes beyond, its peculiar province, and that in the proper religious sphere it must necessarily exist" (80). Therefore, in the constructed narrative histories of the Bible, the human need for explanation (and one could argue, logic) demands the creation of the mythic narrative for causation, genesis, etc. We see this as Strauss attempts to understand the need to create a "narrative" myth of creation, particularly in the form of the biblical narratives. He writes that:

> [i]n adopting the mythical point of view as hitherto applied to Biblical history, our theologians had again approximated the ancient allegorical interpretation. For as both the natural explanations of the Rationalists, and the jesting expositions of the Deists, belong to that form of opinion which, whilst it sacrifices all divine meaning in the sacred record, still upholds its historical character; the mythical mode of interpretation agrees with the allegorical, in relinquishing the historical reality of the sacred narratives in order to preserve to them an absolute inherent truth. The mythical and the allegorical view...equally allow that the historian apparently relates that which is historical, but they suppose him, under the influence of a higher inspiration known or unknown to himself, to have made use of this historical semblance merely as the shell of an *idea*—of a religious conception. (Strauss 65)

This, one could surmise, is the function of literary narrative, for Eliot, in order to create the mythic "narrative" (or as Strauss would argue, allegory) of Britishness. While Strauss' text is primarily concerned with uncovering the creation of biblical (as he argues, supernatural) myths with their historical "Truths," one could understand where Eliot could see in this text a study of the understanding of causal myths, whether of doctrine, theology, or the ideological construction of identity. One could further this assertion in order to locate the function of the "mythic" in Eliot's worldview—the need to find the historical "root" of Englishness, in Eliot's case, found in the heart, or "nature," of the nation's people and their historical traditions, practices, and aesthetic rituals of musical performances.

Eliot addresses the ability to locate the "nature" of a people in her 1856 essay on "The Natural History of German Life." Through a close reading of Wilhelm Heinrich von Riehl's *Die bürgerliche Gesellschaft* and *Land und Leute*, Eliot lays out a mythological/ naturalistic "method" of finding the voice and "nature" of the people. She writes that:

> [i]t is an interesting branch of psychological observation to note the images that are habitually associated with abstract or collective terms—what may be called the picture-writing of the mind, which it carries on concurrently with the more subtle symbolism of language. Perhaps the fixity or variety of these associated images would furnish a tolerably fair test of the amount of concrete knowledge and experience which a given word represents, in the minds of two persons who use it with equal familiarity. (Eliot, "Natural History" 107)

For Eliot, who echoes Strauss, the need to find the nature or identity of a nation lay in the mythic images (and, one could further, the narratives and sounds) constructed by its people. Though examining Riehl's ability to recreate the voice of the German *Volk*, one senses the British ramifications for Eliot's assertions. This is the function of the novel for Eliot: to create the narrative mythology of, in her case, the English people. She writes that:

> … our social novels profess to *represent the people as they are*, and the unreality of their representations is a grave evil … but a *picture of human life* such as a great artist can give, surpasses even the trivial and the selfish into that attention to what is apart from themselves, which may be called the raw material of moral sentiment…. *Art is the nearest thing to life; it is a mode of amplifying experience and extending our contact with our fellow-men beyond the bounds of our personal lot.* All the more sacred is the task of the artist when he undertakes to paint the life of the People. (Eliot, "Natural History" 110, emphasis added)

This novel of the people, according to Eliot, represents the basic, most atomistic building blocks of society and recognizes the citizen who best epitomizes the voice—and in this study, the sonic representations of this voice—of the nation. For Eliot, and one may infer, for Riehl as well, the heart and "nature" of the nation lay in its peasantry. In a rhapsodical tone that anticipates the idyllic romanticism of the English countryside seen in *The Mill on the Floss,* she writes that in:

> ...the peasantry we must look for the historical type of the national *physique.* In the towns this type has become so modified to express the personality of the individual, that even 'family likeness' is often but faintly marked. But the peasants may still be distinguished into groups by their physical peculiarities. In one part of the country we find a longer-legged, in another a broader-shouldered race, which has inherited those peculiarities for centuries. (Eliot, "Natural History" 114, emphasis original)

Though Eliot is describing the physiognomic characteristics of the Germanic "people" found in Riehl's texts, it is clear, as she peoples the village of Hayslope with the peasant-like manual laborer, that the "nature" of the nation lay in the heart of its citizenry—the provincial laborer—of whom she derives her physical characteristics, language, and traditions.

The industrial (and one could argue in Eliot's case, the pre-industrial) manual laborer was the ubiquitous historical symbol of English progress and, one could further posit, supremacy throughout the nineteenth century. Investigating the historical and ideological significance of the imagery of the industrial worker on display at the Great Exhibition, Tim Barringer writes that "...the celebration of labour [was] at the heart of Victorian public discourse: the concept of work was acknowledged as a benchmark of value encompassing the economic, the moral, and the aesthetic" (1). According to Barringer, this "gospel of work" was the very identity of Englishness and shaped every mode of aesthetic and cultural sensibility (1). Thomas Carlyle's early-Victorian seminal work *Past and Present*, lays out the ideological direction for the future of a Victorian industrial society, as he celebrates (as Barringer notes) the common English worker in mythic language that is invocative of Strauss and Eliot's mythic creations of Englishness and identity. Carlyle notes that

> …there is a perennial nobleness, and even sacredness, in Work. Were he never so benighted, forgetful of his high calling, there is always hope in a man that actually and earnestly works: in Idleness alone is there perpetual despair. Work, never so Mammonish, mean, is in communication with Nature; the real desire to get Work done will itself lead one more and more to *truth,* to Nature's appointments and regulations, which are *truth.* The latest Gospel in this world is Know they work and do it. (162–163, emphasis added)

Carlyle "mythically" ties the manual laborer to the glory and honor of the legendary deity. His tone and sentiments echo Strauss' need for creating "mythic" narratives of nobleness and origination. It is little wonder, then, that Eliot turns to the "noble" manual laborer in order to create an English provincial myth. Writing on the nobility of the "gospel of work," Carlyle writes that

> [a]ll work, even cotton-spinning, is noble; work is alone noble; be that here said and asserted once more. And in like manner too all dignity is painful; a life of ease is not for any man, nor for any god. The life of all gods figures itself to us as a Sublime Sadness—earnestness of Infinite Battle against Infinite Labour [sic]. Our highest religion is named the 'Worship of Sorrow.' For the son of man there is no noble crown, well worn, or even ill worn, but is a crown of thorns! (131)

Carlyle's manual worker is the heart of the nation's identity and ideology, just as Eliot's Germanic peasant is the creation and embodiment of all Germanic experience. Thus, we see in Eliot's novel the function of the manual worker, in the form of the historical construction worker and artisan, as the genesis of the English provincial myth, working to build the foundation upon which the industrial laborer could display the supremacy of English culture and industry.

The pre-industrial manual laborer appears from the very outset of *Adam Bede*, as Eliot sets him up as the mythological, noble deity, the very image and representation of Britishness. As she introduces the reader to Adam, Eliot represents him in a mythical tone reminiscent of Carlyle and Strauss. She writes that "[i]n his tall stalwartness Adam Bede was a Saxon, and justified his name; but the jet-black hair, made the more noticeable by its contrast with the light paper cap, and the keen glance of the dark eyes that shone from under strongly marked, prominent, and mobile eyebrows, indicated a mixture of Celtic blood" (Eliot, *Adam Bede* 6). The Adam that Eliot illustrates is the very lifeblood and identity of the British nation; he is a blend of Carlyle's noble worker and Riehl's peasant worker, hard at work in "The Workshop." As if to reiterate the very mythic-ness of Adam's nobleness, Eliot illustrates the way that Adam sees himself, as the epitome of the sacred British manual laborer. Responding to his brother, Seth's, dogmatic fascination with Dinah Morris' public sermons, he says that:

'...it says as God put his sperrit [*sic*] into the workman as built the tabernacle, to make him do all the carved work and things as wanted a nice hand. And this is my way o' looking at it: there's the sperrit o' God in all things and all times—weekday as well as Sunday—and i' the great works and inventions, and i' the figuring and the mechanics. And God helps us with our headpieces and our hands as well as with our souls; and if a man does bits o' jobs out o' working hours...he's doing more good, and he's just as near to God, as if he was running after some preacher and a-praying and a-groaning.' (Eliot, *Adam Bede* 9–10)

For Adam, manual work is sacred; the ability of the laborer to create with his hands (and one could argue, for Eliot, and further, for Carlyle) is a sacred celebration of Nature and the holy. Through his humanistic (and almost romantic/transcendental) aside, we clearly see the "heart" of the British nation, rooted in her peasantry, in this case, revised in her manual laborer. In his statements, Adam echoes Carlyle, who proclaims that "[l]abour is Life: from the inmost heart of the Worker rises his god-given Force, the sacred celestial Life-essence breathed into him by Almighty God; from his inmost heart awakens him to all nobleness,—to all knowledge, 'self-knowledge' and much else, so soon as Work fitly begins" (164). Eliot reiterates this sacredness of work, as Adam Bede sees the very nature of his work as a celebration of the Divine, as a fulfillment of his "duty" not only to himself and his nation, but to his Deity. She writes that:

> [h]is work, as you know had always been part of his religion, and from very early days he saw clearly that good carpentry was God's will—was that form of God's will that most immediately concerned him beyond this daylight reality, no holiday-time in the working-day world; no moment in the distance when duty would take off her iron glove and breastplate and clasp him gently into rest. He conceived no picture of the future but one made up of hard-working days such as he lived through, with growing contentment and intensity of interest, every fresh week.... (Eliot, *Adam Bede* 488)

As Adam "works" himself to distraction, in order to overcome his grief for Dinah Morris' scandal, he turns to his work, as he turns to the Divine comfort associated with the duty of his hard work, theologically, nationally, and personally. In this way, Eliot's manual laborer sees his own function, in creating the mythic ethos of Britishness and ideologically-laden identity. Eliot ties this manual laborer geographically to his location, making him a ubiquitous symbol of the British provincial landscape, perpetuating his very mythic-ness not only in his ethic of work, but every time he opens his mouth.

Eliot turns to extra-textual and extra-visual markers in order to envelope her Hayslope laborer in the identity of provincial Englishness. As the villagers of Hayslope gather to see the spectacle that is Dinah Morris preach in the open green, Eliot draws our attention, sonically, to this provincial "peasant" through the use of dialect. When the "stranger" crosses the path of the Donnithorne Arms, he engages the landlord, Mr. Casson, in conversation. Though primarily interested in provincial theology and doctrine, what is clear in the "stranger's" conversation with Mr. Casson, is that location, geography, and identity are all tied together, all bound in the common, sonic marker of dialect that denotes identity, along with station and class. He says:

> I'm not this country-man, you may tell by my tongue, sir. They're cur'ous talkers i' this country, sir; the gentry's hard work to hunderstand 'em. I was brought hup among the gentry, sir, an' got the turn o' their tongue when I was a bye. Why, what do you think the folks here says for 'hevn't you'?—the gentry, you know, says 'hevn't you'—well, the people about here says, 'hanna yey.' It's what they call the dileck as is spoke hereabout, sir. (Eliot, *Adam Bede* 15–16)

It is clear, then, for Eliot, that this "peasant" laborer, just as Riehl's German peasant, is the identity of the British nation: through his language (and one could argue here, the "sounds" of his language) and through his acts, he embodies the very identity of Englishness. Though the British manual laborer may be the physical and linguistic embodiment of British mythic identity, for Eliot and Carlyle alike, the sounds and "music" that surround this British laborer create the entirety of his mythic Englishness and inform his very embodiment of mythic identity. Carlyle writes that "[t]he Practical Labour of England is *not* a chimerical Triviality: it is a Fact, acknowledged by all the Worlds; which no man and no demon will contradict. It is, very audibly, though very inarticulately as yet, the one God's Voice we have heard in these two atheistic centuries" (143). It is interesting to note that Carlyle connects this noble laborer not to his material output, but to the audible, sonic materialization of his labor. This sonic materialization of labor is the embodiment, for Eliot, of British mythic creation, of, in a Straussian way, a "causal" form of narrative representation of the creative moment of Englishness.

Eliot closely ties the manual dexterity of the British rural laborer to the sounds and "music" associated with his work, creating an all-encompassing sonic "image" of British provincialism, essentially enrobing Carlyle's noble/mythic British laborer within his mythic provincial surroundings. Studying the ability of "soundscape" literature to fully encapsulate the entirety of lived experience and represent national identity, Susan Smith writes that "… the style and form of musical composition—every bit as much as the character and content of landscape painting …—can reproduce ideas about nationhood and national character" (234). Thus, the representation of music in literature evokes extra-musical and extra-textual meanings, as music (and sound) is one of many socio-cultural identity markers. Studying the cognitive and cultural meanings of music, Aniruddh Patel writes that "'[t]one painting' or 'sound painting' refers to the musical imitation of natural phenomena. These can include environmental sounds, animal sounds, or human sounds…. With tone painting, composers are purposefully trying to bring something to mind that lies outside the realm of music" (320). In this way, one can assume that Eliot's representation of the "musical" sounds of provincial life serve as a literary symbol, as a means of encapsulating the noble English provincial worker and tying him to his surroundings, essentially creating an all-encompassing identity that is evoked through Eliot's musical language of work and pre-industrial sounds.[3]

We see this environmental soundscape as Arthur Donnithorne and Rector Irwine venture to Hall Farm to talk to the Poyser family about Dinah's preaching. In Hall Farm, Eliot creates a mythic pastoral provinciality, essentially embedding the farm within the pastoral British mythos. Eliot's description of the farm invokes the "historical" (in a Straussian way) causation of the root of Britishness. She writes that:

> [i]t is a very fine old place, of red brick, softened by a pale powdery lichen, which has dispersed itself with happy irregularity, so as to bring the red brick into terms of friendly companionship with the limestone ornaments surrounding the three gables, the windows, and the door-place…at present one might fancy the house in the early stage of a chancery suit, and that the fruit from the grand double row of walnut trees on the right hand of the enclosure would fall and rot among the grass…. (Eliot, *Adam Bede* 71)

Hall Farm, as majestic and grand as it is, belongs to an older, "simpler" time, yet Eliot's description of Hall Farm reverences (romantically) this very age and mythic-ness. Through her descriptions, Eliot shows that it is this world in which the origination of the myth of

Englishness is rooted. Eliot turns to the sounds embodied in this "natural" landscape in order to root the sonic mythic-ness of nature to the historicity of its embodiment, in Hall Farm. In this way, the sounds and soundscapes that permeate the farm combine with its "ancient"/romantic structure and denote the "originary" location of the British myth of identity, tied directly to its provincial geography and the sounds that envelop it. She writes that

> [t]here is quite a concert of noises: the great bull-dog, chained against the stables, is thrown into furious exasperation by the unwary approach of a cock too near the mouth of his kennel, and sends forth a thundering bark, which is answered by two fox-hounds shut up in the opposite cow-house; the old top-knotted hens scratching with their chicks among the straw, set up a sympathetic croaking as the discomfited cock joins them; a sow with her brood, all very muddy as to the legs, and curled as to the tail, throws in some deep staccato notes; our friends the calves are bleating from the home croft; and, under all, a fine ear discerns the continuous hum of human voices. (Eliot, *Adam Bede* 72–73)

The sounds that permeate the provincial landscape and surround Hall Farm create a "symphony" of nature, as Eliot raises the tenor of farm life to an aesthetic sublime, creating the soundscape that ties the Carlylean laborer to his Eliot/Riehl mythic identity. Eliot uses the rhetoric of high-art music in order to elevate this rustic/mythic landscape, attempting, in a Straussian way, to create the narrative mythos of provincial Englishness. This provincial countryside farm creates the mythic landscape sounds that surround Carlyle's noble worker; however, Eliot's "revision" of this noble worker alters and contributes to the nature of these sounds, essentially tying him to the mythic grand narrative of Englishness.

Throughout *Adam Bede*, Eliot surrounds Carlyle's noble/ mythic worker with the musical sounds of his work. Eliot makes the connection between the "natural" sounds of work and the worker through metaphorical references to high-art music in order to suggest the importance of the sounds of the British laborer, as a means of capturing Englishness. As we are first introduced to Adam Bede, hard at work in "The Workshop," Eliot writes that

> [i]t was to this workman that the strong baritone belonged which was heard above the sound of plane and hammer singing…. Here some measurement was to be taken which required more concentrated attention, and the sonorous voice subsided into a low whistle; but it presently broke out again with renewed vigour [*sic*]…. Such a voice could only come from a broad chest, and the broad chest belonged to a large-boned muscular man nearly six feet high, with a back so flat and a head so well poised that when he drew himself up to take a more distant survey of his work, he had the air of a soldier standing at ease. (*Adam Bede* 5)

This Adam is the epitome of Britishness, filling his work time by singing, whistling, and making various other noises in a "… concert of the tools …" (Eliot, *Adam Bede* 6). What is clear in this representation of Adam is that he is the all-encompassing embodiment of Englishness, providing the sonic and physical representation of what it is to be British. Studying the sounds of industrial labor in the novels of Charles Dickens and Elizabeth Gaskell, Chris Louttit writes that "Dickens was fascinated with the sounds of industry from an early age. It was well known that Dickens experienced menial work at Warren's Blacking Factory at twelve, but there had been an earlier, less immediate encounter with manual labour [*sic*]…. The memory of these experiences remained with Dickens in later life…" and can be seen in the sonic representation of industrial labor in his novels (132–133). While Louttit traces the representation of industrial sounds in Dickens and Gaskell's novels, what is clear is that the two authors fill their novels with the soundscapes of the industrial city. On the other hand, Eliot transcends these industrial soundscapes by illustrating the "musical" representation of pre-industrial work in order to acculturate the mythic ethos of provincial work. Where Dickens and Gaskell are interested in representing the "conditions" of life in (urban) industrial England, Eliot's sonic representations of pastoral life, similarly, create a representation of the "conditions" of life in provincial (historical) England. As Adam heads to a job, he passes the fieldworkers making hay and notes their sounds as they work. Eliot writes that:

> ...when Adam was marching along the lanes, with his basket of tools over his shoulder, he caught the sound of jocose talk and ringing laughter from behind the hedges. The jocose talk of haymakers is best at a distance; like those clumsy bells round the cows' necks, it has rather a coarse sound when it comes close, and may even grate on your ears painfully; but heard from far off, it mingles very prettily with the other joyous sounds of nature. Men's muscles move better when their souls are making merry music, though their merriment is of a poor blundering sort, not at all like the merriment of birds. (*Adam Bede* 207)

Just as Adam "whistles" and sings while he works, so too do the fieldworkers make "musical" noises while they work in the fields, providing the sonic representation of fieldwork that permeate provincial life. Eliot furthers these sounds of "outdoor musicality" just after Adam arrives at his work site. She writes that:

> ...he was coming very near to the end of his walk, within the sound of the hammers at work on the refitting of the old house. The sound of tools to a clever workman who loves his work, is like the tentative sounds of the orchestra to the violinist who has to bear his part in the overture: the strong fibres [*sic*] begin their accustomed thrill, and what was a moment before joy, vexation, or ambition, begins its change into energy. (Eliot, *Adam Bede* 210)

Adam quickly joins the sounds of his fellow workers, adding to them even more, through the use of his hammer and the use of his singing voice. The dichotomy of the representation of the musical fieldworkers with the artisanal "music" of carpentry illustrates the Carlylean mythic-ness of all forms of work and provincial beings. Eliot writes:

> [l]ook at this broad-shouldered man with the bare muscular arms, and the thick firm black hair tossed about like trodden meadow-grass whenever he takes off his paper cap, and with the strong barytone

[*sic*] voice bursting every now and then into loud and solemn psalm-tunes, as if seeking some outlet for superfluous strength, yet presently checking himself, apparently crossed by some thought which jars with the singing … in this rough man, who knew no better lyrics than he could find in the Old and New Version and an occasional hymn; who knew the smallest possible amount of profane history; and for whom the motion and shape of the earth, the course of the sun, and the changes of the seasons, lay in the region of mystery just made visible by fragmentary knowledge. (Eliot, *Adam Bede* 211–212)

Once again, Adam is the embodiment of the deistic, manual British laborer; however, his identity is now rooted in the very rudimentary aesthetic of artisanal "knowledge" and, one could further argue, the identity of the "*Volk*."

Eliot "expands" her representation of the music of the worker to the "*Volk*," as the field workers gather, collectively, to celebrate "The Harvest Supper," which is at once the aural celebration of Carlyle's sacred/mythic laborer, yet also the embodiment of the sounds/soundscapes in which the laborer is surrounded (naturally or aesthetically) during his work. As Adam passes Hall Farm, Eliot writes:

[a]s Adam was going homewards, on Wednesday evening, in the six o'clock sunlight, he saw in the distance the last load of barley winding its way towards the yard-gate of the Hall Farm, and heard the chant of 'Harvest Home!' rising and sinking like a wave. Fainter and fainter, and more and more musical through the growing distance, the falling, dying sound still reached him, as he neared the Willow Brook. The low westering sun shone right on the shoulders of the old Binton Hills, turning the unconscious sheep into bright spots of light; shone on the windows of the cottage too, and made them a-flame with a glory beyond that of amber or amethyst. It was enough to make Adam feel that he was in a great temple, and that the distant chant was a sacred song. (*Adam Bede* 515)

The "temple" of work, as Eliot notes, is the pastoral provincial countryside, a celebration of the Carlylean "noble" laborer, yet also the "root" of the identity of Englishness. The combination of sacred "chanting" and rustic "music" combine in order to create a "holy shrine" of a Straussian English mythic narrative. Adam is overwhelmed by the sensory overload, as he passes Hall Farm. He exclaims "'It's wonderful ... how that sound goes to one's heart almost like a funeral-bell, for all it tells one o' the joyfullest time o' the year, and the time when men are mostly the thankfullest'" (Eliot, *Adam Bede* 515). Though Adam's first "concern" is for his own feelings about Dinah Morris, it is worth noting that Adam's surroundings (whether aurally or naturally) inspire his willingness to "internalize" his thoughts (in a typically Eliot-esque manner) and root both his feelings and his sense of identity in the "temple" landscape of Hall Farm and the "musical" celebration of the harvest feast. We get a more direct connection between the representation of aurality in the workers' celebration and the union of music (directly) to the ethic of work as Adam joins the workers in their celebratory festivities. After celebrating the harvest feast, the evening's (temple sermon) entertainment passes on into congregational-like singing of "traditional" English songs. Eliot writes that:

> *[n]ow,* the great ceremony of the evening was to begin—the harvest song, in which every man must join: he might be in tune, if he liked to be singular, but he must not sit with closed lips. The movement was obliged to be in triple time; the rest was *ad libitum.* As to the origin of this song—whether it came in its actual state from the brain of a single rhapsodist, or was gradually perfected by a school or succession of rhapsodists, I am ignorant. There is a stamp of unity, of individual genius, upon it, which inclines me to the former hypothesis, though I am not blind to the consideration that this unity may rather have arisen from that consensus of many minds which was a condition of primitive thought, foreign to our modern consciousness. (*Adam Bede* 519)

The traditional songs that the workers sing, according to Eliot, are as old as the English countryside itself; they are the embodiment of British identity and the voice of its heart—the British agricultural (Carlylean) laborer, seen in the temple of British provincialism, Hall Farm. The harvest celebration at Hall Farm—as it vacillates between political, economic, and social debates and the traditional songs of Englishness—is at once a celebration of the mythic representation of English identity, through the "noble" produce of hard work and the sounds of the British nation itself.

The provincial community of Hayslope is the all-encompassing embodiment of British mythic identity. Relying on her studies of the construction of the mythological, George Eliot fills *Adam Bede* with symbols to create a narrative mythology of Englishness. The Hayslope that Eliot constructs is full of idyllic, pastoral symbols, evoking the "fairy land" of British historical provinciality that surrounds Carlyle's noble laborer, the very embodiment of British identity. The manual laborer of Hayslope is surrounded not only by the pastoral provincial village but is enveloped in the musical sounds of his work. This mutual representation of the romantic countryside and the sounds and music of the pre-industrial laborer create an all-encompassing English identity and, in a Strauss-ian vein, allow Eliot to locate the causality of Englishness, tied to the noble worker of the legendary English countryside. Through these aural/musical soundscapes, Eliot effectually ties this noble laborer to his provincial countryside, making the provincial soundscape that surrounds the ubiquitous, legendary pre-industrial laborer part and parcel of British mythic identity. Eliot's use of high-art musical language rhetorically ties the manual Carlylean laborer to his provincial countryside, at once rooting him in the identity of Britishness, yet elevating his rudimentary identity on an aesthetic, historical, and mythical level. Where traditional Eliot scholarship examines the author's representations of music and musical performances as windows into Victorian culture, studying her illustrations of soundscapes expands on the musicological scholarship of the author's work and allows us to understand that the aural potpourri that enveloped nineteenth-century Britons informed their definitions of identity, location, and character.

Notes

1. John Picker argues that this type of all-encompassing representation of music and sound in literature is the basis of the "soundscape."

This form of representation allows sounds (and music) to infiltrate all areas of lived cultural experience.

2.   Likewise, Eliot's 1854 translation of Feuerbach's *The Essence of Christianity* makes a similar claim. Feuerbach argues that:

> [r]eligion is the dream of the human mind. But even in dreams we do not find ourselves in emptiness or in heaven, but on earth, in the realm of reality; we only see real things in entrancing splendour [sic] of imagination and caprice, instead of in the simple daylight of reality and necessity. Hence, I do nothing more to religion—and speculative philosophy and theology also—than to open its eyes, or rather to turn its gaze from the internal towards the external, i.e., I change the object as it is in the imagination into the object as it is in reality. (xi)

3.   For Eliot, the burgeoning realist author, such a goal of theology/ philosophy is crucial in understanding the causal nature of human understanding (or in the case of this inquiry, the genesis of the mythic identity of Englishness). Where Feuerbach's work in Higher Criticism is interested in the (human) creation of an ideological doctrine, we can see where such a doctrine can transfer into Eliot's idea of the creation of a mythic ideology of Britishness.

4.   Eliot's close friend, Herbert Spencer, investigated the emotional and psychological effects of music on the individual in his 1857 essay "The Origin and Function of Music." Though discussing the physical stimuli of vocal music on the individual, Spencer writes that "…what is the *function* of music? Has music any effect beyond the immediate pleasure it produces? Analogy suggests that it has. The enjoyments of a good dinner do not end with themselves, but minister to bodily well-being" (69).

Works Cited

Barringer, Tim. *Men at Work: Art and Labour in Victorian Britain.* New Haven, CT: Paul Mellon Centre for Studies in British Art, Yale UP, 2005.

Bonaparte, Felicia. "'Middlemarch': The Genesis of Myth in the English Novel: The Relationship between Literary form and the Modern

Predicament." *Notre Dame English Journal* 13:3 (Summer 1981): 107–154. *JSTOR.* Web. 29 Apr. 2013.

Byerly, Alison. "'The Language of the Soul': George Eliot and Music." *Nineteenth-Century Literature* 44:1 (June 1989): 1–17. *JSTOR.* Web. 10 Oct. 2013.

Carlyle, Thomas. *Past and Present.* Rockville, MD: Serenity Publishers, LLC, 2009.

Clapp-Intyre, Alisa. *Angelic Airs, Subversive Songs: Music as Social Discourse in the Victorian Novel.* Athens, OH: Ohio UP, 2002.

_____. "Indecent musical displays: Feminizing the pastoral in Eliot's *The Mill on the Floss.*" *The Idea of Music in Victorian Fiction.* Ed. Sophie Fuller & Nicky Losseff. Burlington, VT: Ashgate, 2004.

Conrad, Peter. "The Englishness of English Literature." *Daedalus* 112.1 (Winter 1983): 157–173. *JSTOR.* Web. 10 Oct. 2013.

Correa, Delia da Sousa. *George Eliot, Music and Victorian Culture.* New York: Palgrave Macmillan, 2003.

Eliot, George. *Adam Bede.* Ed. Valentine Cunningham. Oxford, UK: Oxford UP, 1996.

_____. "History of 'Adam Bede.'" *Adam Bede.* Ed. Valentine Cunningham. Oxford: Oxford UP, 1996.

_____. "The Natural History of German Life." *Selected Essays, Poems, and Other Writings.* Ed. A.S. Byatt & Nicholas Warren. London: Penguin Books, 1990.

_____. "Silly Novels by Lady Novelists." *Selected Essays, Poems, and Other Writings.* Ed. A.S. Byatt & Nicholas Warren. London: Penguin Books, 1990.

Feuerbach, Ludwig. *The Essence of Christianity.* Trans. George Eliot. Cambridge, UK: Cambridge UP, 2012.

Fleishman, Avrom. *George Eliot's Intellectual Life.* Cambridge, UK: Cambridge UP, 2010.

Fuller, Sophie & Nicky Losseff. "Introduction." *The Idea of Music in Victorian Fiction.* Ed. Sophie Fuller & Nicky Losseff. Burlington, VT: Ashgate, 2004.

Hill, Susan. "Translating Feuerbach, Constructing Morality: The Theological and Literary Significance of Translation for George

Eliot." *Journal of the American Academy of Religion* 65.3 (Autumn 1997): 635–653. *JSTOR.* Web. 1 Oct. 2012.

Jones, Miriam. "'The Usual Sad Catastrophe:' From the Street to the Parlor in *Adam Bede.*" *Victorian Literature and Culture* 32.2 (2004): 305–326. *MLA International Bibliography.* Web. 10 Oct. 2012.

Levine, George. "Introduction: George Eliot and the Art of Realism." *The Cambridge Companion to George Eliot.* Ed. George Levine. Cambridge, UK: Cambridge UP, 2001.

Losseff, Nicky. "The Voice, the Breath and the Soul: Song and Poverty in *Thyrza, Mary Barton, Alton Locke* and *A Child of the Jago.*" *The Idea of Music in Victorian Fiction.* Ed. Sophie Fuller & Nicky Losseff. Burlington, VT: Ashgate, 2004.

Louttit, Chris. "The Sounds of Industry in Dickens and Gaskell." *Victorian Soundscapes Revisited, Leeds Working Papers in Victorian Studies.* Vol. 9. Ed. Martin Hewitt & Rachel Cowgill. Leeds, UK: Leeds Centre for Victorian Studies, 2007.

McDonagh, Josephine. "The Early Novels." *The Cambridge Companion to George Eliot.* Ed. George Levine. Cambridge, UK: Cambridge UP, 2001.

Mitchell, Sally. *Daily Life in Victorian England.* 2nd ed. Westport, CT: Greenwood Press, 2009.

Patel, Aniruddh. *Music, Language, and the Brain.* Oxford, UK: Oxford UP, 2008.

Picker, John. "*Victorian Soundscapes* Revisited." *Victorian Soundscapes Revisited, Leeds Working Papers in Victorian* Studies. Vol. 9. Ed. Martin Hewitt & Rachel Cowgill. Leeds, UK: Leeds Centre for Victorian Studies, 2007.

Putzell, Sara Moore. "The Search for a Higher Rule: Spiritual Progress in the Novels of George Eliot." *Journal of the American Academy of Religion* 47.3 (Sept. 1979): 389–407. *JSTOR.* Web. 29 April 2013.

Smith, Susan. "Soundscape." *Area* 26.3 (Sept. 1994): 232–240. *JSTOR.* Web. 19 Oct. 2012.

Solie, Ruth. "Music." *The Cambridge Companion to Victorian Culture.* Ed. Francis O'Gorman. Cambridge, UK: Cambridge UP, 2010.

Spencer, Herbert. "The Origin and Function of Music." *Literary Style and Music, Including Two Short Essays on Gracefulness and Beauty.* New York: Philosophical Library, 1951.

Strauss, David Friedrich. *The Life of Jesus, Critically Examined.* Trans. George Eliot. London: Swan Sonnenschein & Co., n.d.

Stwertka, Eve Marie. "The Web of Utterance: *Middlemarch.*" *Texas Studies in Literature and Language* 19.2 "An Issue Devoted to the Nineteenth Century" (Summer 1977): 179–187. *MLA International Bibliography.* Web. 19 Oct. 2012.

Tongson, Karen. "Thomas Carlyle and the grain of the voice." *The Idea of Music in Victorian Fiction.* Ed. Sophie Fuller & Nicky Losseff. Burlington, VT: Ashgate, 2004.

Young, Percy. "George Eliot and Music." *Music and Letters* 24.2 (Apr. 1943): 92–100. *JSTOR.* Web. 2 Oct. 2012.

George Eliot: Unsung Poet of Sympathy_____

Wendy S. Williams

Although George Eliot is best known for her novels, she also wrote poetry. By the time she published the poem *The Spanish Gypsy* in 1868, she had already attained wealth and fame through the publication of five successful novels: *Adam Bede* (1859), *The Mill on the Floss* (1860), *Silas Marner* (1861), *Romola* (1863), and *Felix Holt, the Radical* (1866). Eliot turned to poetry at this late stage in her career because she believed that poetry had a "superiority over all the other arts" ("Notes on Form in Art," *Essays* 435), and she aspired to a calling greater than that of a popular novelist. Poetry offered cultural prestige and the opportunity to achieve literary greatness as a moral sage.[1] Many of Eliot's contemporaries perceived her as achieving such renown. The philosopher Herbert Spencer called her the "female Shakespeare," and businessman Henry Doulton said she was "the Shakespeare among woman" (Collins, *Interviews* 104, 140). After her death, however, her novels overshadowed her poetry, and over the years, critics dismissed her poetry as inferior verse. Thus, Eliot's readership overlooked a significant portion of her writing for more than a century because of critical dismissal and inaccessibility (Williams 4). However, recent scholarship reveals a renewed interest in this important aspect of Eliot's career.[2] Studies of Eliot's poetry not only contribute to a better understanding of Eliot's work as a whole but also provide a more accurate picture of one of the era's greatest writers. In this chapter, I will first summarize Eliot's poetic career and her ethic of sympathy. Then I will explain her adoption of a poetess persona— one that associated with spirituality and feminine piety—to further her artistic aim of enlarging readers' sympathies. I will also discuss ways she emphasized the value of understanding difference through versatility in poetic form and content. Throughout, I will analyze a number of her poems to show how Eliot promoted her ethic of sympathy in poetry in ways unseen in her prose works.

Eliot's Poetic Career

In the 1860s and 1870s, Eliot published her poems in prominent periodicals such as *Blackwood's Magazine*, *Macmillan's Magazine*, and *The Atlantic Monthly*, and she oversaw two editions of her collected poems: *The Legend of Jubal and Other Poems* (1874) and *The Legend of Jubal and Other Poems, Old and New* (1878). Eliot wrote poetic fragments, lyric poems ("In a London Drawingroom," "Two Lovers," "In the South," "Ex Oriente Lux," "I grant you ample leave"); a sonnet sequence ("Brother and Sister"); elegies ("Erinna," "Arion"); hymns and ballads ("O May I Join the Choir Invisible," "Sweet Evenings Come and Go, Love"); narrative verse ("A Minor Prophet," "Agatha," "How Lisa Loved the King," "The Legend of Jubal," "Stradivarius," "The Death of Moses"); philosophical dialogues ("Self and Life," "A College Breakfast Party"); lengthy dramatic poems (*Armgart* and *The Spanish Gypsy*); and ninety-six original poetic epigraphs for prose chapters.[3] She demonstrated poetic versatility by masterfully employing blank verse, free verse, heroic couplets, and irregular rhyme schemes, and she addressed a number of themes that also permeate her novels: suffering and renunciation, death and immortality, community and isolation, and artistic ambition. When Eliot submitted *The Legend of Jubal and Other Poems* to her publisher John Blackwood, she wrote: "every one of those [poems] I now send you represents an idea which I care for strongly and wish to propagate as far as I can" (*Letters* 6: 26).

Eliot's Promotion of Sympathy via Prose

Eliot's poetry was meaningful to her and offered a vehicle through which she could further her deeply held belief that sympathy led to a moral and better society. Throughout her works, she urged readers to open their minds to people's differences and to extend their feelings based on such understanding. But her mode of persuasion changed as she developed as a writer—first as an essayist, then as a novelist, and finally as a poet.

As an anonymous essayist for the *Westminster Review* in the 1850s, Eliot appealed to her readers for sympathy by exposing those who failed to show it. For example, in her essay, "Evangelical

Teaching: Dr. Cumming" (1855), she condemns Reverend John Cumming's antipathetic religion that fostered hate and presents an alternate view of God as one who "sympathizes with all we feel and endure for our fellow-men, [and] who will pour new life into our too languid love" (461). This God, she argues, "is an extension and multiplication of the effects produced by human sympathy" (461). In another essay, "Worldliness and Other-Worldliness: The Poet Young" (1857), Eliot bemoans the "vicious imagery resulting from insincerity" and "disruption of language from genuine thought and feeling" in Edward Young's poem, "Night Thoughts" (27, 30) and explains that in the poem, "there is hardly a trace of human sympathy, of self-forgetfulness in the joy or sorrow of a fellow-being" (31). For Eliot, art was "a mode of amplifying experience and extending our contact with our fellow-men beyond the bounds of our personal lot," and the "task of the artist" was "sacred when he undertakes to paint the life of the People" ("The Natural History of German Life" 54).

As a writer of fiction in the 1850s and 1860s, Eliot engendered sympathy more gently, by depicting realistic characters with rich inner lives, with whom readers could identify. Additionally, in her fiction, she employed narrators who directly addressed readers to appeal to their sympathetic understanding. In "The Sad Fortunes of the Reverend Amos Barton," a short story in *Scenes of Clerical Life* (1857), the narrator entreats the reader to "see" the human condition: "Depend upon it, you would gain unspeakably if you would learn with me to see some of the poetry and the pathos, the tragedy and the comedy, lying in the experience of a human soul that looks out through dull grey eyes, and that speaks in a voice of quite ordinary tones" (137). The narrator urges readers to "learn with me," look into the "dull grey eyes," "see" beyond "ordinary tones," and discover the lives and experiences that differ from their own. Similarly, "Janet's Repentance," another story in *Scenes*, concludes with a call to hear, feel, and strive to understand others by looking beyond outward appearances: "the only true knowledge of our fellow-man is that which enables us to *feel with* him—which gives us a *fine ear* for the *heart-pulses* that are *beating* under the mere clothes of circumstance and opinion" (279, emphasis mine). This description of human sympathy associates knowing with listening (with a "fine ear") and feeling ("the heart-pulses"). This text echoes a number of similar passages in her novels, the most famous of which appears in *Middlemarch*: "If we had a *keen vision* and *feeling* of all ordinary human life, it would be like *hearing* the grass grow and the squirrel's *heart beat*, and we should die of that *roar* which lies *on the other side of silence*. As it is, the quickest of us walk about well wadded with stupidity" (180, emphasis mine). Despite the difficulty of the task, the narrator explains, "we" must endeavor to *see* (with "keen vision"), *feel* with ("all ordinary human life"), and *listen* for the usual, frequent tragedies of all of those around us. Even the most sympathetic ("quickest") of us are relatively deaf and blind ("well wadded with stupidity") to the silent suffering of our fellow human beings. For Eliot, sympathy required seeing and listening to know (i.e., sympathize with) one another, and though "our frames could hardly bear much" of the world's suffering (180), she urges readers to make every effort to do so.[4] Throughout the 1850s and 1860s, Eliot persuaded her readers to see, listen, and feel through realistic characterization and narrative voice in her fiction.

Eliot's Promotion of Sympathy via Poetry and the Poetess Tradition

In the late 1860s and 1870s, Eliot took periodic breaks from her novel writing and turned to poetry to arouse sympathy. She thus offered a means to experience sympathy sensorily through prosody (rhythm and meter), rhyme, and form, which could move readers to see, hear, and feel the cadences that create meaning and bring about sympathetic understanding. To awaken sympathy via poetic form and meaning, Eliot assumed the role of a moral guide to the nation, refashioning herself as a poetess—a stance associated with feminine spirituality in her society. In *George Eliot, Poetess*, I argue that readers of her novels would have viewed her poems as works of moral instruction rather than entertainment, and they would have understood Eliot's role as that of a public novelist taking on a poetess identity to voice a guiding message for her readership. Eliot adopts "stereotypically feminine poetic models as an influence that should change the cultural landscape, and even have a guiding influence akin to that of the Bible" (LaPorte 159). She was famous, influential, and prominent in changing the thought in Victorian England via her literary works. As a poetess, she used her influence to write with a moral imperative in the highest form of art to make a better society (Williams 136).

Eliot's Poetry: Sympathy for Women

The poetess stance offered a measure of disguise behind feminine expression and within the confined quarters of verse form that allowed Eliot to take risks that she could not as a novelist. In her poetry, she made bold claims that she could not make in her more widely circulated novels. By fashioning herself as a poetess with spiritual authority, Eliot appeared to promote middle-class values while subtly inserting transgressive views about sympathy and society in her poems. For example, in "Brother and Sister" (1869), she ostensibly relays a simple story about two siblings who happily grow up together in an idyllic setting but actually inveighs against societal restrictions that hinder women. Throughout the sequence of eleven sonnets, the sister-narrator, speaking as a grown woman looking back at her childhood, describes her youthful idolization of her older brother:

> I held him wise, and when he talked to me
> Of snakes and birds, and which God loved the best,
> I thought his knowledge marked the boundary
> Where men grew blind, though angels knew the rest. (Eliot, *Complete Shorter Poetry*, 2:5)[5]

The sister appears contented in her obedience to her all-knowing and commanding brother. However, the sonnet form, which thematizes confinement within both social and poetic rules, and the poem's imagery and language related to measurement and constraint woven throughout the poem, reveal another view—that of a sister discontent with the rigid patriarchal gender roles that eventually distance her from her brother.[6] In a formal, controlled setting, the narrator demonstrates her ability to translate past female obedience to present poetic obedience and set her own boundaries as an artist. As an adult poet, she engraves the past with authority and control, within the confines of the metered sonnet form, and produces a "thought-tracked line" (*CSP* 2:11) that will guide future readers toward sympathetic relations (Williams 90–92).

Similarly, in "How Lisa Loved the King" (1869), Eliot challenges nineteenth-century marriage practices in a poem that appears to extol the institution of marriage. The poem, adapted from Giovanni Boccaccio's *The Decameron* (1353), tells of a common girl in medieval Europe who falls in love with a king, pines for him, and expresses her love to the king who marries her to another man and declares her marriage a sacrament that benefits the entire nation (102). Eliot employs heroic couplets and epic conventions to exalt the love of Lisa, whom the reader perceives as an epic heroine who is greatly influential in matters of love. However, Lisa has no influence over her own love life and ends up in a loveless marriage. Eliot criticizes the male-controlled institution of marriage by presenting Lisa's marriage as a financial contract between men. Lisa's father seeks to elevate his social status by marrying her to a man of higher birth and lesser fortune than himself. The narrator says of Lisa's father:

> He loved his riches well,
> But loved them chiefly for his Lisa's sake,
> Whom with a father's care he sought to make
> The bride of some true honorable man,—
> Of Perdicone (so the rumor ran),
> Whose birth was higher than his fortunes were (*CSP* 1:144–5)

Once her father's property, Lisa becomes her husband's property after marriage, and marriage merely transfers her from one owner to another (Williams 102–3).[7] Through the poem, Eliot criticizes the commodification of women without directly stating her non-traditional views.

In "Erinna" (ca. 1873–6) Eliot again employs feminine voice and conventions to comment on gender restrictions in Victorian society. The poem is a lament for the ancient Greek poetess, Erinna, who died in her youth after her mother chained her to a spinning wheel. By choosing Erinna, a well-known poetess, for the subject of her poem, Eliot identified with the ancient poetess tradition. And in choosing the elegy verse genre, one that called attention to the feminine ability to mourn and sympathize, Eliot used and embodied the feminine poetic voice that she invited readers to experience through feeling (Williams 29–30). In the poem, Erinna labors at a spinning wheel in "insect labour" (*CSP* 2:114). The insect imagery and the steady iambic rhythm, like that of the tedious spinning wheel, allow the reader to see and hear Erinna's domestic imprisonment (Williams 31). Through her imagination, Erinna escapes the monotonous labor. As she spins silk, she spins stories of "Gods and men" (*CSP* 2:114) that inspire her art (her tapestry and her poem). Erinna's imagination awakens her emotion ("passion"), which allows her to pour her "lonely pain" into her song ("melodic cries") (*CSP* 2:114).[8] Eliot describes this process of creating poetry in "Notes on Form in Art" (1868): "*Poetry* begins when passion weds thought by finding expression in an image" (*CSP* 2:182). As the spinning wheel provides rhythmic inspiration, Erinna's passion and imagination find expression in her song (Williams 33). Erinna will ultimately die, but her inspired work will endure; she will craft "in speech/Harmonious a statue" (*CSP* 2:114) for others to behold for years to come. In "Brother and Sister," "How Lisa Loved the King," and "Erinna," Eliot relies on poetic form and prosody, while also embracing the feminine conventions of the poetess tradition, to advocate sympathy in a society stifled by rigid gender roles and limited choices for women.

Eliot's Poetry: Sympathy and Difference

Although Eliot was able to successfully refashion herself as a poetess with vatic authority in the later years of her career, society did not always venerate her. Eliot suffered the rejection of her family and society when she eloped with George Henry Lewes in 1854. Lewes was legally married to another woman and could or would not divorce. Society deemed Eliot a "fallen woman," and she lived as an outsider for many years. By the time she began to write poetry, her fame was more influential than her breach of societal decorum, and she was able to adopt a poetess stance without attracting attention to her personal life. But her experience living as a social outcast who longed to be understood and accepted influenced her writing. She transformed her own pain into a catalyst to awaken sympathy in her readership. She championed sympathy not only for women, as the abovementioned poems demonstrated, but for all who, like herself, were different. She wrote to her friend Charles Bray: "If Art does not enlarge men's sympathies, it does nothing morally...and the only effect I ardently long to produce by my writings, is that those who read them should be better able to imagine and to feel the pains and the joys of those who differ from themselves" (*Letters* 3:111). For Eliot, sympathy required difference—difference in gender, beliefs, religion, lifestyle. In her prose works, she challenged readers to enter into the lives and minds of characters who acted and thought in ways that readers did not. Through poetry, Eliot invited readers to experience difference not via psychological realism but rather via the poem itself. In "Versification," Eliot explains that "rhythmic and tonic relations are used as a means of moving men's souls" and that "versification shall be to the meaning as the mythical wings to the strong quadruped" (*CSP* 2:188). Victorian scholar Herbert Tucker elucidates, "For poetry is the literary domain where 'form' and 'idea' are coderterminant, where the structure not only delivers the content but constitutes it. This is most obviously the case when prosody's performative devices execute a meaning by fulfilling it" (24). The poem's artistry draws the reader into the life of the poem. And for Eliot, variety in poetic artistry offered the reader the greater possibility of pleasure. "Every irregularity," she states, "is good if it can be shown to be the secret of a higher pleasure than the unbroken observance of a rule" (*CSP* 2:188). Eliot's poems celebrate difference through their versatility in form and content.

Eliot's Poetry: Sympathy for the Other

Through poetic versatility, Eliot sought to move readers toward a better understanding of others' lives. In a variety of verse forms and through imagery and artistry, she engenders sympathy for outcasts and outsiders: a wandering tribe of pagan gypsies in the dramatic epic poem, *The Spanish Gypsy*; the biblical character Jubal, who created the lyre, brought music to the world, and was ultimately rejected by his own community in the narrative poem, "The Legend of Jubal"; an egotistical opera singer who loses her voice, career, and options as a single woman in nineteenth-century society in the dramatic poem, *Armgart*; a poor, old woman who never married or had children but served as a mother to her community in the narrative poem, "Agatha." She even urges sympathy for all of Asia, a part of the world Britons held as inferior, by extolling the region as the birthplace of civilization in the lyric poem, "Ex Oriente Lux."

Eliot's poems create a sensory experience that summons the reader to see, hear, and feel the meaning of the poem. The poems demonstrate the value of difference through diversity in form, prosody, and imagery. In "A London Drawingroom" (1865), she implicitly pronounces the beauty of difference by painting a dreary world lacking in variety. The dark imagery and uniform blank verse (with only two of nineteen lines varying in meter)[9] depict industrial London as a place of monotony and sameness, devoid of sympathy. Looking out the window of a London drawing room, the narrator sees a row of houses "Cutting the sky with one long line of wall/ Like solid fog: far as the eye can stretch" creating a "Monotony of surface and of form/Without a break to hang a guess upon" (*CSP* 2:91). Monotony creates darkness which inhibits wonder about the outside world ("Without a break to hang a guess upon"). People on the street fail to look at one another and miss their chance to connect and experience life: "No figure lingering/Pauses to feed the hunger of the eye/Or rest a little on the lap of life" (*CSP* 2:91). Rather, they are apathetic to one another: "All hurry on and look upon the ground,/ Or glance unmarking at the passers by" (*CSP* 2:91). Even the vehicles hurry through the streets with their passengers closed inside and oblivious to the world: "The wheels are hurrying too, cabs, carriages/All closed, in multiplied identity" (*CSP* 2:91). London feels like "one huge prison-house" in which inmates live monotonous, self-involved lives, giving and receiving no sympathy.

Because the citizens do not see and feel with one another, they live without "colour, warmth and joy" (*CSP* 2:91). By contrast, in the lyric poem "O May I Join the Choir Invisible" (1867), the narrator describes the world as a sanctuary in which people (past and present) live "In pulses stirred to generosity,/ In deeds of daring rectitude, in scorn/For miserable aims that end with self" (*CSP* 2:85). The musical imagery and lively blank verse with metrical irregularities[10] animate a world in which "discords" caused by selfishness ("Rebellious flesh") are extinguished by kindness and forgiveness ("quenched by meeting harmonies") and "Die in the large and charitable air" (*CSP* 2:85). Instead of passively looking out a window into a dark city of people who do not see one another, this narrator strives to understand fellow suffering, to "be to other souls/The cup of strength in some great agony," and improve the lives of others: "Enkindle generous ardour, feed pure love,/ Beget the smiles that have no cruelty—/ Be the sweet presence of a good diffused" (*CSP* 2:86). Through the music of the poem, the narrator invites the reader to join the "choir invisible," look into and feel with the lives of others, and in so doing, make music that is "the gladness of the world" (*CSP* 2:86).

"A College Breakfast Party" (1874), a blank verse poetic dialogue, demonstrates through its form and content the relationship between harmony and discord (i.e., sympathy and difference). The characters vigorously debate a range of philosophical perspectives including how to live in the world and what constitutes "human good" (*CSP* 2:35–40). The poem presents multiple perspectives but offers no resolution to the problems discussed; however, the conflict itself offers harmony: "As these different worldviews collide, it becomes increasingly clear that the glue holding this community together is not intellectual agreement but rather a spirit of amical discord" revealing Eliot's belief that "the most advanced 'form'—whether one is speaking of a literary production or a social body—must be heterogeneous in make-up" (Stern 97). Intellectual consensus is a sort of "feeling together (*con-sensus*) that is fostered not by a spirit of general agreement but rather by ideological difference" (97). Interestingly, the poem introduces a debate about the function of poetry through which Eliot furthers her own artistic agenda. One character, Osric, naively argues that poetry "knows nought" of the world's suffering ("bitter strife, denial, grim resolve,/ Sour resignation") (*CSP* 2:45). Rather, like a lake, poetry "Images all things, yet within its depths/Dreams them all lovelier—thrills with sound" (*CSP* 2:45). In his idealistic view, poetry transforms all forms of atrocity into a singular beauty and composes unifying music ("a harp") from the "plenteous liquid chords" of life (*CSP* 2:45). "Hatred, war, vice, crime, sin" and "human storms" provide "contrast" for art and aid the artist by giving "grander touch/ To the master's pencil and the poet's song" (*CSP* 2:45). Art turns a "fleckless mirror to the various world,/ Giving its many-named and fitful flux/An imaged, harmless, spiritual life" (*CSP* 2:46). For Osric, art subsumes the human suffering of a "mongrel globe" and reflects a perfect, pure, spiritual beauty that is free from ugly variety (*CSP* 2:46). Another character, Guildenstern, argues (Eliot's view) that poetry should not portray an idealized, homogenous view of the world but should reflect the world as it really is and find beauty in its diversity:

> Join in a war-dance with the cannibals,
> Hear Chinese music, love a face tattooed,
> Give adoration to a pointed skull,
> And think the Hindu Siva looks divine:
> 'Tis art, 'tis poesy. (*CSP* 2:47)

This passage suggests that the "mongrel globe" is indeed a "precarious sphere, one that is in continual flux and always at risk of falling apart. Yet it is ultimately the very tenuousness of the connections between individuals ... that makes sympathy possible" (Stern 101). Through the poetic dialogue in "a College Breakfast Party," Eliot demonstrates the value of listening to others' perspectives and urges readers to strive for harmony while embracing difference.

Eliot also employs dialogue in "Self and Life" (date unknown) to contrast the opposing perspectives of two "characters," "Self" and "Life." Near death and disillusioned, Self demands justification from his "Changeful comrade, Life" for "What thou hast been and art" (*CSP* 2:57). Self complains of the fear and suffering experienced in life, but Life justifies such "anguish" and "discontent" as growth, "the elemental strife/ Towards feeling manifold with vision blent/ To wider thought" (*CSP* 2:57–8). In other words, Life argues, difficulty in life opened Self's eyes to the diverse suffering of the world and urged a broader sympathy with humanity. After a series of alternating rejoinders, Self ultimately comes to see the truth of Life's view: "Yea, I embrace thee, changeful Life!/ Far-sent, unchosen mate!" (*CSP* 2:60) and they find harmony following their disagreement: "Self and thou, no more at strife,/ Shall wed in hallowed state" (*CSP* 2:60). Self and Life reconcile after nine stanzas of strict yet non-traditional verse. Self's stanzas all contain six lines with an *ababcc* rhyme pattern and Life's stanzas comprise twelve lines with an *ababcdcdeeff* rhyme scheme. Conflict and resolution within the boundaries of a rigid, yet creative verse form demonstrate the delicate balance between discord and harmony.

"A Minor Prophet" (1865) is a narrative poem with some dialogue through which Eliot criticizes the narrow-minded character, Elias Baptist Butterworth, a "harmless, bland, disinterested man" whose ancestors insisted on uniformity: "coats and hats/... of one pattern, "books and songs/ All fit for Sundays" (*CSP* 1:169). Butterworth has no original ideas but "On all points he adopts the latest views" to grasp "higher truths" (*CSP* 1:170). Like Osric, he believes in a utopian world in which "All will be harmony of hue and line,/ Bodies and minds all perfect, limbs well-turned,/ And talk quite free from aught erroneous (*CSP* 1:173). The poem's narrator, Colin Clout, rejects Butterworth's vision of "perfect future times" that "Will not know half the dear imperfect things," the "fine old incongruities," and the "twists and cracks in our poor earthenware,/ That touch me to more conscious fellowship" (*CSP* 1:173–4). Clout, like Guildenstern, advocates for beauty in variety:

> I cleave
> To nature's blunders, evanescent types
> Which sages banish from Utopia.
> "Not worship beauty?" say you. Patience, friend!
> I worship in the temple with the rest;
> But by my hearth I keep a sacred nook

For gnomes and dwarfs, duck-footed waddling elves
Who stitched and hammered for the weary man
In days of old. (*CSP* 1:174)

He pities those in Butterworth's future world who will not know "A keen experience with pity blent,/ The pathos exquisite of lovely minds/ Hid in harsh forms" (*CSP* 1:174). Unlike Osric, Butterworth exits the scene and does not have the benefit of the narrator's more evolved view. However, readers understand through dialogue and disagreement the importance of experiencing the beauty of different and "harsh forms."

Through poetic versatility, Eliot sought to show the beauty in difference and thereby widen the scope of sympathy for others. For her, the world needed to understand difference and sympathize with Otherness to improve. Readers in the nineteenth century could learn not only to expand their sympathies by entering the minds of characters and engaging narrators in her novels; they could also see, hear, and feel her message of sympathy through the experience of poetry. Eliot turned to poetry—then considered the highest art form—late in her career because she sought to achieve literary greatness and leave a guiding message for future generations. She was one of the most famous and influential figures of her time, and she used her influence to write with moral authority. Today, she still influences readers through her novels. By also studying Eliot's poetry, readers can gain a better understanding of the author, her artistic vision, and her work as a whole. In addition, readers of her poetry open themselves to the influence of a great mind who sought to "Be the sweet presence of a good diffused" and bring music that is "the gladness of the world" (*CSP* 2:86).

Notes

1. Nancy Henry explains: "To a Victorian author—even one whose novels were influential in transforming realist fiction into high art— the most serious form of writing was poetry" and "By freeing herself from the restrictions of realism and conforming to the metrical requirements of poetry," Eliot conveyed her beliefs through the

highest form of expression and thus associated not with the realist novelists but with the great poets of the age (174–5).

2. See Antonie Gerard van den Broek's scholarly editions of Eliot's poems: *The Complete Shorter Poetry of George Eliot* (2005) and *The Spanish Gypsy* (2008); Charles LaPorte's "George Eliot, the Poetess as Prophet" (2003); the special issue of the *George Eliot-George Henry Lewes Studies*, Isobel Armstrong's "The Cultural Place of George Eliot's Poetry" (Sept. 2011); Gregory Tate's, *The Poet's Mind: The Psychology of Victorian Poetry 1830–1870* (2012); Herbert F. Tucker's "Poetry: The Unappreciated Eliot" (2013); and Wendy S. Williams's *George Eliot, Poetess* (2014).

3. Of the 225 epigraphs in her novels, ninety-six are original and 129 are borrowed from fifty-six identified authors and eight anonymous authors (Higdon 128–9).

4. She wrote to Charles Bray in 1857: "My own experience and development deepen everyday my conviction that our moral progress may be measured by the degree in which we sympathize with individual suffering and individual joy" (Eliot, *Letters* 2:403).

5. Hereafter *The Complete Shorter Poetry* will be referred to as *CSP*.

6. See Williams 82, 85–7.

7. Compare Eve Sedgwick's model of marriage in which women serve as objects of exchange between homosocial men in *Between Men: English Literature and Male Homosocial Desire*.

8. Kyriaki Hadjiafxendi aptly observes that Eliot writes poetry (elegy in particular) as a way of reproducing meaning through sound: "Erinna's melodious cries transform not only her pain into singing but also her response to the images she weaves into sound, and hence she herself becomes the elegy—an inter-communicative poetic body whose rhythmic processes the reader shares" ("Aural Sensibility" 110).

9. The first foot in line 3 shifts from iambic to trochaic meter to emphasize the severity of the obstruction of the light by houses that are "*Cut*ting the sky with one long line of wall" (3, emphasis mine). The first foot in line 11 also shifts from iambic to trochaic meter. Line 10 (…"No figure lingering") rushes to line 11 and shifts from iambic to trochaic meter (*Pau*ses to feed the hunger of the eye") to demonstrate the people's lack of pausing (10–11, emphasis mine).

10. Lines 9–10 (To vaster issues./ So to live is heaven") together read as one blank verse line. However, because of the division, the reader

visually and mentally pauses to see and feel the emphasis of such a lofty claim—that living a life of sympathy in "the choir invisible" is heaven on earth. Lines 34–35 follow a description of the "better self" living until the end of time when the sky will gather like a scroll inside a tomb ("Unread forever./ This is life to come"). Like lines 9–10, lines 34–35 create a visual and aural pause that accentuates a similar arresting idea—that the sympathetic life (described as heaven on earth) leads to a heavenly existence after human time. See also the metrical irregularities in lines 14, 19, 21, 34–35, 42, and 44.

Works Cited

Armstrong, Isobel. "The Cultural Place of George Eliot's Poetry." Special Issue of *George Eliot-George Henry Lewes Studies*. Ed. Kyriaki Hadjiafxendi. 60–61 (Sept. 2011): 7–16.

Boccaccio, Giovanni. *The Decameron, Or Ten Day's Entertainment of Boccaccio*. Trans. Walter Keating. London, UK: Henry G. Bohn, 1855.

Collins, K. K. *Interviews and Recollections*. Houndmills, UK: Palgrave Macmillan, 2010.

Eliot, George. *The Complete Shorter Poetry of George Eliot*. Ed. Antonie Gerard van den Broek. 2 Vols. London, UK: Pickering & Chatto, 2005.

_____. *Essays of George Eliot*. Ed. Thomas Pinney. New York, NY: Columbia UP, 1963.

_____. "Evangelical Teaching: Dr. Cumming." *Westminster Review* 64. London: John Chapman, 1855.

_____. *The George Eliot Letters*. Ed. Gordon Sherman Haight. 9 vols. New Haven, CT: Yale UP, 1954.

_____. *Middlemarch*. Ed. Gregory Maertz. Ontario, Canada: Broadview Press, 2004.

_____. "The Natural History of German Life." *Westminster Review* 66. London: John Chapman, 1856.

_____. *Silas Marner and Scenes of Clerical Life*. Boston: Fields, Osgood, & Co., 1869.

_____. *The Spanish Gypsy*. Ed. Antonie Gerard van den Broek. London: Pickering & Chatto, 2008.

_____. "Worldliness and Other-Worldliness: The Poet Young." *Westminster Review* 67. London: John Chapman, 1857.

Hadjiafxendi, Kyriaki. "Voicing the Past: Aural Sensibility, the Weaver-Poet, and George Eliot's 'Erinna.'" *Studies in the Literary Imagination* 43.1 (2010): 95–118.

Henry, Nancy. *The Life of George Eliot: A Critical Biography*. Chichester, UK: Wiley-Blackwell, 2012.

Higdon, David Leon. "George Eliot and the Art of the Epigraph." *Nineteenth-Century Fiction* 25.2 (1970): 127–51.

LaPorte, Charles. "George Eliot, the Poetess as Prophet." *Victorian Literature and Culture* 31.1 Victorian Religion (2003): 159–79.

Stern, Kimberly. "The Poetics of Criticism: Dialogue and Discourse in George Eliot's Poetry." *The Cultural Place of George Eliot's Poetry*. Ed. Kyriaki Hadjiafxendi. Special issue of *George Eliot-George Henry Lewes Studies* 60–61 (Sept. 2011): 91–106.

Tate, Gregory. *The Poet's Mind: The Psychology of Victorian Poetry 1830–1870*. Oxford: Oxford UP, 2012.

Williams, Wendy S. *George Eliot, Poetess*. Burlington, VT: Ashgate, 2014.

"The world must be romanticized":
Tracing George Eliot's German Influences_____

Gareth Hadyk-DeLodder

> But this general disenchantment with the world … only intensified her sense of forlornness; it was a visibly sterile distance enclosing the dreary path at her feet, in which she had no courage to tread.
>
> (Eliot, *Daniel Deronda* 333)

> By giving the common a higher meaning, the everyday, a mysterious semblance, the known, the dignity of the unknown, the finite, the appearance of the infinite, I *romanticize* it.
>
> (Novalis, 1798)

Writing to her friend Maria Lewis on March 23, 1840, a twenty-year-old Mary Ann Evans noted, "I have just received my second lesson in German" (*Letters*, March 23, 1840). Such was the humble beginning of what would become a lifelong pursuit for George Eliot intellectually, spiritually, and personally. Within months of beginning her studies, she was reading Schiller and Goethe and beginning to translate German poetry ("Question and Answer" Oct. 1840). Her letters over the following two years reveal an explosive growth of her studies in German language and literature, and she often addressed her correspondents with German flourishes, textual references, and more. She would become, as many critics have contended, one of the preeminent translators and cultural bridges between England and Germany during her lifetime. Indeed, such was the pervasive influence and merit of German thought for her that she marked *Daniel Deronda*'s Lord Grandcourt, one of the most pernicious villains in her fiction, as one who "embraced all Germans … as brutes" (Eliot, *Daniel Deronda* 645). Similarly, she suggests that *Middlemarch*'s Casaubon, another odious husband (though not as malevolent as Grandcourt), fails in his own intellectual pursuits in part for not having familiarized himself with German historicism ("And therefore it is a pity that it should be thrown away, as so much

English scholarship is, for want of knowing what is being done by the rest of the world. If Mr. Casaubon read German he would save himself a great deal of trouble" [Eliot, *Middlemarch* 208]). She was evidently in agreement with her beloved George Henry Lewes, who, in 1858, boldly stated that:

> Great are the achievements of the German mind, and incalculable the debt which Europe owes Germany. In every department of literature, art, and science, he who has mastered the German language finds himself in possession of a key which will unlock costly cabinets. ("Realism in Art" 489)

A perusal of her critical pieces and fiction highlights the degree to which Lewes' remark is emblematic of her work as well. In addition to her excellent translations of prominent German thinkers, beginning with David Friedrich Strauss' *Das Leben Jesu, kritisch bearbeitet* [*The Life of Jesus, Critically Examined*] in 1844, many of her protagonists are conversant in German (Will Ladislaw from *Middlemarch*, Daniel Deronda, and others), and many of her critical pieces delve into German thought and philosophy. As critics like Hans Ulrich Seeber have argued, Eliot's works require "extraordinary demands on the intellectual capacity of her reader" (Rignall 20). She moves effortlessly between languages, textual references, and historical moments in her writing, creating a wonderfully dialogic space in which she engages and disseminates many different aspects of German literature and philosophy. It is, in part, the intention here to chart some of the different modes in Eliot's work that reflect her lifelong study of German thought. Because of the scope of her writing, this represents quite an undertaking—and one that has been carried out successfully and more comprehensively by other scholars. Consequently, this essay is framed around three different sections, each of which attempts to synthesize some of her reading and writing around a central theme growing out of her German studies. This structure, which prioritizes breadth over depth, has a two-fold importance: it organizes loosely some of the different themes that Eliot revisits in her major works, and it also serves to introduce some of the critical vocabulary associated with German and European romanticism in the nineteenth century.

For Eliot, the role of German ideas was fundamentally active in her fiction, and many of her characters would come to model the principles she found in the writings of Strauss, Ludwig Feuerbach, Goethe, and others. As she writes after reading W. H. Riehl's *Die bürgerliche Gesellschaft* (1851) [*Civil Society*] and *Land und Leute* (1856) [*Land and People*], "We wish to make these books known to our readers, not only for the sake of the interesting matter they contain, and the important reflections they suggest, but also as a model for some future or actual student of our own people" (Eliot, "Natural History" 31). This is a clear assertion of the value that she places on texts like Riehl's and others, and it becomes the dual logic in much of her writing: she embraces the ability to elucidate and to "model" the ideas therein. Similarly, although on a much smaller scale, this essay seeks to "make known" some of the principal themes in Eliot's works and the nature of their relationship with German philosophy. Using excerpts from *The Mill on the Floss* (1860), *Middlemarch* (1871–72), and *Daniel Deronda* (1876), I will address the secularization of religion in her translations and fiction and how it afforded her a means of moving beyond "outworn teaching,"[1] transcendental and literal homesickness, and the role of sympathy in what Goethe termed "elective affinities" (*Die Wahlverwandtschaften*, 1809). All three are foundational in addressing one of the primary roles of her fiction: "getting a clearer conception and a more active admiration of those vital elements which bind men together and give a higher worthiness to their existence" (Eliot, *Letters* IV: 472). Ultimately, I hope that this essay can serve both to introduce the important role that German romanticism played in the philosophical and spiritual development of Eliot—especially in terms of nuancing her social critiques—and to point to the rich vein of insight offered by engaging her works and ideas alongside those of the "great German masters."

*   *   *

In the years surrounding her introduction to German, Evans broke from the Evangelical religious practice of her family, almost breaking completely from Christianity. In a letter to Maria Lewis dated November 13, 1841, she wrote, "My whole soul has been engrossed in the most interesting of all inquiries for the last few days, and to what result my thoughts may lead I know not—possibly to one that will startle you, but my only desire is to know the truth, my only fear to cling to error..." (Eliot, *Letters* 18). The ellipsis at the end of the sentence is revealing, even more so when we stop to consider its context. As Gordon Haight supplies, Evans was referring to Charles Hennell's *Inquiry Concerning the Origin of Christianity* (Eliot, *Letters* 18). Not only was Hennell the brother of Sara, who would become one of Evans' closest confidantes for many years of her life, but he was also the author of this rather polemical text, one that purported to analyze the New Testament as a historical document. Her shifting perception of religion is wonderfully manifest in a later letter to Sara:

> I am inclined to think that such a change of sentiment is likely to happen to most persons whose views on religious matters undergo a change early in life. The first impulse of a young and ingenuous mind is to withhold the slightest sanction from all that contains even a mixture of supposed error. When the soul is just liberated from the wretched giant's bed of dogmas on which it has been racked and stretched ever since it began to think, there is a feeling of exultation and strong hope. (Oct. 9, 1843)

Her language is unambiguous in connecting her previous Evangelical beliefs with a register at once injurious and unhealthy—so much so, in fact, that there is little surprise when Maggie Tulliver assumes a similarly militaristic approach to her faith as a young girl in *The Mill on the Floss*.

Mary Ann Evans' interest in more historically-oriented biblical interpretation, in tandem with her growing skills in German, led to an offer to assume the duties of translating Strauss' *Das Leben Jesu* in 1844, which was similar to Hennell's text in spirit, although more rigorous in critiquing the historical reality of biblical narratives. For Strauss, "After many centuries of tedious research, [the modern world] has attained a conviction, that all things are linked together by a chain of causes and effects which suffers no interruption" (Strauss 59). This "linked ... chain" would become foundational in her writing—and it should be familiar to readers of *Middlemarch*, with its iconic web metaphor for human relations—and established a framework that Eliot would develop further through her readings of Spinoza, Feuerbach, and others.

For the next two years, Evans worked exhaustively on the translation, steeping herself in a mode of criticism that, as Anthony McCobb writes, many Victorians felt was "sacrilegiously rationalistic" (9). Following the success of her translation in 1846 and her stewardship as editor of the *Westminster Review* between 1851–1854, she began working first on a translation of Baruch Spinoza's *Ethics* and then Ludwig Feuerbach's *Das Wesen des Christentums* (*The Essence of Christianity*) in 1854. Spinoza's work, as others have commented, proved to be tremendously influential for Evans in articulating her break from Christian dogma. Similarly, Feuerbach's work also helped her to move away from strict doctrinal understandings of faith and goodness. As Rosemary Ashton argues, "Most important of all for George Eliot was Feuerbach's allowance for goodness in human beings as a spontaneous emotion, not one extracted from them by fear of an angry God" (*The German Idea* 160). Spinoza and Strauss afforded her a model for the secularization of religious affect, which, as we will see presently, figured prominently in her female protagonists. More importantly, perhaps, both also figured into her own understanding of personal and sexual relations and moralities.

Maggie, Dorothea, and Gwendolen suffer the most grievously from a "wretched giant's bed of dogmas" in their respective stories, and so it is fitting that each, in varying degrees, is afforded a similar spiritual awakening as Eliot herself was. The characters are quite different from each other, which becomes apparent as each story progresses. We might argue that Maggie Tulliver is Eliot's closest biographical analogue, as various critics have commented in the past. Like Eliot, she is cast off by society because she transgresses normative boundaries in her failed attempt to run off with a man (the charismatic Stephen Guest) and is thereafter shunned by her brother.

Similarly, Maggie adopts a strict, almost ascetic religious habitus as a young woman that, crucially, is challenged by those around her and by her own spiritual maturation. In spite of their differences, all three women undergo a marked evolution, using ideas and language from Feuerbach.

Not only do Maggie and Dorothea break away from radical religious thinking—Maggie from her "utter privation of joy" (Eliot, *Mill on the Floss* 378) through self-negation and Dorothea from her strict "hereditary strain of Puritan energy" (Eliot, *Middlemarch* 8)—but Gwendolen also comes to adopt a more comprehensive understanding and sympathy for others. Arguably, Gwendolen's transformation is the more surprising, given that she does not reject clearly constructed religious "outdated teaching[s]" as do Maggie and Dorothea, but instead arrives at an understanding of sympathy derived from Spinoza and Feuerbach. The latter wrote,

> The relations of child and parent, of husband and wife, of brother and friend—in general of man to man—in short, all the moral relations are *per se* religious. Life as a whole is, in its essential substantial relations, throughout of a divine nature. (Feuerbach 271)

Thus when Eliot writes that Gwendolen has regained a "spiritual breath" in the companionship of Deronda, it is another example of how she elevates human relationships. Eliot writes, "For the first time since that terrible moment on the sea a flush rose and spread over her cheek, brow, and neck, deepened an instant or two, and then gradually disappeared" (Eliot, *Daniel Deronda* 840). For Gwendolen, both survival (in her festering marriage to Grandcourt) and salvation after his death and the role she fears she played in it are arrived at through Deronda's sympathy. In place of a religious sympathy as mediated by practice and protocol— and given that, for her, "Church was not markedly distinguished in her mind from the other forms of self-presentation ... than that of unexplained and perhaps inexplicable social fashions" (666)—it is her connection with Deronda that fashions her "outer conscience" (833). This is a crucial point; Eliot locates her "higher purpose" through a burgeoning awareness of others, which reflexively allows

Gwendolen to understand herself better (and leads to, among other developments, Gwendolen's newfound familial commitments). For Maggie, Dorothea, and Gwendolen, the repudiation of "wretched giant's bed of dogmas" allows each woman to find a greater sense of self and community.

*   *   *

The violence of repudiating artificial or false conventions and teachings in the previous section often precipitates a loss that can be felt on multiple levels. For Eliot, the liberation from "wretched … dogmas" almost always leads initially to a domestic division or rupture. Maggie is shunned by her brother after her failed attempt to elope with Stephen, Silas is cast away from his religious community when he breaks from them theologically, Dorothea and Will face public rebuke after Casaubon's death and the issue of his will, and more. In these examples, Eliot's characters become outcasts or exiles of one sort or another, and each yearns for some kind of return or resolution to their unhappy status. Maggie idealizes the space and people of her childhood, for example, embodying a kind of *Heimweh* (homesickness) that afflicts many characters in Eliot's work. That we see this often in her writing is perhaps unsurprising, given her own history of being exiled from family members and elements of "respectable" society following her decision to live openly with Lewes. As she writes in a letter to Sara, "I have a little *Heimweh* 'as it regards' my friends, I yearn to see those I have loved the longest" (Eliot, *Letters* I: 177).

Heimweh thus becomes an important register in her works, given that the affect or mood often signifies a vital loss or status outside of the norm; it is something that must be understood or reoriented in order for the character to grasp the redeeming influence of human relationships. Read in this light, Eliot's own *Heimweh*, revealingly, is not for her family or home, but instead for a different community in which she loves and feels loved. We learn that Deronda's general homesickness reflects his liminal position as both Jewish and English, while Maggie's homesickness conceals the rupture of her family and her status within the community, for example.

This homesickness for a lost object is not to be confused with a more idealized nostalgia for an innocent past, however. She opines, "I never will believe that our youngest days are our happiest. What a miserable augury for the progress of the race and the destination of the individual if the more mature and enlightened state is the less happy one" (Eliot, *Letters* [to Miss Sara Hennell, dated May 1844]). Eliot is shrewd enough to recognize some of the pitfalls with the retrospective gaze, as it can obscure or even elide social or personal problems. A few lines from her excellent "The Natural History of German Life" illustrate this vividly, in which she critiques W. H. Riehl's *Die bürgerliche Gesellschaft* (1851) [*Civil Society*] and *Land und Leute* (1856) [*Land and People*]:

> The aristocratic dilettantism which attempts to restore the 'good old times' by a sort of idyllic masquerading, and to grow feudal fidelity and veneration as we grow prize turnips, by an artificial system of culture—none of these diverging mistakes can coexist with a real knowledge of the people, with a thorough study of their habits, their ideas, their motives. (Eliot, "Natural History" 31)

Very much in the same vein as Feuerbach and Spinoza, then, "artificial systems of culture" must be rejected in favor of the human elements.

This classed awareness of historical consciousness extends into a political arena. Undermining the twin axes of German historical power, church and throne, Eliot writes,

> He [the peasant] has the warmest piety toward the old tumble-down house which his grandfather built, and which nothing will induce him to improve, but toward the venerable ruins of the old castle that overlooks his village he has no piety at all, and carries off its stones to make a fence for his garden, or tears down the gothic carving of the old monastic church, which is "nothing to him," to mark off a foot-path through his field. It is the same with historical traditions. ("Natural History" 34)

The breakdown of religious and aristocratic markers is thus literal and ideological. The peasant's "warmest piety" towards immediate community (and the lost family) is wholly absent in his feelings about his country's noble lines, just as the religious signifier ("carving of the old monastic church") is similarly evacuated of authority. Both the castle's ruins and religious carvings are recycled into serviceable structures, signaling at once their nature as commodity as well as their potential to be appropriated by the proletariat, Marx's term for the working classes. Indeed, the language of the past is omnipresent throughout her observations. The "tumble-down house" is a relic of the grandfather's era, while the castle is described as "venerable," "old," and "ruin[ed]." Similarly, the church is "old" and "Gothic," and its austerity is no longer capable of inspiring fear or reverence as the peasant "tears [it] down"—a much more violent action than simply "carrying off" some of the castle's stones. Importantly, this offers Eliot another register in the shift from the romanticized "robber barons" of old that she mentions in *The Mill on the Floss* towards the "sordid life" of the "tragic comic": the life of the Tullivers and the Dodsons, which are "irradiated by no sublime principles" but still reveal the "strongest fibres" of their hearts (Eliot, *Mill* 362–63).

While Eliot's narrators sometimes articulate a longing for the past, her female characters often demonstrate the precariousness of women's societal roles in ways that challenge traditional (patriarchal) understandings of *Heimweh*. Gwendolen, Mary Garth (*Middlemarch*), and Maggie, for example, all must deal with the harsh realities for unmarried women, as they each are forced to consider leaving their homes to become a governess when their families are faced with economic hardships. The loss of home and liminal social standing are framed as trying and distressing dislocations. As Mr. Gascoigne attempts to comfort Gwendolen on the prospect, he relates that "It [a position in the house of a Mrs. Mompert] *is really a home*, with a continuance of education in the highest sense: 'governess' is a misnomer" (Eliot, *Daniel Deronda* 313, emphasis added). His cheery rhetoric conceals a truth far grimmer than he can understand. Despite his protestations, "governess" points to the murky conflation of labor and the artificial domestic. Eliot's narrator takes Mr. Gascoigne to task for this misunderstanding immediately following his line—"The Rector's words were too pregnant with satisfactory meaning to himself for him to imagine the effect they produced on the mind of his niece" (313). There is a poignancy to these lines, similar to what Mary Garth hints at in *Middlemarch* as she considers the vocation of being a governess: "I thought it would always be part of my life to long for home" (408).

* * *

Goethe held a special place for Eliot; she speaks of him in her letters from the time of her first introduction to his writing and the language spanning 1840 to an admiring response about his poetic nature in a letter to Harriet Beecher Stowe in 1874 ("I am writing to your dear husband as well as to you, and in answer to his question about Goethe, I must say, for my part, that I think he had a strain of mysticism in his soul—of so much mysticism as I think inevitably belongs to a full, poetic nature"). Perhaps most significant, however, was that Goethe was the object of lifelong study for Lewes. Indeed, she helped him research and edit his manuscript (the very successful *The Life of Goethe*, published in 1855), which took the couple frequently to Germany, a second home for both, given the wider acceptance of her relationship with Lewes. Goethe's influence on Eliot and her writing cannot be overstated, as well as the relationship between Goethe and other German thinkers. Eliot was quick to point this out: in a letter to Sara Hennell on October 28, 1865, she noted that "As Goethe said long ago about Spinoza, 'Ich zog immer vor von dem Menschen zu erfahren *wie er dachte* als von einem anderen zu hören *wie er hätte denken sollen*'" ["I always preferred to learn from the man himself *what he thought*, rather than to hear from someone else *what he ought to have thought*"]. She must have felt the same about Goethe, given the numerous epigraphs from his work that frame multiple chapters in her novels as well as different essays that she published on his writing.

Middlemarch derives some of its emotional charge from Goethe's *Die Wahlverwandtschaften* [*Elective Affinities*]—a technical title that refers to the tendency of chemicals to attract and combine with other substances. The title suggests an operating metaphor for the makeup and changes to the personal relationships in the novella. His work, which Eliot writes "brings us into the presence of living, generous humanity—mixed and erring, and self-deluding," establishes a blueprint that she would eagerly adopt in her own work ("The Morality of Wilhelm Meister"). It is not only *Middlemarch* that follows this trajectory (especially in the slow development of the relationships between Dorothea and Will Ladislaw and between Lydgate and Rosamond); most of her fiction is based on "comfortable issues allowed to questionable actions and questionable characters," as she wrote of Goethe in 1855.

Chapter 6 in volume III of *The Mill on the Floss* is entitled "Illustrating the Laws of Attraction"—a clear reference to Goethe's work. The chapter deals with the feelings of desire and attraction that Maggie and Stephen cannot articulate. Eliot writes, "Each was oppressively conscious of the other's presence, even to the finger-ends. Yet each looked and longed for the same thing to happen the next day. Neither of them had begun to reflect on the matter, or silently to ask, 'To what does all this Tend'" (Eliot, *Mill* 516)? Similar to the language that she uses for the charged pairings in *Middlemarch* and *Daniel Deronda*, Eliot follows her own observations of Goethe: "He quietly follows the stream of fact and of life; and waits patiently for the moral process of nature as we all do for her material processes" ("Morality of Wilhelm Meister"). The connections between the characters are not forced or sudden; dozens of chapters chart the development for each major pairing, as readers are party to a slow unfolding of the different moods and feelings that shape the attraction. This organic relationship is perhaps most clearly outlined in *Daniel Deronda*:

> That was the sort of crisis which was at this moment beginning in Gwendolen's small life: she was for the first time feeling the pressure of a vast mysterious movement, for the first time being dislodged from her supremacy in her own world, and getting a sense that her horizon was but a dipping onward of an existence with which her own was revolving. (876)

The line is arresting in both its emotional power and its vivid imagery. The "crisis," similar to the emotional response(s) of homesickness discussed in the previous section, is nonetheless a catalyzing agent for Gwendolen, who is gradually becoming aware of her own egoism through her feelings for Deronda. For Gwendolen and Maggie, it is this sympathetic connection with another person that ultimately reorients their worldview (*Weltanschauung*) through Eliot's understanding of Goethe's "moral process of nature."

* * *

As Eliot herself recognized, romanticism was a "spreading movement" (*Middlemarch* 188) in the nineteenth century to combat the disenchantment (*Entzauberung*) that Gwendolen (and others) felt so keenly, and the "upheaval" at its ideological core raises a number of questions in terms of how we understand its many and varied influences (Lowy & Sayre 8). What is clear is that, despite her narrator's protestations in *Middlemarch* that the story (and others like it) trace "unhistoric acts," Eliot's work embodies a reimagining of history that sought to dislodge (or at least shift) an entrenched way of blotting out the proletariat: for Eliot, the "obscure hearths" (*Mill* 363). In thus uncovering and throwing the varied sympathies that connect *all* of her characters into relief, Eliot puts the ideas and theories of Strauss, Spinoza, and Feuerbach into practice in ways that invite further speculation about the reverberations of her fiction and criticism. Scholars like Nancy Cervetti have examined some of the shared ideas between Eliot and Karl Marx, for example—lines of inquiry that work particularly well in *Silas Marner* and several other of her novels.

In offering a relatively broad overview of how Eliot brought to bear several different aspects of German thought, this essay sought both to complement other entries in this collection and to establish an important lens through which to appreciate the nuance and depth of her artistic expression. Eliot's fiction, criticism, and translation constitute a dense and complex body of works; accordingly, whatever signposts we can use to better understand her writing become all the more valuable heuristics. When choosing these three areas, I tried to pick several ideas that comprised an important emotional trajectory prominent in her fiction, in her nonfiction, and in her personal life. Hopefully, these brief vignettes can, at the very least, point to the kinship between Eliot's writings and German literary and philosophical traditions, illuminating a number of critical and interpretive paths to follow.

Note

1. In a letter to Clifford Thomas Allbutt in 1868, she wrote that her chief motivation to write was "[P]resenting our human life as to help my readers in getting a clearer conception and a more active admiration of those vital elements which bind men together and give a higher worthiness to their existence; and also to help them in gradually dissociating these elements from the more transient forms on which an outworn teaching tends to make them dependent."

Works Cited

Ashton, Rosemary. *The German Idea: Four English Writers and the Reception of German Thought, 1800–1860.* Cambridge, UK: Cambridge UP, 1980.

_____. *George Eliot: A Life.* London: Penguin, 1996.

_____. *G. H. Lewes: A Life.* Oxford, UK: Clarendon Press, 1991.

Eliot, George. *Middlemarch.* Ed. Rosemary Ashton. London: Penguin, 2003.

_____. *The Mill on the Floss.* Ed. A. S. Byatt. Harmondsworth, UK: Penguin Books, 1985.

_____. *Silas Marner.* New York: Bantam Books, 1992.

_____. *Daniel Deronda.* Ed. Barbara N. Hardy. Harmondsworth, UK: Penguin Books, 1967.

_____. "Natural History of German Life." *Westminster Review* Vol. 66 (July/Oct. 1856): 28–43.

_____. *Selections from George Eliot's Letters.* Ed. Gordon S. Haight. New Haven, CT: Yale UP, 1985.

Feuerbach, Ludwig. *The Essence of Christianity.* Trans. Marian Evans. London: Trüber & Co., Ludgate Hill, 1881. Digital.

Fleishman, Avrom. *George Eliot's Intellectual Life*. Cambridge, UK: Cambridge UP, 2010.

Lewes, George Henry. "Realism in Art: Recent German Fiction." *Westminster Review*. Vol. 14 (Jul./Oct. 1858): 488–500.

Löwy, Michael & Robert Sayre. *Romanticism against the Tide of Modernity*. Durham, NC: Duke UP, 2001.

McCobb, Anthony. *George Eliot's Knowledge of German Life and Letters*. Salzburg, AT: Institut für Anglistik und Amerikanistik, Universität Salzburg, 1982.

Pfau, Thomas. *Romantic Moods: Paranoia, Trauma, and Melancholy, 1790–1840*. Baltimore, MD: Johns Hopkins UP, 2005.

Rignall, John. *George Eliot and Europe*. Aldershot, Hants, UK: Scholar Press, 1997.

Röder-Bolton, Gerlinde. *George Eliot and Goethe: An Elective Affinity*. Amsterdam, NL: Rodopi, 1998.

Strauss, David Friedrich. *The Life of Jesus, Critically Examined*. Trans. Marian Evans. New York: Calvin Branchard, 1860. Digital.

Doubt, Devotion, Duty: George Eliot, the Death of God, and the Quest to Combine Transcendence and Coherence_____

Shandi Stevenson

George Eliot's novels present a uniquely rich exploration of the late-Victorian struggle to absorb the impacts of Darwinism, Biblical criticism, and the "death of God" movement. Eliot's fiction, like her life, captures a brief, momentous window of time during which a generation of intellectuals and artists rejected the theological certainties of a previous era, yet sought a worldview in which a transcendent ethic and a coherent, unified vision of man's place in the world still defined human life. The faith Eliot and others struggled to maintain in such ideals as duty, love, honor, and sacrifice collapsed, for many, on the blood-soaked battlefields of World War I, and after that cultural cataclysm, a new and much more pessimistic set of ideas—of which the darkest, most anguished late-Victorian meditations of Hardy, Arnold, and Swinburne were only a foreshadowing—came to dominate culture and literature. During Eliot's lifetime, however, the same search for transcendence and coherence that preoccupied her was the still-hopeful quest of many Victorian rationalists. The best of the new (progress in knowledge through scientific explanations and the possibility of defeating such ancient demons as poverty, crime, and war) was to be blended with the best of the old (the sense of wonder and mystery that stimulated art and imagination, and the robustly transcendent morality that, many believed, held society together and enabled it to progress).

Those late-Victorians who were philosophically or temperamentally pessimistic—Ruskin, Carlyle, and Hardy spring to mind—already believed this project was ultimately impossible, and that much would inevitably be lost in the sacrifice of the old religious worldview. T. H. Huxley, though opposing this group himself, aptly described their experience:

The consciousness of this great truth [material explanations of the universe] weighs like a nightmare ... upon many of the best minds of these days. They watch what they conceive to be the progress of materialism, in such fear and powerless anger as a savage feels when, during an eclipse, the great shadow creeps over the face of the sun. The advancing tide of matter threatens to drown their souls; the tightening grasp of law impedes their freedom; they are alarmed lest man's moral nature be debased by the increase of her wisdom. (qtd. in Beer 142)

Such thinkers feared that the one-two punch of Darwinism (which seemed to eradicate the supernatural from the material universe) and the "higher" textual criticism of the Bible (which, by studying the Bible as a collection of imperfect ancient documents rather than a divinely inspired message, seemed to eliminate the supernatural from Scripture) had finished off any possibility of belief in a meaningful universe. Together these developments, along with other trends in philosophy and science, had created what was known as "the death of God" movement—a school of thought that considered rational belief in the supernatural no longer possible, but feared the moral, philosophical, and existential ramifications of sacrificing that belief.

Victorian optimists, in contrast, envisioned humanity on the threshold of a new age, ready to throw off the shackles that had made its progress slow and painful and achieve its moral, cultural, and intellectual potential. The progress of reductionist, materialist scientific analysis, not only of the physical universe but of human psychology and society, would give mankind power to realize all that was best in the human mind and spirit. The moral aspirations and obligations once fueled by Christianity would not vanish, but would be strengthened by a new, rationalist foundation. Science would prove the savior, not the destroyer, of human values, once integrated with and supported by ethics, education, and the arts. As Terry Eagleton explains:

As the power of religion begins to fail, its various functions are redistributed like a precious legacy to those aspiring to become its heirs. Scientific rationalism takes over its doctrinal certainties, while radical politics inherits its mission to transform the face of the earth. Culture in the aesthetic sense safeguards something of its spiritual depth…. Meanwhile, culture in the wider sense of the word retains something of religion's communitarian ethos. (174)

This great rebuilding of the world shaped the literature of late-Victorian Britain. The novel, in particular, was reaching its artistic and philosophical apex just in time to capture the conflicts of the era and explore their effects on individuals and communities. George Eliot, who read the books and knew the people reshaping the consciousness of Europe, is an especially compelling chronicler of her time. As Gertrude Himmelfarb writes, "Eliot was the rare novelist who was also a genuine intellectual, whose most serious ideas found dramatic expression in her novels" (154). And Neil Roberts points out:

[I]n her writing we hear the sincere and intelligent voice of profound human experience in an age which for the sensitive and intelligent was one of uncertainty, contradiction and conflict…. Because of her honesty and intelligence, the central conflicts of her age impressed themselves directly upon her life … of the moral and spiritual experience of educated people, she is a uniquely complete witness…. Of all great English novelists … she was most of an intellectual. Her imaginative achievement was prepared for and accompanied by a passionate and informed interest in the most up-to-date philosophy, theology, sociology, and natural science. (9–10)

Eliot's fiction thus captures a moment of transition in Anglo-American thought. Unlike such predecessors as Austen, Gaskell, Dickens, and Thackeray, Eliot fully incorporates into her fiction what A. N. Wilson describes as an impulse to "reconcile the advancements of modern thought with the religious instincts of human kind" (337). She weights her words, as Gillian Beer writes, "with the fullest concerns of the time—those concerns in which emotion and intellect are not kept apart but most completely imply each other" (140). Eliot thus anticipates the coming generation of novelists, for whom the most controversial ideas of the Victorian period had become unquestioned assumptions. Yet unlike such subsequent authors as Hardy and Forster, Eliot rejects the dark and disorienting moral universe that would become a hallmark of modernism. She continues to believe in the possibility of a coherent worldview, comprising both high ideals of morality and human potential, and a rigorous understanding of modern science and philosophy. Thus, her work is unsettling and complex in comparison with that of her predecessors, yet oddly innocent and nostalgic beside that produced only a few decades later.

Eliot is the last great novelist to hope for that elusive combination of transcendence and coherence, the possibility of which was taken for granted by the novelists who preceded her, and the impossibility of which was a fundamental assumption for those who followed her. After the "death of God," thinkers and artists tended to divide into two groups. One prioritized coherence over transcendence, ultimately willing, however reluctantly, to sacrifice religious, ethical, and aesthetic ideals to a scientific materialism, which alone seemed to offer the certainty and consistency of a worldview grounded in scientific objectivity. The other was unwilling to accept what seemed to them a harsh, uninspiring worldview, and believed such intangibles as wonder, faith, and unselfish love were essential to the human spirit and must be retained even if they contradicted the true nature of the universe. Such thinkers feared that the loss of the emotional; aesthetic; and, most especially, moral undergirding Christianity had once given society would, at best, drain the color from human experience and, at worst, plunge society into unrestrained selfishness and immorality.

Eliot's fiction portrays examples of both groups, and some of her most compelling (and, one suspects, most autobiographical) characters find themselves forced to choose between them, or to struggle for a coherent synthesis of both. In *Middlemarch*, Dorothea marries Casaubon because she longs to dedicate herself to his scholarly work, which for her embodies the pursuit of truth itself. Just as Dorothea begins to suspect the futility of Casaubon's work, however, she comes to know Will Ladislaw, who not only criticizes Casaubon's outdated methods, but rejects knowledge and systematization as ends in themselves. His declaration that it would be a loss to mankind if the sources of the Nile were discovered is the opposite of Casaubon's and Lydgate's determination to trace their own subjects to their ultimate sources. The young Dorothea initially believes that, as in the Christian worldview, truth and knowledge will lead to moral and emotional fulfillment, but she is forced to question that assumption and to face the possibility that human beings may have to choose between what is true and what is beautiful. Ladislaw's fear that the ultimate tendency of scientific knowledge may be to rob the world of something human beings need contrasts with the confidence of Casaubon and Lydgate that advances in, and systematization of, knowledge can only improve the lot of human beings in every way—physically, morally, imaginatively, and intellectually. Dorothea, who desires a great, unifying narrative to give meaning and consistency not only to her ideas and beliefs but to her feelings and actions, is torn between instinctive sympathies for both views and dissatisfied with the limitations of both—unable to conform to the narrowness of Casaubon's worldview, but unable (at least initially) to agree with Ladislaw that truth is inadequate to shape a complete life.

Another of Eliot's most compelling female characters, Maggie Tulliver in *The Mill on the Floss*, shares with Dorothea the compulsion to seek a defining purpose for her life. Like Dorothea, Maggie is torn between her strong affections and emotions, represented in different ways by Tom and by Stephen, and her intellectual and imaginative life liberated by Philip. The tragic end of the novel leaves it unclear what would have become of Maggie had her heroic death not cut short her struggle to reconcile the competing forces of her strong, passionate nature, which, like Dorothea's and Eliot's own, was incapable of doing, feeling, or believing anything halfheartedly.

It is this power of grappling with the competing claims of mind, heart, and conscience—claims which, after centuries of apparent harmony, had begun to seem like warring entities dividing, rather than uniting, the human psyche—that gives Eliot's work its distinctive impact. Her unique perspective stems not simply from her grasp of the human longing for transcendence, or of the human need for coherence—both of which she shared with other writers of the period—but from her struggle to combine the two. She shared her commitment to intellectual honesty and inquiry with the boldest materialists and rationalists of the day, adopting the ideas of Lyell, Darwin, Spencer, Comte, Feuerbach, and others. Yet she shared a reverent tenderness toward religious tradition and a demanding ethic of self-sacrifice with those who most fiercely resisted them. It is this dichotomy, embodied in both her life and her fiction, which makes George Eliot the great voice of her age.

Thus, Eliot's fiction explores the quest for transcendence—the longing for some great, ennobling purpose, which Eliot herself experienced throughout her life. Her poem "O May I Join the Choir Invisible" speaks of her desire to live with "scorn/of miserable aims that end with self," and "thoughts sublime that pierce the night like stars/and with their mild persistence urge men's minds/ to vaster issues" (5–9). Bernard Paris refers to "Eliot's need for a sense of religious orientation in the cosmos" (11) and explains, "The great question for Eliot ... was, how can man live a meaningful, morally satisfying life in an absurd universe" (12). Even when her abandonment of Christianity was complete, Eliot was drawn to systems of thought that resembled it in their comprehensiveness and their ethical dimension. As Oliver Lovesey points out, Eliot was "enticed" by "grand narratives and totalizing systems such as those of Auguste Comte, Ludwig Feuerbach, Herbert Spencer and Baruch Spinoza" (239). Such characters as Dorothea in *Middlemarch*; Deborah in *Adam Bede*; and Romola, Felix Holt, and Daniel Deronda in the novels of the same names are driven to seek a larger life, to discover some transcendent truth to give meaning to their brief time on earth. They cannot accept the small, self-centered motives that satisfy their contemporaries; they cannot dismiss, as other characters do, moments of illumination that make them aware of larger claims upon their lives.

Yet Eliot's most compelling characters are not satisfied with a sense of transcendence that avoids difficult truths. They are also driven by the need for coherence, for intellectual honesty and rigor, and for an informed and consistent understanding of reality. Dorothea can no more ignore the unwelcome fact of Casaubon's failure as a scholar, Silas Marner can no more set aside the inconsistencies that shatter his early faith, and Felix Holt can no more align himself with the comfortable perspectives of his friends than Dorothea or Maggie can be content with the narrow lives of the women around them. Eliot's greatest characters are profoundly affected by cognitive dissonance, as Eliot herself was. All her life, ideas had life and power for Eliot; she changed both her beliefs and her actions in response to ideas. Like Lydgate, who seeks the essence of the human body, and Casaubon, who seeks the common root of world mythologies, Eliot instinctively sought a cohesive understanding of the world and of human life.

The search for a worldview that combines transcendence and coherence is, then, the distinctive quest of Eliot's life and fiction, and it is this that makes her the voice of an era. She was both a pioneer, distilling in her fiction the latest developments in scientific, philosophical, political, and religious thought, and the last survivor of an endangered species, defending a moral vision many were already rejecting as untenable. Much of her greatness lies in the uniquely transitional world she creates for us, in which the values and impulses of a dying age are preserved and celebrated, yet in which the fast-approaching disillusionment and disorientation of the next literary generation are foreshadowed.

Eliot's fiction explores three avenues to the synthesis of transcendence and coherence: doubt, devotion, and duty, or the intellectual, the emotional, and the moral. First, then, Eliot captures the experience of doubt, portraying with unparalleled ability the impact on thoughtful minds of encountering new ideas. Her description of Lydgate's intellectual passion for medical science and its awakening by his childhood reading is especially moving and evocative. In particular, however, her sympathetic, insightful portrayals of intellectual and religious crisis are characteristic of Eliot. She is not alone in treating a subject few novelists of her era could avoid, but, combining as she does the sympathy of Elizabeth Gaskell or the great Russian novelists with the hard-edged, clear-sightedness of Thomas Hardy, Eliot is the great chronicler of the struggle between sincere, even passionate religious belief and intellectual doubt that was so characteristic of her time.

Much of Eliot's insight into this struggle stemmed from her own experience. As a young woman of exceptional intelligence and education, Eliot grappled with the great intellectual currents of her day in a way relatively few women could have done. Like her characters Dorothea and Romola, Eliot was concerned with far larger issues than those that preoccupied most young women. As a child, Eliot shared the conventional religious attitudes of her family, and as a young woman, she went a step further and embraced a fervent evangelical devotion that was more rigorous and more enthusiastic than her family's Anglican belief and practice. A few years later, however, exposed through new acquaintances and wider reading to biblical criticism, free thought, and theological modernism, Eliot rejected her Christian upbringing with the same fervent, wholehearted enthusiasm with which she had once pursued it and, for a time, caused a mutually painful estrangement in her family by refusing to accompany her father to church (Jacobs par. 1–4). Ultimately, Eliot agreed to return to church and outwardly conform to her father's expectations, on the clear understanding that she was not a Christian. Later in her life, she would regret the youthful zeal that had made her harsh and contemptuous in her attitude toward the religious belief of others (Jacobs 4). In such stories as *Silas Marner* and *Adam Bede*, Eliot portrays Christianity with a genuine sympathy and respect.

Yet Eliot's rejection of Christianity and commitment to intellectual inquiry are fundamental to her life and work. Always in search of a grand truth about the universe, the young Eliot was strongly influenced by the quasi-pantheistic views of Wordsworth, by the positivist system and the "religion of humanity" of Comte, by the philosophies of Spinoza and Herbert Spencer, and by the theology of Feuerbach. As Roberts notes, "George Eliot was an intellectual in the deepest sense, in that she demanded the assent of her intellect before accepting any proposition about how to live and what to live for… (11). Eliot believed in making any sacrifices reason might demand. Oliver Lovesey notes that "a willingness to live in the presence of uncomfortable truths without recourse to opium—intellectual or otherwise—is admired everywhere in her fiction" (241). Eliot believed "those who have strength to wait and endure, are bound to accept no formula which their whole souls—their intellect as well as their emotions—do not embrace with entire reverence" (*Letters* 217–218). And she speaks reverently of "that patient watching of external fact, and that silence of preconceived notions, which are urged upon the mind by the problems of physical science" (qtd. in Roberts 14). The love of truth as an intellectual, ethical, and aesthetic concept unified Eliot's thought, underlying not only the specific ideas but also the commitment to realism that characterized her fiction (Henry 79).

Thus, Eliot writes sympathetically of all whose intellectual struggles stem from a commitment to intellectual integrity. She is somewhat less gentle with those who abandon the struggle for truth, whether religious hypocrites, such as Bulstrode, or incompetent scholars, such as Casaubon. Eliot is far too gifted an observer of human beings to fall into the error of suggesting that most people are preoccupied with intellectual inquiry, or that it is somehow better to be an intellectual than to be occupied with one's own work and community—as are Caleb Garth and Adam Bede, two of her most lovable characters. Indeed, Eliot makes it clear that such characters as Celia in *Middlemarch* and Pastor Irwine in *Adam Bede*, with their instinctive empathy, their common sense, and their acceptance of daily life, have a wisdom that eludes such characters as Dorothea. Yet Eliot's major characters face confrontation with a threatening truth of some kind—some fact, idea, or insight that does not fit their current picture of the world. At this point, characters must respond by embracing, however painfully, an enlargement of their world, a shifting of the self out of the center of things—as, in their different ways, Daniel Deronda, Maggie, Romola, Dorothea, Adam Bede, Silas Marner, and Arthur Donnithorne do—or find a way to close their minds defensively against the new thought and draw their small, self-centered world more closely around them. Casaubon and Tito take this response to its extreme. Such characters as Lydgate and Amos Barton, in smaller, more gradual ways, accept the lessening of their lives' potential in exchange for the comfort that comes with abandoning the costly commitment to truth. And such characters as Gwendolyn, Arthur Donnithorne, and Godfrey Cass must tread an excruciating road back from the denial of unpalatable truths. "The great division among George Eliot's characters is between egoists and those who approach reality objectively" writes Paris (26).

Yet Eliot rejects the idea that life can be fulfilled or truth discovered through reason alone. Like her fellow Victorians Coleridge, Carlyle, and Butler, she was temperamentally incapable of satisfaction with the amoral, mechanistic universe of materialism and utilitarianism. As Roberts explains, "[I]t would be a mistake to call [Eliot] a rationalist. 'The truth of feeling' and 'the mystery that lies under the processes' are examples of the phrases that recur throughout her writing expressing the final impotence of 'reason' to explain the ends of life, or, still more important, to understand other people" (11). Characteristically, Eliot's first important literary undertaking, the translation of an important work of German biblical criticism, was marred by her frustration at the author's insensitivity to the aesthetic and emotional beauty and power of the Gospels, even though she agreed with most of his views (Henry 53–54). Maggie Tulliver and Dorothea, Eliot's most compelling female characters, journey in their different ways from hope that the liberated intellect will discover truth, to a painful recognition of the limitations of the life of the mind. While her commitment to the rigorous pursuit of truth is absolute, Eliot always seems to be feeling her way toward a concept of "truth" much wider than the purely intellectual, one that includes the ethical, the emotional, and the aesthetic. Ironically, the truth for which Eliot seems to be searching is, essentially, the Christian one, in which belief and practice, intellectual and moral assent, are inseparable.

Human relationships—affection, empathy, emotion, and connection to other people—are the second avenue Eliot tries in her search for transcendence and coherence. For Eliot, "human relationships are by their very nature religious" (Paris 25), and, in a pattern common to many Victorian novelists, such characters as Dorothea, Maggie Tulliver, Adam Bede, Daniel Deronda, and Silas Marner find meaning and redemption through their connection to, first, one human being and then, more broadly, the human community. Some of these transformative relationships are romantic, but others, such as the love of Silas Marner for a mysterious orphan or the devotion of Daniel Deronda to his friend and mentor Mordecai, are not. Indeed, Henry notes that it was ties of birth, rather than the contractual obligation of marriage, which Eliot seems to have earliest and longest recognized as a primary source of obligation and object of sacrifice (51)—perhaps not surprisingly in view of Eliot's devoted, though conflictual, relationships with her father and siblings and the long, lonely years in which she relied on intense friendships while drifting from one disappointing romantic attachment to another before her alliance with fellow intellectual Lewes, whom she loved but could not marry. For Eliot, human connection is indeed the great goal and good of life, but personal fulfillment in a happy romantic relationship is only one of several forms this connection can take and perhaps not the most likely to achieve its end.

Thus, Dorothea ultimately achieves happiness by marrying the man she loves, after a disastrous first attempt to marry out of idealism and self-sacrifice. But Lydgate, whose story parallels Dorothea's, exemplifies through his marriage the opposite error—the mistaken belief that an emotionally satisfying relationship can exist without an intellectual and moral dimension. Daniel Deronda, who, like Dorothea, longs for a unifying purpose in life, finds fulfillment in his growing connection to the Jewish people long before he marries Mirah. Yet Gwendolen, the other main character in the same novel, is Eliot's most complex and intriguing example of one who invests a human relationship with more power than it should have. Gwendolen can ultimately grow into her moral potential only by accepting that she must seek her duty apart from Daniel, and it is not entirely clear at the end of the novel that she will be able to do this.

For Eliot, even the most precious human relationships must connect to, not isolate from, the larger human community. Silas Marner must love Eppie not so he can be happy, but so he can return to the community. Adam Bede and Deborah must suffer through their compassion for others before they can relinquish their different kinds of separateness and find fulfillment, not only in marriage, but as part of their community. Maggie Tulliver, torn by conflicting loyalties to her brother; her cousin; her first love, Philip; and the love of her life, Stephen, must recognize that no happiness is possible in a single relationship that violates the network of connections and obligations surrounding each human being. Romola must find meaning after betrayal and tragedy by caring for those who need her most. And the redemptive meaning in Mrs. Barton's sad story must come, like Maggie's and Romola's, from sacrificial commitment to an ideal of duty, compassion, and self-denial. For Eliot, personal relationships should be a reflection of and means to the sacrificial subordination of self to the love of one's fellow human beings.

As Eliot warns through Theophrastus Such:

> Not for one moment would one willingly lose sight of the truth that the relation of the sexes and the primary ties of kinship are the deepest roots of human wellbeing, but one cannot make them by themselves the equivalent of morality...being necessarily in the first instance a private good, there is there is always the danger that individual selfishness will see in them only the best part of its own gain.... (ch. xvi)

This, then, brings us to the third and most characteristic approach Eliot takes in her quest for synthesis: duty. All her life, Eliot longed for a transcendent morality to give shape and meaning to the universe. She had a special tenderness for the time in her life when she nursed her dying father, despite their difficult relationship and the sacrifice of her time and ambition (Hardy 138). Indeed, as many critics have pointed out, Eliot clings more fiercely to the Christian virtues of sacrifice, integrity, endurance, and duty as she rejects the historical, doctrinal basis of those ideals—becoming, in Alan Jacobs' words, "ever more passionate about the moral life as her belief in anything transcendent evaporates" (par. 20). In this, too, Eliot is typical of her time; Himmelfarb writes "[the Victorians] affirmed moral principles all the more strongly as the religious basis of those principles seemed to be disintegrating ... morality became

... a surrogate for religion" (26). Himmelfarb goes on to describe as "the classic statement of this secular ethic" Eliot's famous declaration that, while God was inconceivable and immortality unbelievable, duty was both peremptory and absolute (27). "To do and be good," writes Henry, "and to sublimate self for the sake of others was a goal and motivation of her life, evident from her earliest letters to her late journal entries" (236); Henry also notes that, for Eliot, "Duty replaced God as the abstraction for which she would willingly suffer injury and subdue ambition" (Henry 51).

Eliot could not relinquish the idea that individuals have a purpose on earth greater than themselves—one they must sacrifice to fulfil. In George Cooke's view, "[Eliot] stands out as the deepest, broadest, and most catholic illustrator of the true ethics of Christianity; the most earnest and persistent expositor of the true doctrine of the Cross, that we are born and should live to something higher than the love of happiness" (234–235). The characters with which Eliot compels us to identify most powerfully seek a great cause, a worthy sacrifice, a chance to transcend self. Dorothea, Lydgate, Maggie Tulliver, Romola, Felix Holt, Deborah, Adam Bede, Daniel Deronda—all share this sense of duty.

Dorothea learns to understand herself and, eventually, to find love and happiness, yet only after passing through an agonizing struggle to commit herself to carrying on her husband's work—work in which she no longer believes. His death delivers her from the life of drudgery she envisions, but her self-sacrifice to this perceived duty is real and is a transformative moment for Dorothea. Similarly, Maggie Tulliver spends a night of desperate misery wrestling with the temptation to accept a happiness to which she does not feel entitled. This time, it is her own death that delivers Maggie from the prolonged sacrifice she has brought herself to face. And Adam Bede endures what is, for him, the ultimate sacrifice—the choice to forgive, to pity, to endure, and to accept, when he longs instead for action, revenge, and hope. Only through this devastating experience can Adam achieve his potential and find his purpose. Eliot rejects both heavenly reward and the example of a historically incarnate God, both the mandate of a divinely inspired Scriptural command and the reality of a supernatural rebirth, as foundation for her passionate commitment to duty and sacrifice. Yet the Scriptural resonances that permeate Eliot's work are never more striking than when, again and again, she takes her characters through a Gethsemane in which the ultimate sacrifice of happiness, identity, and hope is demanded of them. And nothing is more characteristic of Eliot than the strangely fruitful conflict between her rationalist rejection of any comprehensible motive or justification for this sacrifice and her celebration of it as the truest human fulfillment.

It is no small part of Eliot's greatness that her fiction keeps alive the moral orientation that shaped Victorian literature, even as it incorporates the ideas that were undermining it. Like Austen, Gaskell, and Dickens, Eliot assumed no human being has the right to live his or her own life for personal comfort, or happiness. Indeed, this conviction undergirds and unites both her commitment to intellectual integrity and her commitment to empathy and compassion. By laboring to give a strictly secular orientation to this ethic, Eliot prepares the way for the postwar literary generation for whom, in D. H. Lawrence's words, all the "great, dynamic words" had been cancelled (63).Yet by creating a world in which her characters confront new struggles with old values, she builds a bridge over the chasm that separates us from a generation who believed in those great, dynamic words.

Works Cited

Beer, Gillian. *Darwin's Plots: Evolutionary Narrative in Darwin, George Eliot and Nineteenth-Century Fiction.* 1983. 2nd ed. New York: Cambridge UP, 2000.

Brown, John Crombie. "The Ethics of George Eliot's Work." *George Eliot Ultimate Collection.* Ed. Darryl Marks. Everlasting Flames Pub. 2013. Kindle.

Cooke, George. *George Eliot: A Critical Study of Her Life, Writings, and Philosophy.* 1895. *Google Book.* 2009. Web. 15 Sept. 2015.

Eagleton, Terry. *Culture and the Death of God.* New Haven, CT: Yale UP, 2014.

Eliot, George. *The Writings of George Eliot: George Eliot's Life as Related in Her Letters*. Houghton Mifflin, 1908 *Google Book*. Web. 14 Jul. 2015.

_____. "Impressions of Theophrastus Such." *George Eliot Ultimate Collection*. Ed. Darryl Marks. Everlasting Flames Pub. 2013. Kindle file.

_____. "O May I Join the Choir Invisible." 1895. *The Literature Network*. Jalic, Inc. 2000–2015. Web. 14 Jul. 2015.

Hardy, Barbara. *George Eliot: A Critic's Biography*. New York: Bloomsbury Academic. 2006.

Henry, Nancy. *The Life of George Eliot*. Malden, MA: Wiley-Blackwell, 2012. Blackwell Critical Biographies Ser.

Himmelfarb, Gertrude. *The Demoralization of Society: From Victorian Virtues to Modern Values*. New York: Knopf, 1994.

_____. *The Jewish Odyssey of George Eliot*. New York: Encounter Books. 2009.

Jacobs, Alan. "Good Without God." *First Things*. First Things, April 2000. Web. 14 July 2015.

Lawrence, D. H. *Lady Chatterley's Lover*. New York: New American Library, 1959.

Lovesey, Oliver. "Religion." *George Eliot in Context*. Ed. Margaret Harris. New York: Cambridge UP, 2013. 238–247.

Paris, Bernard. "George Eliot's Religion of Humanity." *George Eliot: a Collection of Critical Essays*. Ed. George Creeger. Englewood Cliffs, NJ: Prentice-Hall, Inc., 1970. 11–36.

Roberts, Neil. *George Eliot: Her Beliefs and Her Art*. Pittsburgh, PA: U of Pittsburgh P, 1975.

Wilson, A. N. *God's Funeral*. New York: W.W. Norton. 1999.

"How Was a Man to Be Explained?": Masculinity, Manhood, and Mothering in *Silas Marner*_____

Danny Sexton

In November 1860, George Eliot records in her journal how a new story "thrust itself between me and the other book I was meditating" (Harris & Johnston, *Journals*). The "new story" causing the interference was *Silas Marner: The Weaver of Raveloe*, and the "other book" was *Romola*, an ambitious historical novel set in fifteenth-century Florence. Four months later, in a February 1861 letter to John Blackwood, her publisher, she echoes her journal entry, explaining how the story "came to me first of all, quite suddenly, as a sort of legendary tale, suggested by my recollection of having once, in early childhood, seen a linen-weaver with a bag on his back" (Haight & Johnston 382). Similar to how the story interrupts George Eliot's contemplation on *Romola*, critical reception of *Silas Marner* also indicates a disturbance in terms of how to place the work in George Eliot's canon. Attempting to make space for it, F. R. Leavis in *The Great Tradition* calls it a "moral fable" and "that charming minor masterpiece" (62). So influential was Leavis' work that his labels remained the prevailing ones for a number of years until scholars begin to note in *Silas Marner* the same issues that preoccupied Eliot in her "major masterpieces."

Felicia Bonaparte has asserted that "the question, which entails all others, to which Eliot addressed herself, is the perennial riddle of the Sphinx: What is man?" (xii). Similar to Oedipus, who leaves Corinth to find a new home in Thebes, Silas journeys from his home in Lantern Yard to the village of Raveloe. Interestingly, *Romola* also begins with a major male character's entrance to a new city and the struggles that both the character and the citizens find in allowing this new man into their community. In *Silas Marner*, this struggle is put to the forefront when the narrator expresses the way in which Silas Marner disturbs the citizens of Raveloe: "No one knew were wandering men had their homes or their origin; and how was a man to be explained unless you at least knew somebody who knew his father and mother?" (Eliot 5). At the heart of the villagers' uneasiness about Silas Marner are questions concerning his masculinity and how it compares to other masculinities in Raveloe.

These questions are associated with two different meanings of masculinity. On one hand, it can describe without judgment or evaluation the actions and thoughts of biological males, such as in the following: "Peter saw his emotional sensitivity as a key component of his masculinity." On the other, masculinity can function as a code of conduct for male behavior specific to a particular culture. For instance, if someone were to state, "masculinity is being strong and facing one's challenges head on," this person is expressing a code of conduct. This singular form is also known as "hegemonic masculinity," a "model of masculinity which a culture privileges above others, which implicitly defines what is 'normal' for males in that culture, and which is able to impose that definition of 'normality' upon other kinds of masculinity" (Mangan 13). Returning to the earlier example of Peter, his masculinity could be labeled as one of those "other kinds." His culture may then impose upon him their code of conduct for male behavior.

Although the Victorians did not use the term "masculinity," they did have a code of conduct for the expected behavior of males. It was called "manliness," which placed emphasis "on moral courage, sexual purity, athleticism, and stoicism" (Roper & Tosh 2). However, manliness was not defined the same for all males. There were different codes based on classifications, such as class, race, or religious affiliation. For instance, moral courage for a working-class man involved a different set of expectations than those for a man of the gentleman class. Regardless of these various codes, "each version claimed an exclusive authority" by which the man who fulfilled and continued to live up to those standards was rewarded with having achieving manhood (Tosh 2). Similar to masculinity, manhood has both an individual meaning and a social one. In its individual context, it implies that the male has achieved a personal goal that he associates with manhood. In terms of the social, the man must achieve what his peers have designated as an accomplishment for men. Manhood, however, is precarious because once rewarded, it can also be lost if the man does not continue to live up to those expectations set by his society (Sussman 47).

More than a charming minor masterpiece, *Silas Marner* is significant because it presents a view of gender that is radically different from the binary one that was the norm in Victorian England. A binary gender system allows for only two gender markers (the masculine and the feminine) that are viewed as distinct and separate. Furthermore, it assigns the masculine gender to the biological male and the feminine one to the biological female, using these designations to regulate male and female behavior, including what clothing to wear, what type of work to pursue, and what spaces to occupy. Often referred to as the separate sphere theory when applied to the Victorians, it is an ideology that situated women's proper place in the home (i.e., the private), fulfilling domestic duties, and men's outside the home (i.e., the public), where he must do "rough work in the open world" (Ruskin 102).

In order to work against the strict Victorian binary gender system, George Eliot sets *Silas Marner* in a remote part of England at the dawn of the nineteenth century, recalling an age prior to the Industrial Revolution. New manufacturing techniques not only transformed how goods were produced, but they also led to a gender division of labor. Prior to industrialization, the home and the workplace were situated in the same space with family members of both sexes working alongside one another. Creation of factories led to a gendered separation of labor, with men working outside the home and women working within it. This division provided a basis for the further distinction between men and women in nearly every other facet of daily life. In *Silas Marner*, George Eliot anticipates current scholarship on gender that emphasizes how meanings are socially established and constructed to create "stable identity or laws of agency from which various acts follow" (Butler 140). Similarly, the novel rejects these attempts at identity stability, by removing those restrictions about public and private spaces, detaching sex from gender, and dismantling the binary gender system.

Masculinity and manhood in their social contexts are based largely on a binary system that views them as being opposite than femininity and womanhood. However, this binary system is also used against men who are perceived as not measuring up to an ideal masculinity. A present-day example is the expression "man up," which chastises any man who displays a perceived weakness while also shaming him into aligning his behavior or thoughts with a conceived masculine idea. If a culture promotes a certain type of physicality as an identifying mark of masculinity and manhood, any man who does not possess it may be ridiculed, ostracized, and even demonized. Any men traveling through Raveloe, including Silas Marner, find themselves victims of this mode of thinking. They are often described as "pallid undersized men, who, by the side of the brawny country-folk, looked like the remnants of a disinherited race" (Eliot 5). These unexplained men not only disturb the citizens, but they cause unrest among animals and are read as bad omens portending evil: "The shepherd's dog barked fiercely when one of these alien-looking men appeared on the upland, dark against the early winter sunset" (Eliot 5). The narrator explains that although the shepherd knows that the bags these men carry hold "nothing but flaxen thread," a fear still grips him that he could not carry the bag "without the help of the Evil One" (Eliot 5).

Although most of the citizens of Raveloe are good-natured, they are also traditional and superstitious, which has much to do with Raveloe's isolated location: "it was nestled in a snug well-wooded hollow, quite an hour's journey on horseback from any turnpike, where it was never reached by the vibrations of the coach-horn, or of public opinion" (Eliot 7). Matters are made worse by Silas' own self-alienation, which affects how his masculinity and manhood are perceived. He establishes his home in a stone cottage "near the village of Raveloe" (Eliot 6) and does not attempt to make any deep attachments: "he sought no man or woman, save for the purposes of his calling, or in order to supply himself with necessaries" (Eliot 8). Additional fodder to feed the Ravelonians' superstitions and anxieties concerning Silas is the cataleptic[1] fits and seizures that he often experiences. Jem Rodney observes one of these fits and recounts to others how he found the weaver standing with dead-set eyes and stiffed limbs, failing to respond to verbal and physical contact. Just as Jem determines that the weaver has died, Silas comes "all right again, like, as you might say, in the winking of an eye, and said 'Good night,' and walked off" (Eliot 8). Others discuss the account at length with an effort to make sense of what Jem witnesses, which leads them to read a defect in Silas' body. Mr. Macey, the parish clerk, reasons that Marner's soul occasionally leaves his body, and the "lassies ... declare that they would never marry a dead man come to life again" (Eliot 8).

A cataleptic fit was also what led to Silas' exile from his original home. Similar to Raveloe, Lantern Yard is a close-knit community with one major difference: it is a small Calvinistic dissenting sect. In the context of Lantern Yard, the church serves as a marker of achieved manhood, which Silas has accomplished because he is highly respected as "a young man of exemplary life and ardent faith" (Eliot 9). He is engaged to marry Sarah, a young servant woman, and has a close friendship with another young man, William Dane, who was also "regarded as a shining instance of youthful piety" (Eliot 10). Silas' achieved manhood, however, is lost when William Dane and Sarah betray him. William views himself as one having the authority to evaluate and confirm manhood upon others for he is "somewhat given to over-severity towards weaker brethren, and to be so dazzled by his own light as to hold himself wiser than his teachers" (Eliot 10). After witnessing one of Silas' fits during a prayer meeting, William comments that the "trance looked more like a visitation of Satan than a proof of divine favour" (Eliot 11), an observation that reads as a negative criticism of Silas' masculinity.

This criticism is soon followed by Silas having his manhood stripped from him. Around the time that William first witnesses Silas' fit, a senior deacon falls seriously ill and is tended by the young members of the congregation, among them Silas and William. Silas wakes from one of his fits to find that the deacon has died. Worse yet, he is accused of stealing a bag of the church's money kept in the Deacon's bureau. On the night of the deacon's death, William was supposed to come to relieve Silas; however, he claims a sudden sickness kept him away. Although it is not directly stated, it is strongly implied that William not only stole the money but also set Silas up to take the blame. It is no coincidence that it is William who discovers the empty moneybag in Silas' chambers. Found guilty of the theft, Silas is "suspended from church-membership" (Eliot 13) with the proviso that once he confesses his crime and returns the money he can then be restored back into the church. His emasculation is further evident when on the following day, a deacon informs him that Sarah has broken off the engagement. Less than a month later, William and Sarah are married and Silas departs Lantern Yard. The manhood that he had achieved in Lantern Yard has been lost to him, and his masculinity is rendered deficient.

In addition to his experiences in Lantern Yard explaining his self-alienation in Raveloe, they also feed his determination to create masculinity and manhood on his own terms, ones where the authority to grant them resides with the individual instead of society. Ironically, money comes to signify manhood and masculinity for Silas. The money is the fulfillment of a personal achievement that elevates Silas' masculinity above those of other men because it would allow him to "buy up 'bigger men' than himself" (Eliot 9). Furthermore, he associates the money with his very being: "He began to think it was conscious of him, as his loom was, and he would on no account have exchanged those coins, which had become his familiars, for other coins with unknown faces" (Eliot 19). More than viewing the money as his constant companions, he treats it as if it were his progeny: "[He] thought fondly of the guineas … as if they had been unborn children—thought of the guineas that were coming slowly through the coming years, through all his life" (Eliot 21).

Silas' alienation and hoarding conflicts with how citizens of Raveloe evaluate masculinity. They expect men to be active members in the life of the community. In distancing himself from public life, Silas sets himself as "Other." However, for fifteen years, he is successful in creating a masculinity and manhood that thrives, even in opposition to the social requirements. Donald Hall associates Silas' obsession with his gold to a masturbatory instinct[2] where we often see Silas "alone in his hovel at night, caressing his coins, fingering them repeatedly, loving them intensively" (182–183). It leads to what he identifies as the "primary ill" of the novel that must be cured: "That of pleasing oneself by oneself" (Hall 184). Silas' masturbatory instincts do not serve the public good because he is hoarding his money instead of spending it in the community, which eventually leads to his individual manhood also failing. While in one of his cataleptic fits, his money is stolen by the unscrupulous Dunstan Cass, a younger son of the local squire. This second theft similar to the first one in Lantern Yard is significant because both reveal the precarious nature of masculinity as something not inherent, but as something external that can be either achieved or lost.

Despair over the dual loss causes him to seek assistance from the men of Raveloe at the Rainbow, a pub that is designated as a masculine space of "luxurious resort for rich and stout husbands" (Eliot 45) to be among men and participate in masculine discourse. Earlier in the novel, Godfrey Cass, the eldest son of the squire, retreats there to "hear the talk about the cock-fighting" (Eliot 33). In Silas' view, "it was the place where he was likely to find the powers and dignities of Raveloe, and where he could most speedily make his loss public" (Eliot 45). Despite Silas' years of fostering an individual masculinity and manhood, he still attributes authority to the social element, one that grants manhood and also punishes those men who go against the code. Upon Silas' entry into the Rainbow, the landlord asks him "in a conciliatory tone, what's lacking to you? What's your business here?" (Eliot 55). While the landlord's tone indicates a willingness to allow Silas into this masculine space, the questions imply both evaluation and judgment of Silas' manhood. The two questions asked before Silas has even uttered a word are directly related to his lack of manhood, which by extension excludes him from this masculine space. In coming to the Rainbow, Silas is partly acknowledging that he has erred in not following the social codes for masculine behavior in Raveloe:

> Left groping in darkness, with his prop utterly gone, Silas has inevitably a sense, though a dull and half-despairing one, that if any help came to him it must come from without; and there was a

slight stirring of expectation at the sight of his fellow-men, a faint consciousness of dependence on their goodwill. (Eliot 81)

In these thoughts, awareness is dawning on Silas that his individual masculinity and manhood have failed and that if he is to reclaim them, they must be through the social instead of the individual.

Achievement of masculinity and manhood for Silas, however, comes when he becomes mother to a newly orphaned young girl, who finds her way to his hearth. When the girl awakes and the mother is not present, Silas is first forced and then assumes willingly the role of mother: "The child had awaked, and Marner stooped to lift it on his knee. It clung round his neck, and burst louder and louder into that mingling of inarticulate cries with 'mammy' by which little children express the bewilderment of waking" (Eliot 111). At her young age, the child has not been instructed by society to associate the role of the mother with the biological female. Having not been educated in a gender binary system, the child simply identifies mother, regardless of sex, as anyone who provides those basic needs. Mothering, as Nancy J. Chodorow avers in *The Reproduction of Mothering: Psychoanalysis and the Sociology of Gender*, has social and political causes as well as natural and biological ones. She explains, "women's mothering perpetuates itself through social-structurally induced psychological mechanisms. It is not an unmediated product of physiology. Women come to mother because they have been mothered by women" (Chodorow 211). In other words, women also learn to mother; it is not completely by nature and instinct, even though many cultures, particularly the Victorians, have held and promoted this view. Given that mothering also involves learned behaviors, Chodorow posits that "primary parenting," her term to describe the parent who takes the main responsibilities for the day-to-day existence of a child, can be learned and performed by either man or woman.

In having Silas unquestioningly assume the role of primary parent, George Eliot dismantles the binary gender system. Silas ignores the codes of his society and publicly announces his intention to be mother to the child. He goes to the Red House, Squire Cass' home, to inform them of the found child and the death of her mother. When it is suggested that he leave the child there, he refuses and impulsively decides to keep her: "His speech, uttered under a strong sudden impulse, was almost like a revelation to himself: a minute before, he had no distinct intention about the child" (Eliot 115). Furthermore, when Godfrey Cass assumes that Silas will take the child to the parish, Silas responds by stating that since the child's mother is dead and there is no father present, the child, like him, is alone, and he will keep her. After this declaration, "the child ... began to cry and call for 'mammy,' though always clinging to Marner" (Eliot 116). His explanation is a further illustration of the mother association. He observes the father is absent and implies that he will not take that role because this person may still reappear. However, in stating that the mother is dead, he indicates that it is this role that he will assume in the child's life. As to reaffirm Silas' statement, the child once again calls for "mammy" while clinging to him.

Additionally, the women of Raveloe take it upon themselves to provide Silas with maternal wisdom: "Notable mothers ... [and] lazy mothers were equally ready with their suggestions" (Eliot 120). Dolly Winthrop, a "notable mother," accepts his role as mother as if it were the most natural relationship between man and child. When she brings him some of her son's old clothes for the girl, Dolly notices the fondness the child has for him and insists that Silas dress her: "'She wants to go o' your lap, I'll be bound. Go, then: take her, Master Marner; you can put the things on, and then you can say as you've done for her from the first of her coming to you'" (Eliot 122). Not only does Dolly accept Silas' motherhood, the other citizens of Raveloe do as well. They come to understand that a person can easily perform a role that has been traditionally associated with one gender without losing the other, as evident in one of the comments that Silas receives concerning his motherhood: "'Why there isn't many lone men 'ud ha' been wishing to take up with a little un like that: but I reckon the weaving makes you handier than men as do out-door work—you're partly as handy as a woman, for weaving comes next to spinning'" (Eliot 130). Although this comment indicates an acceptance of Silas' motherhood, it also reveals that remnants of the gender binary system remain. The speaker distinguishes between men's work (i.e., "out-door work") and women's work (i.e., weaving and spinning), reasoning incorrectly that Silas takes so well to mothering because his work as a weaver is more aligned with the feminine than the masculine. This view, however, is not one that George Eliot endorses or encourages. To understand the significance of this comment to the dismantling of the binary gender system, let us return to the young child's unquestioned association of Silas with mother. As mentioned previously, she has not been indoctrinated to make the associations that the system promotes. However, patience is required for adults who must unlearn the system, and this is an emphasis that George Eliot makes repeatedly in *Silas Marner*.

One important example of this unlearning is the conversation that was occurring in the Rainbow before Silas' appearance to make known his stolen money. Mr. Macey was telling a story of the old Rector, Mr. Drumlow, who when performing a wedding ceremony mixed up the vows: "But when he come to put the questions, he put 'em by the rule o' contrary, like, and he says, 'Wilt thou have this man to thy wedded wife?'... and then he says, 'Wilt thou have this woman to thy wedded husband'" (Eliot 50). Mr. Drumlow has associated the man with the wife and the woman with the husband thus blurring gender markers. For Mr. Macey, it is not so much that Mr. Drumlow confused the vows, but that "nobody took any notice on it" (Eliot 50). Although no one else took notice, Mr. Macey was troubled by the mixed up vows, fearing that the couple might not have been married because the words were uttered incorrectly. He questions whether it's the words or the meaning that matters. He first decides it's the meaning but then thinks it's the glue that makes the meaning stick. The "glue" that Mr. Macey speaks of stands in for society, and he cannot imagine that the marriage conducted under incorrect words is a valid one. So distraught, he voices his anxiety to Mr. Drumlow who makes light of the "mistake," indicating to Mr. Macey that as long as everything works out well, the words and meanings are trivial and insignificant.

Everything works out well for Silas and the little girl, whom he names Eppie. For the next sixteen years, he fulfills the duties of both father and mother; yet, the narrative emphasizes Silas' mothering. In *Family Fortunes*, Leonore Davidoff and Catherine Hall explain, "mothers were to be relied upon for personal care and emotional rather than economic support" (335). Silas furnishes Eppie with all three and takes on "that presence of the ... mother which is the fountain of wholesome love and fear" (Eliot 24). The domestic happiness created by Silas is in direct contrast to the sad state of affairs of the Red House, in which Godfrey and Dunstan grew up without a mother figure: "the hearth had no smiles, and ... the daily habits were not chastised by the presence of household order" (Eliot 31). In the above quotation, it should be noted that the narrator does not prescribe these duties exclusively on the biological female. Mothering could have been performed by anyone, allowing Dunstan and Godfrey to have more stable lives.

Godfrey's marriage to Nancy Lammeter provides him with the stability lacking in his youth, yet he experiences discontent at not being a parent. The discovery of Dunstan's remains and Silas' gold prompts Godfrey to disclose that he is Eppie's biological father. However, given the opportunity to become daughter to Godfrey and Nancy, Eppie chooses to remain with Silas because of the bond between them: "He's took care of me and loved me from the first, and I'll cleave to him as long as he lives, and nobody shall ever come between him and me" (Eliot 172). Her mature declaration here has the same effect as her childish cries of "mammy" while clinging to Silas sixteen years previously. She speaks of a maternal bond, one that makes the two of them inseparable because she is as much a part of Silas as he is a part of her. Although Nancy feels that Eppie should accept their offer, she states, "It's natural you should cling to those who've brought you up ... but there's a duty you owe to your lawful father" (Eliot 172). Her choice of using "lawful" to describe Godfrey and "natural" to describe Silas are revealing; Nancy, unconsciously, gives more weight to the bond between Silas and Eppie than that of Godrey and Eppie. Godfrey's "choosing" to be involved in Eppie's life, while Silas being "naturally" in her life is an illustration of Davidoff and Hall's distinction between fathers and mothers: "While for fathers involvement with their children's lives was a matter of choice, it was regarded as natural for women to take up the whole duty of motherhood" (335). Davidoff and Hall's statement should not be read as their approval of such division; they are merely explaining the belief of the period.

Biographical scholarship on George Eliot provides some insight into her approach on gender. In an analysis of *Daniel Deronda*, Marianne Hirsch associates the central struggle between the novel's protagonists to Eliot's own issues within a binary gender system: "Gwendolyn and Daniel, both occupying (and competing for) the position of the novel's protagonist, enact the battle between Eliot's own self-representation as Marian and as George" (70). Implicit in Hirsch's statement is the conflict between a feminine identity (George Eliot was born Marian Evans) and a masculine one (the masculine nom de plume that she assumed as her public identity) as well as the roles that society assigns to each. Labeling Eliot's personal conflict a "gender dysfunction," U. C. Knoepflmacher explains that it "began at an early stage of her emotional development as she turned from a precarious mother love and an identification with sisters and female teachers to a strong attachment to father, brother, and other father-surrogates" (131). This dysfunction is the result of a system that couples the male with the masculine, the female with the feminine, and allows no space for people to behave or think outside those couplings. Dysfunction occurs when a person attempts to live within these systems, such as with Silas, who experiences failures early in the narrative. George Eliot reveals the tensions that are inherent in such a rigid system. *Silas Marner* challenges this system by illustrating that gender identity is never stable but always evolving and developing, undergoing "continual redefinition" (Mangan 247). Furthermore, she uncouples gender roles from biological sex, revealing that mothering and fathering are not restricted to a particular sex. Similar to *Silas Marner* intruding on Eliot's contemplation on *Romola* and Silas' entry into Raveloe, George Eliot disturbs those views that Victorians held and promoted about public and private spaces, sex-gender couplings, and the binary gender system.

Notes

1. Symptoms of catalepsy may include the body going rigid, fixed posture, and no response to external stimuli, leading uninformed observers to assume that the sufferer has died.

2. Masturbation was a social concern for the English in the nineteenth century. Advice and medical literature of the day warned against "spermatorrhea," a disease that was supposedly caused by masturbation. Epilepsy, similar to Silas' cataleptic fits, was linked to masturbation. See Tim Hitchcock and Lawrence Stone for further discussion of the anxiety surrounding masturbation in nineteenth-century England. See also Jeff Nunokawa for an analysis of masturbation in *Silas Marner*.

Works Cited

Bonaparte, Felicia. *Will and Destiny: Morality and Tragedy in George Eliot's Novels.*New York: New York UP, 1975.

Butler, Judith. *Gender Trouble: Feminism and the Subversion of Identity.* New York: Routledge, 1990.

Chodorow, Nancy J. *The Reproduction of Mothering: Psychoanalysis and the Sociology of Gender.* Berkeley: U of California P, 1999.

Davidoff, Lenore & Catherine Hall. *Family Fortunes: Men and Women in the English Middle Class, 1780–1850.* Chicago: U of Chicago P, 1987.

Eliot, George. *Silas Marner: The Weaver of Raveloe.* 1861. London: Penguin Books, 1996.

Haight, Gordon, ed. *The George Eliot Letters.* 9 vols. New Haven: Yale UP, 1954–78.

Hall, Donald. "The Private Pleasures of Silas Marner." *Mapping Male Sexuality: 19th Century England.* Ed. Jay Losey & William D. Brewer. Madison, NJ: Fairleigh Dickinson P, 2000. 178–97.

Harris, Margaret & Judith Johnston, eds. *The Journals of George Eliot.* Cambridge, UK: Cambridge UP, 1998.

Hirsch, Marianne. *The Mother/Daughter Plot: Narrative, Psychoanalysis, Feminism.* Bloomington: Indiana UP, 1989.

Knoepflmacher, U. C. "Unveiling Men: Power and Masculinity in George Eliot's Fiction." *Men and Women*. Ed. Janet Todd. New York: Holmes & Meier, 1981. 130–46.

Leavis, F. R. *The Great Tradition: George Eliot, Henry James, Joseph Conrad*. 1949. New York: Doubleday Anchor Books, 1954.

Hitchcock, Tim. *English Sexualities, 1700–1800*. New York: St. Martins P, 1997.

Mangan, Michael. *Staging Masculinities: History, Gender, Performance*. Basingstoke, UK: Palgrave MacMillan, 2003.

Nunokawa, Jeff. *The Afterlife of Property: Domestic Security and the Victorian Novel*. Princeton, NJ: Princeton UP, 1994.

Roper, Michael & John Tosh. Introduction. "Historians and the Politics of Masculinity." *Manful Assertions: Masculinities in Britain Since 1800*. Ed. Michael Roper & John Tosh. London: Routledge, 1991. 1–24.

Ruskin, John. *Sesame and Lilies*. 1864–65. New York: John Wiley & Sons, 1890.

Stone, Lawrence. *The Family, Sex and Marriage in England, 1500–1800*. New York: Harper & Row, 1977.

Sussman, Herbert. *Victorian Masculinities: Manhood and Masculine Poetics in Early Victorian Literature and Art*. Cambridge, UK: Cambridge UP, 1995.

Tosh, John. *Manliness and Masculinities in Nineteenth-Century Britain: Essays on Gender, Family, and Empire*. Harlow, UK: Pearson Longman, 2005.

Missing Mother: Eliot's Philosophy of Sympathy and the Effect of Loss in *The Lifted Veil*_____

Emilia Halton-Hernandez

Criticism of Eliot's *The Lifted Veil* (1859) has tended to focus on the supernatural and pseudoscientific elements of the novella. More recently, Jane Wood has shifted attentions to the gendered discourses at play in the narrative. However, I would like to approach *The Lifted Veil* by drawing attention to the loss of the maternal figure in the text. I think that a deeper understanding of Eliot's conceptions of melancholia, egoism, and her philosophy of sympathy can be gained through this type of analysis. From a close reading of *The Lifted Veil*, I will first identify the specters of Latimer's idealized mother that permeate the text. I will then explore the ways in which such an absence or loss might have affected Latimer's representation of women in the novel and his relationship with his male relatives, also referring to what is known about Eliot's own familial experiences. Next, I will interrogate the ways in which Eliot's portrayal of Latimer's melancholy and egoism closely parallels Freud's later notions of such a condition in Freud's "Mourning and Melancholia" (1917). I will also look at the ways Eliot's notion of the development of the psyche and the importance of childhood experience to this development influenced and broke away from contemporary understandings. Finally, with these insights in mind I will question how Eliot's notions of maternal loss, melancholia, and egoism play into her philosophy of sympathy and human intersubjectivity.

The Significance of Maternal Loss
Latimer—Eliot's misanthropic character, who presents us with his sorry autobiography—details the course of his life, from his early origins in England (we presume) to the greater part of his adolescence in Geneva, back to his adulthood in England. Although he speaks fondly of his early childhood with his mother, he furnishes the narrative with few real details of this period, instead providing a

somewhat cursory glance at such a formative period. His childhood remains the happiest time by which other periods in his life are compared: "My softened feeling towards my father made this the happiest time I had known since childhood" (Eliot, *Lifted* 28). The main reason for his childhood happiness, he explains, is his "tender mother," who provides him with an "unequalled love" (4). He describes longingly the comfort he derived from her physical presence, one that contained and loved him:

> even now, after the dreary lapse of long years, a slight trace of sensation accompanies the remembrance of her caress as she held me on her knee—her arms round my little body, her cheek pressed on mine. I had a complaint of the eyes that made me blind for a little while, and she kept me on her knee form morning till night. (Eliot, *Lifted* 4)

Echoing the second stanza of 'Life' from Eliot's poem 'Self and Life' (1878), Ruby Redinger reads it as "one of her most personal utterances" (Redinger 43). Eliot writes: "I was thy warmth upon thy mother's knee/When light and love within her eyes were one;/ We laughed together by the laurel-tree,/ Culling warm daisies 'neath the sloping sun" (Eliot qtd. in Redinger 43). Here, Eliot is emphasising the importance of the mother-child relationship to the development of the Self. It is worth noting that Redinger describes these lines as a "remarkable recall of symbiotic love; the child is not distinct from the mother, but an actual part of her sentient being" (Redinger 43), whereas in Latimer's description of his mother's love, he does not seem to partake in this organic union. Instead, his mother gazes upon him, bestowing him with affection, which he recalls missing. During Latimer's temporary blindness, he relies solely on his mother's love and gaze, but we get no sense of his returning her affections. Latimer is, in fact, aware of how he may be idealizing his childhood and the mother figure of this period. He writes that "My childhood perhaps seems happier than it really was, by contrast with all the after-years" (Eliot, *Lifted* 4). Similarly, in a letter to Sarah Hennell in 1844, Eliot writes that "Childhood is only the beautiful and happy time in contemplation and retrospect—to the child it is full of deep sorrows, the meaning of which is unknown" (Eliot qtd. in Redinger 50). Latimer's idealization of his childhood and the mother figure from this period suggests that Eliot is drawing attention to an idealization that is most probably due to the early maternal loss Latimer suffers. Such a love:

> soon vanished out of my life, and even to my childish consciousness it was as if that life had become more chill. I rode my little white pony with the groom by my side as before, but there were no loving eyes looking at me as I mounted, no glad arms opened to see me when I came back. Perhaps I missed my mother's love more than most children of seven or eight would have done, to whom the other pleasures of life remained as before; for I was certainly a very sensitive child. (Eliot, *Lifted* 4)

Throughout the narrative of *The Lifted Veil*, Eliot portrays the effects of maternal loss on the adult psyche with relation to her own experiences of loss. Redinger and U. C. Knoepflmacher have drawn attention in their biographical sketches of Eliot to both how the author and Latimer suffered from the same effects of maternal deprivation and neglect. Though her mother died in Eliot's own adulthood, accounts from both Eliot herself and her biographer John Cross describe the early withdrawal of both warmth and availability from Christiana Evans. As a young child, Eliot became estranged from her mother, sent to school far from the family home, despite her mother's 'pet'—Eliot's older brother Isaac—being permitted to stay (Knoepflmacher 108). From early on, Eliot had an instinctive recognition that "she occupied at best second place in the affections of her mother, the fountainhead of her very life" (Redinger 39). As Knoepflmacher observes, her portraits of inadequate mothers throughout her novels suggest that Eliot indeed "never fully weathered the withdrawal, at such an early stage of development, of that maternal "warmth" she poignantly dramatized in "Self and Life" (Knoepflmacher 108). However, unlike Eliot, who partnered with G. H. Lewes and who was able both to give and receive love, Latimer's mother remains the only person in the narrative whom he feels loved by, and whom he can remember without the usual disillusionment or contempt others produce in him. His father's inability to mourn his wife's death is deeply troubling for Latimer. Indeed, he can only feel compassion and sympathy when they both participate in a long overdue period of mourning when his brother dies: "As I saw into the desolation of my father's heart, I felt a movement of deep pity towards him, which was the beginning of a new affection—an affection that grew and strengthened in spite of the strange bitterness with which he regarded me" (Eliot, *Lifted* 28).

It is significant that Latimer's father is portrayed in stark contrast to the unknown and idealized mother figure. Whereas he recollects his mother as providing unfaltering affection and warmth, his father was a "firm, unbending, intensely orderly man, in root and stem a banker" whose disapproval of his youngest son's effeminate nature is resented by Latimer (Eliot, *Lifted* 5). Nonetheless, Latimer's feelings towards his father are linked to real experiences and events, whereas his mother is more a concept rather than a fully realized person. In a startling image of male and paternal potency, Latimer describes the "mingled trepidation and delicious excitement" he felt when he heard "the trampling of the horses on the pavement in the echoing stables, by the loud resonance of the grooms' voices, by the booming bark of the dogs as my father's carriage thundered under the archway of the courtyard" (5). In comparison to his memories of "riding the little white pony" associated with his mother, the contrast between benign mother and malignant father is heightened. Again, critics have likened such an uncompromising paternal figure as resembling Eliot's own misgivings about her father's unbending personality. Latimer's complicated relationship with his father is expressed in his clairvoyant vision of Prague, showing the ways in which such preoccupations with familial ties pervade the text. Rather than his vision of Prague providing an extra eye of insight, the scene at the bridge is primarily characterized by his disturbance at the lifelessness of the fatherly statues: "It is such grim, stony beings as these, I thought, who are the fathers of ancient faded children … who worship wearily in the stifling air of the churches, urged by no fear or hope" (9).

Such a split in Latimer's affections and perceptions of those around him is heightened in his relationship to Bertha, the monster to Latimer's mother's angel. The maternal ideal induced by loss also illuminates Latimer's portrayal of Bertha in the novella. As critics Gilbert and Gubar have observed, the splitting of characteristics between two women is a common approach to the paradox of femininity, often produced by a lost, idealized mother (Gilbert & Gubar 244). Latimer's mother's love is likened to tender nature: "it seemed to me that the sky, and the glowing mountain-tops, and the wide blue water, surrounded me with a cherishing love such as no human face had shed on me since my mother's love had vanished out of my life" (Eliot, *Lifted* 7). Whereas Bertha is the demonic nixie, the "fatal-eyed woman, with the green weeds, looked like a birth from some cold, sedgy stream, the daughter of an aged river" (12). Indeed, Latimer himself compares Bertha to the characteristics of the pure, angelic woman, whose only manifestation in the text is in the form of his remembered mother. Bertha, he tell us, was:

> was the very opposite, even to the colour of her hair, of the ideal woman who still remained to me the type of loveliness; and she was without the enthusiasm for the great and good, which, even at the moment of her strongest dominion over me, I should have declared to be the highest element of character. (Eliot, *Lifted* 17)

Bertha is "a bearer of meaning" for Latimer rather than a "maker of meaning" in the novella, acting as the archetypal Lucrezia Borgia femme fatale that Latimer holds in both disdain and erotic fascination (Dever 166). Although both Carolyn Dever and Gilbert and Gubar think about the angel/monster split as more representative of a trope in Victorian fiction due to the pervading gendered stereotypes of the time, I think Eliot is also demonstrating a nuanced psychological understanding of the ways in which something like maternal loss might affect our conceptions of sexuality and subjectivity. As I will go on later to explore, Eliot was influential in the late nineteenth century with regards to her understanding of childhood experiences and its effect upon adult life.

The Portrait of a Melancholic

Latimer is disturbed by his father's inability to mourn, or at least to show any signs of the loss he remembers so painfully: "he married my mother soon after; and I remember he seemed exactly the same, to my keen childish observation, the week after her death as before. But now, at last, a sorrow had come" (Eliot, *Lifted* 27). But Latimer is also unable to mourn properly and closely resembles Freud's conception of the melancholic in his seminal 1917 work, "Mourning and Melancholia." Though theories of melancholia had advanced considerably in the nineteenth century to an interest in non-delusional melancholia, Freud broke away from previous explanations of the emotions by emphasizing psychic loss rather than physical imbalance or defect (Lawlor 45). For example, in 1883, an Edinburgh physician defined melancholia as a form of mental disease that would usually run "a somewhat definite course, like a fever" (Coulston, qtd. in Jansson 1). Freud, on the other hand, departed from this model by explaining how the lost object of the melancholic became established within the ego: "the shadow of the object fell upon the ego, and the latter could henceforth be judged by a special agency, as though it were an object, the forsaken object" (Freud 249). Indeed, Eliot's protagonist shares many of the same characteristics as Freud's prototypical melancholic, demonstrating a prescience on Eliot's behalf in her nuanced and sophisticated portrayal of the condition. The melancholic—as opposed to the mourner, who has been able to give up the lost object—is unabashedly communicative with regards to his feelings of lack of self-worth: "One might emphasize the presence in him of an almost opposite trait of insistent communicativeness which finds satisfaction in self-exposure" (Freud 248). Latimer continually reminds the reader of his inadequacies, almost to the point of indulging in self-flagellation. He compares himself to his brother as a "fragile, nervous, ineffectual self" (Eliot 14) and such self-reproaches characterize the text. In fact, one could consider Latimer's autobiographical account itself as a performative exercise in self-exposure. Masochism's counterpart, sadism, is also prevalent in Latimer's account of his relations, as with humiliating his brother and refusing to relinquish Bertha from a failed marriage. Freud writes that the "The self-tormenting in melancholia, which is without doubt enjoyable, signifies, just like the corresponding phenomenon in obsessional neurosis, a satisfaction of trends of sadism and hate which relate to an object" (Freud 251). That this melancholic state is triggered by loss, but that this is not necessarily known by the sufferer is a crucial component to the phenomenology of both Latimer and Freud's patient's melancholia: "the patient cannot consciously perceive what he has lost either. This would suggest that melancholia is in some way related to an object-loss which is withdrawn from consciousness, in contradiction to mourning, in which there is nothing about the loss that is unconscious" (Freud 245).

Eliot, in her inclusion of Latimer's "vanished" mother provides the protagonist with the loss that might have affected him so profoundly in childhood and beyond. In *The Lifted Veil*, Eliot is engaging with different notions of the time as to the origins of adult disturbances and the theory of development. As I have mentioned earlier, Eliot's conceptions of childhood and psychology had a profound influence on psychiatrists and medical practitioners in the Victorian period and beyond. Leonard Guthrie, whose 1907 book *Functional Nervous Disorders in Childhood* was one of the first full-length child psychiatry studies, drew upon Eliot's work to understand better the psychological complexity of childhood (Shuttleworth 16). From Eliot's *The Mill on the Floss*, he quotes her passage on the emotional life of the child: "Every one of those keen moments has left its trace and lives in us still, but such traces have blent themselves irrevocably with the [finer] texture of our youth and manhood; and so it comes [to pass] that we can look on at the troubles of our children with a smiling disbelief in the reality of their pain" (Eliot qtd. in Shuttleworth 16). Shuttleworth writes that:

> Guthrie draws on Eliot to suggest that it is not only happiness in later life which is determined by childhood experience but also mental health. Suffering in childhood is not only real but has a permanent impact on the psyche. *The Mill on the Floss* was clearly a formative work for Guthrie. (Shuttleworth 16)

Like Eliot, in his 1856 article 'Hereditary Influence, Animal and Human,' her partner G. H. Lewes sought to weaken notions that the origins of insanity were always hereditary and necessarily inherent. With Latimer, Eliot is thinking about the phenomenon of loss; its effects on the psyche; and, as I will later explore, its effects on the ability to sympathize and relate to others. *The Lifted Veil* shows the way in which Eliot might be thinking about complicated developmental questions, the nature/nurture problem that dominated the thinking at the time, and still does today. Eliot presents Latimer's own accounting for his character with one that believes in his own innate qualities or 'nature.' For example, Latimer describes himself as possessing a particularly 'sensitive' nature various times throughout the text. His depressed state is very much an embodied one: "I saw in my face nothing but the stamp of a morbid organisation, framed for passive suffering" (Eliot, *Lifted* 14). In relation to others, Latimer also justifies his inability to relate to his constitution. About his bother Alfred, he writes that "There must always have been an antipathy between our two natures" (14) and with regards to his father, "the radical antipathy between our natures made my insight into his inner self a constant affliction to me" (27). It is important to identify this aspect of Latimer's notion of himself and others because it is in great contrast to the way in which Eliot considers human growth and relatedness as dependent on individual agency and free will. In one example of her expressing these sentiments, in *Adam Bede* the narrator writes: "What greater thing is there for two human souls than to feel that they are joined-to strengthen each other ... to be at one with each other in silent, unspeakable memories" (Eliot, *Adam* 300). Latimer, on the other hand attributes his general inability to relate to people to "This disposition of mine," which "was not favourable to the formation of intimate friendships among the numerous youths of my own age" (Eliot, *Lifted* 7).

Eliot's Philosophy of Sympathy

Eliot's philosophy of sympathy is made richer through an analysis of how she conceives of melancholia as later articulated by Freud, the narcissism that is involved with it, and therefore the importance of the mother-child relationship to the development of the psyche. Eliot's understanding of sympathy is crucially dependent on a capacity for recognizing difference, an ability to separate the Self from Other. Elizabeth Deeds Ermarth writes of Eliot's conception as involving "The ego as well as the other, the I as well as the Thou, are [the] required participants in the life of sympathy" (Deeds Ermarth 30). These thoughts were greatly influenced by Eliot's work on German philosopher Ludwig Feuerbach. Scholars like Moira Gatens have found evidence for Feuerbach's influence on Eliot's philosophies of knowledge and sympathy—in a letter written by Eliot, she asserts that "with the ideas of Feuerbach I everywhere agree" (Eliot qtd. in Gatens 89). Similarly, Ermarth acknowledges Feuerbach's influence on Eliot, who translated Feuerbach's magnum opus from German in 1854: "A glance at Feuerbach's *Essence of Christianity* will help to suggest the psychic conditions for sympathy" (Deeds Ermarth 24). Importantly, Feuerbach's critique of religion involved the assertion that God is the outward projection of human nature, rather than a deity separate from mankind (Deeds Ermarth 26). Rather than directing our love and devotion towards theological abstractions, like the idealized Madonna, such human feelings should be directed towards real objects and people, like our relatives and friends, as for Eliot and Feuerbach "It is these natural, concrete, embodied, living relationships that immanently and spontaneously generate our love for others, our sympathy for them, and our moral obligations towards them" (Feuerbach qtd. in Gatens 78). In order to form these ethical relations, both Feuerbach and Eliot firmly believe that every person must first overcome an inborn egoism (Gatens 81). Difference is the keyword here—an ability to recognize a difference between the Self and the Other, or I and thou for Feuerbach meant the sovereign individual of Christianity was dethroned (Gatens 78). Feuerbach writes that every individual exists "only by virtue of the conditions which constitute him a member of the whole, or relative whole" (Feuerbach qtd. in Gatens 78). Therefore, Feuerbach is proposing a relational model that is central to his notions of moral and ethical life, and whose influence is evident in works such as *The Lifted Veil* and Eliot's highly ethical novel, *Adam Bede*. For Eliot, the capacity to recognize the differences between I and thou demands the ability to take an imaginative leap into the experience of the Other. As critics like Thomas Albrecht have shown in relation to *The Lifted Veil*, Eliot's belief that art can help its reader with such a task is put to the test. With relation to Latimer, it is his inability to recognize the difference between I and thou that characterizes his failed relationships with others and with his world at large. Indeed, Latimer is also unable to become a poet himself because of this egoism he is unable to transcend. He recognizes that he has "the poet's sensibility without his voice," lacking the imaginative capacity to universalize his personal feelings (Eliot 7). Talking in relation to the character Gwendolen Harleth of *Daniel Deronda,* A. S. Byatt and Ignes Sodre explain why she may be unable to enjoy art: "if you're totally narcissistic you can't enjoy art because you want to be its creator all the time" (Byatt & Sodre 113). Latimer also has difficulties taking in and viewing art in his adulthood: "I could never look at many pictures in succession; for pictures, when they are at all powerful, affect me so strongly that one or two exhaust all my capability of contemplation" (Eliot, *Lifted* 18). Whether or not Latimer wants to consciously be art's creator, his "diseased consciousness" projects so heavily onto the outside world that he inevitably constructs his own reality. Similarly, Latimer has problems taking in other people, not only in his ability to read minds as felt to impinge on his sense of self, but also in his 'real' rather than psychic dealings with people, even those he thinks of with some fondness, like Charles Meunier. When Meunier would unload his intimate dreams and desires to Latimer, he writes that "I listened dreamily to the monologues ... I mingled them confusedly in my thought ... He knew quite well that my mind was half-absent" (8). Latimer is never able to equally confide in Meunier about his psychic qualities despite desiring to do so.

As Freud elucidates in his study of the melancholic, the egoism that is caused by object-loss denies the I and thou separation by identifying with the lost object itself. Freud writes that "This substitution for object-love is an important mechanism in the narcissistic affections.... It represents, of course, a *regression* from one type of object-choice to original narcissism" (Freud 249). The shadow of loss on the ego therefore characterizes the psyche's construction of the Other, projecting these shadows onto its experience of the Other, the external world. Key to Eliot's moral and ethical philosophy is the notion of free will, the importance of the individual's capacity to enact change and growth within itself and beyond. With regards to their egoism, Redinger writes that all of Eliot's "major feminine characters were to struggle [with it] before they either triumphed or succumbed to it" (Redinger 42). Indeed, the growth of characters like Gwendolen Harleth and Romola de'Bardi relies upon their ability to overcome their predispositions towards an egotistical world view through their challenges and suffering, which causes them to questions their notions of themselves and the Other, the first step to being able to sympathize and relate to other beings in a meaningful way. Ted Zenzinger explains that Eliot's view of sympathy is one "that incorporates transformative pain as a key role for the imagination," requiring the ability to overcome loss and suffering that doesn't take on the egoism of the melancholic, but the transcendence of the mourner (Zenzinger 438). That Latimer remains the melancholic, trapped in his destructive worldview and relations to others signifies his incapacity for development through suffering. Latimer himself describes his pain as "passive suffering," incapable of learning from his experience of loss, which Eliot highly values as a characteristic of the human with agency and free will.

The Supernatural

The role of Latimer's psychic or supernatural abilities in the narrative can also be better understood in their relation to Latimer's experience of maternal loss/object-loss and the melancholic egoism this produces. Latimer's clairvoyance and telepathy is a narrative device for portraying his "diseased" inner life, an image of the shadow of loss on the ego that Freud describes. Rather than providing access to other people's consciousness's through his mind-reading, Eliot provides us with another insight into Latimer's own internal state. As with his depressed visions of Prague and the scenes of his future marriage with Bertha, neither the reader nor Latimer really learns anything new from such previsions. Instead, they function as more concrete examples of scenes of projection of the kind that the melancholic might produce. Object-relations theorist Melanie Klein has called this process 'projective identification' where "aspects of the self or an internal object are split off and attributed to an external object" (*Melanie Klein Trust*). In many ways, Latimer's visions more closely resemble dreams, though he denies this: "Was this a dream—this wonderfully distinct vision ... No, it was not a dream" (Eliot 10). Though Latimer might indeed have a crystalline vision of Prague and be able to read clearly the thoughts of others, neither to the reader nor himself is he able to present this knowledge in a way that is separate from his own sneering and depressed internal and unconscious state.

As I mentioned earlier, Latimer's clairvoyant vision of Prague is steeped in associations of his disliked father. The definition of a clairvoyant 'one who sees clearly.' Really though, Latimer is a highly incompetent clairvoyant and telepathist. Latimer is instead in Bertha's thoughts a "miserable ghost-seer," whose visions are wholly inextricable from the internal. If one of the ways Latimer's extrasensory perception in the novella functions as a way for Eliot to externalize the internal, I think this is where *The Lifted Veil* is a less accomplished work of art than her later works. As Eliot's capacity as a novelist grows throughout her career, Byatt writes of *Daniel Deronda* that:

> What we have here is a perfect novel full of violent action in which a murder almost takes place, in which jewels are scattered, vengeance is taken" but that nevertheless "what we most care about is what Edward Dowden described as George Eliot's greatest innovation—she took all the action *inside*. (Byatt & Sodre 116)

Many critics would agree that Eliot achieves this to its highest degree in her 1874 masterpiece *Middlemarch*. In her earlier work in *The Lifted Veil*, the use of the supernatural is used as a narrative and psychological tool for facilitating this inside action. I would also like to draw attention to an interesting passage in Freud's "Mourning and

Melancholia." Clark Lawlor has identified "some echoes of older traditions" in Freud's account of melancholia when he writes that the melancholic might have greater abilities of insight than others in certain matters (Lawlor 145). Such beliefs also applied to Victorian medical discourses linking mesmerism, clairvoyance, and telepathy to mental illness. Freud uses the example of Hamlet, stating that he "has a keener eye for the truth than other people who are not melancholic" (Freud 246). Yet Eliot demonstrates how such insight is invariably colored by Latimer's own narcissism. Rather than Latimer using his own imagination for insight, he has to rely on a "pitiable peculiarity" (Eliot, *Lifted* 13) that does not require the imaginative powers necessary for developing sympathy or insight. This "exceptional mental character" is not really owned by Latimer, instead it forces itself upon him without his consent.

Conclusion

Many critics writing about *The Lifted Veil* have rightly shown how Eliot is experimenting with her idea of what the artist does and "whether they can raise sympathies" (Swann 46). Eliot referred to her novels as "simply a set of experiments in life—an endeavour to what our thought and emotion may be capable of" (Eliot qtd. in Gatens 48). I have pointed to how *The Lifted Veil* might have been for Eliot also an experiment in thinking about the effects of loss on a psyche, and what happens when this loss takes over and manifests itself into something destructive, tarnishing our grasp on reality. The emotional context in which Eliot wrote *The Lifted Veil* is significant. The novella was written in interruption of Eliot's novel, *The Mill on the Floss* (1860). In Beryl M. Gray's words, there is the "sense that she had to write story of Latimer to be able to continue with her story of Maggie Tulliver and her tender reconciliation with her brother" (Gray 407). Maggie, the novel's central character, undergoes a series of traumatic experiences, including the death of her father. Despite her suffering and alienation from her relatives, at the end of the novel, she is able to make amends with those closest to her. Although she faces a tragic end, her ability to rekindle these intimate connections redeems her in the eyes of Eliot and the other characters.

As one of the most autobiographical of her novels, Maggie's struggle with her father and brother has elements resembling Eliot's own relationship with Isaac and her father, and her ability to enter a loving relationship with Lewes was important. Indeed, *The Lifted Veil* was written early on in her relationship with Lewes and could be seen as Eliot working through the alternative—not being able to overcome loss and learning from experience, which leaves Latimer alone and unfulfilled. Indeed, Bertha is also an orphan, presumably suffering in ways similar to Latimer. Latimer writes of Bertha: "I asked myself how that face of hers could ever have seemed to me the face of a woman born of woman, with memories of childhood, capable of pain, needing to be fondled?" (Eliot, *Lifted* 40). His inability to conceive of this pain in another and indeed see it in himself more clearly prevents him from acquiring the kind of redemptive and agentic sympathy that Eliot so highly esteems.

Works Cited

"Projective Identification." *Melanie Klein Trust.* Melanie Klein Trust, 2014. Web. 17 Dec. 2014.

Byatt, A. S. & Ignes Sodre. *Imagining Characters: Six Conversations About Women Writers: Jane Austen, Charlotte Bronte, George Eliot, Willa Cather, Iris Murdoch, and Toni Morrison.* New York: Vintage Books, 1997.

Deeds Ermarth, Elizabeth. "George Eliot's Conception of Sympathy." *Nineteenth-Century Fiction.* 40.1 (1985): 23–42. Web.

Dever, Carolyn. *Death and the Mother from Dickens to Freud: Victorian Fiction and the Anxiety of Origins.* Cambridge, UK: Cambridge UP, 2006.

Eliot, George. *Adam Bede.* Hertfordshire, UK: Wordsworth's Editions, 1997.

_____. *The Lifted Veil.* Ed. Helen Small. Oxford: Oxford UP, 1999.

Freud, Sigmund. "Mourning and Melancholia." *Standard Edition of The Complete Psychological Works of Sigmund Freud—On the History of the Psycho-Analytic Movement, Papers on Metapsychology and Other Works.* Vol. 14. London: Vintage Classics, 2001.

Gatens, Moira. "The Art and Philosophy of George Eliot." *Philosophy and Literature*. 33.1 (2009): 73–90. Web.

Gilbert, Sandra M. & Susan Gubar. *The Madwoman in the Attic: The Woman Writer and the Nineteenth-Century Literary Imagination*. New Haven, CT: Yale, 2000.

Gray, Beryl M. "Pseudoscience and George Eliot's *The Lifted Veil*." *Nineteenth-Century Fiction*. 36.4 (1982): 407–423.

Jansson, Asa. "Melancholia, Melancholy, and Suicidality: Normal and Pathological Mental Pain in Victorian Medicine." *Seen*. Academic, 13 Dec. 2014. Web. 15 Jan. 2016. <www.academia.edu/8654113/ Melancholia_Melancholy_and_Suicidality_Normal_and_ Pathological_Mental_Pain_in_Victorian_Medicine_draft_paper_>.

Knoepflmacher, U. C. "On Exile and Fiction: The Leweses and The Shelleys." Ed. Ruth Perry & Martine Watson Brownley. *Mothering the Mind: Twelve Studies of Writers and their Silent Partners*. Boulder, CO: Lynne Rienner, 1984.

Lawlor, Clark. *From Melancholia to Prozac: A History of Depression*. Oxford, UK: Oxford UP, 2012.

Redinger, Ruby. *George Eliot: The Emergent Self*. New York: Alfred A. Knopf, 1975.

Shuttleworth, Sally. *The Mind of the Child: Child Development in Literature, Science, and Medicine 1840–1900*. Oxford, UK: Oxford UP, 2013.

Zenzinger, Ted. "Spinoza, *Adam Bede*, Knowledge, and Sympathy: A Reply to Atkins." *Philosophy and Literature*. 36.2 (2012): 424–440. Web. 15 Jan. 2016.

Casaubon's "Highly Esteemed … Fable of Cupid and Psyche"; Or, Can We Take Myth Seriously in *Middlemarch*?

Erin A. Spampinato

Although *Middlemarch* claims via its subtitle to be a "study of provincial life," it is also, of course, a novel of ideas. Of all the systems for understanding the world that the novel forces into conversation with each other, the most easily dismissed is that of myth. This is because myth is the province of Mr. Casaubon, the novel's most heavily ironized and morally problematic major character. That said, the multitude of mythological references in the novel beg to be considered. This essay proposes that myth be considered an epistemological system—a way of knowing the world—in the same way that scientific inquiry, religious faith, or artistic interpretation are in the novel. I trace the significance of the myth of Cupid and Psyche in *Middlemarch*, arguing that its subtle but insistent presence in the novel allows us to reconsider the power and value of myth itself.

When we meet him, Mr. Casaubon is years into a project of Sisyphusian proportions, having "undertaken to show … that all the mythical systems or erratic mythical fragments in the world [are] corruptions of a tradition originally revealed" (Eliot 22). The novel invokes two definitions of the word 'mythology.' The first is Casaubon's, for whom 'myths' are the Greco-Roman mysteries (pre-Christian religious systems) that he studies. He seeks to find Christian antecedents in the Greco-Roman mysteries, thus reconciling the Greek and Roman traditions with Christian 'Truth.' As Ladislaw suggests in Rome, Casaubon's project is old-fashioned; German folklorists, anthropologists, and philologists had already begun to look beyond the Greco-Roman into other mythological traditions and were theorizing broad continuities between mythological systems in all different ages and cultures. (The radical element of such projects was the treatment of Christianity as one mythical tradition among many.) The other meaning of 'myth' that the novel offers is what I will call mythic repetition: the stories that recur throughout and across human culture and time. The fact that myths, the "religious and proto-scientific perceptions of differing cultures," often structurally and thematically resemble one another was widely recognized in Eliot's day (Beer 162). The paradox of such mythic repetition is that it both suggests continuities and highlights differences between cultures and times. As Gillian Beer writes, "myths ... survive because they tell stories ... which satisfy the need for recurrence. Cultures are defined by their myths but myths outlive the cultures which produced them" (162). Casaubon's project actually presupposes—in its attempt to discover an original myth—that myths, in this anthropological and narratological sense, are not real. I read the novel as conducting a quiet dialogue with this perspective, suggesting that there are stories that recur but cannot be located in one culture, location, or moment. I will argue that the novel puts the mythic into conversation with the allegorical. Here I use 'allegory' to refer to texts in which meaning is constructed through the use of interpretive 'keys.' Of course, *Middlemarch* offers us an interpretive key in its Prelude, inviting us to read Dorothea as a new Teresa[1]. I will argue, however, that we are meant to read beyond this allegorical interpretation, to muddy the waters that the Prelude seems to clear for us. By juxtaposing the mythic and the allegorical, the novel shows the value of thinking 'mythically'; that is, recognizing structural similarities without assigning meaning or fixing interpretation.

That our generous narrator is unwilling, even for a moment, to share Casaubon's conception of myth suggests the novel's implicit critique of his position. This is the same narrator who devotes pages to embodying Dorothea's religious feeling and Lydgate's fervor for scientific exploration. This narrative silence—the unwillingness to either critique, or momentarily embody—Casaubon's "under[taking]" suggests that the novel's position on myth stands in profound antithesis to that of Casaubon (Eliot 22). Although the novel continually ironizes Casaubon's project, it simultaneously sets up a counter-narrative, which entertains the possibility that there is, in fact, mythic recurrence in human life. The work of this paper will be to describe the value of tales of such recurrence in the world of the novel. Although they are obscured rather than highlighted by the text, the novel's many subtle references to the myth of Cupid and Psyche allow us to read this counter-narrative.

The story of Cupid and Psyche is first invoked and then dismissed by Casaubon, who mentions it in passing while discussing sightseeing prospects in Rome. The narrator describes a scene that we are told is becoming typical on Dorothea's honeymoon:

> When he said, "Does this interest you, Dorothea? Shall we stay a little longer?..."—it seemed to her as if going or staying were alike dreary. Or, "Should you like to go to the Farnesina, Dorothea? It contains celebrated frescoes designed or painted by Raphael, which most persons think it worth while to visit."
>
> "But do you care about them?" was always Dorothea's question.
>
> "They are, I believe, highly esteemed. Some of them represent the fable of Cupid and Psyche, which is probably the romantic invention of a literary period, and cannot, I think, be reckoned as a genuine mythical product…." (Eliot 184–5)

The narrator's "Or," before Casaubon's question about the Farnesina implies that Casaubon's suggestion is just one of many bloodless suggestions he has made regarding their sight-seeing prospects; this is a representative rather than particular comment. And yet, this moment is also particularly, painfully ironic: the frescoes he has coolly mentioned were famous for their luscious eroticism. Furthermore, Casaubon's account of the myth's derivation is so narrow as to be incorrect. The written tale of Cupid and Psyche is first found in the Latin writer Apuleius's second-century novel *The Golden Ass*, but the pairing of Cupid and Psyche appears in Greek and Roman sculpture much earlier than that. Apuleius's version of the tale evolved two figures who were already well known in connection with one another, although earlier iterations of the pairing in art and sculpture were simpler, often symbolically demonstrating "the union of Cupid (Love) and Psyche (Soul)" as a kiss shared

(Kingsley-Smith 163). While Casaubon is probably right that the myth of Cupid and Psyche never took on religious cult status, as the myths of Demeter and Persephone did, his dismissal of the myth speaks to his narrow conception of the way mythical and religious 'truths' are formed.

There are a number of structural similarities between the myth of Psyche and the story of Dorothea's marriage. In the Apuleius version, Psyche is a woman of exceptional beauty, willingly sacrificed to the Gods by her family, who believe her destined to marry a monster. Rather than be killed, she is taken to a palace where she can see none of the servants who attend her, but can hear their voices and feel their ministrations. A man whom she cannot see comes to her at night, and—this is the phrase used by most translations—"makes her…his wife" (Adlington 205). He comes every night and leaves before the sun rises, and although she at first fears him, she ultimately comes to love him. Nevertheless, she is haunted by her inability to know his identity. She secretly brings a lantern into their bedchamber and discovers that, instead of a monster, he is the God Cupid. For this betrayal, he abandons her and leaves her to be punished by his mother Venus, who sets for her a number of seemingly insurmountable tasks. Ultimately, she is sent on an errand into the Underworld and must be rescued by Cupid. In the end, Jupiter allows her to drink ambrosia and become immortal, thus making it possible for her to marry Cupid. She gives birth to a child called Pleasure. (The frescoes in Rome which Dorothea and Casaubon discuss visiting depict the wedding banquet of Cupid and Psyche.

The story bears a striking resemblance to that of Dorothea on the psychological level: Psyche willingly submits to a fate (marrying a monster) that others perceive as horrible. Her marriage is imagined by many (including herself) to be a kind of death. While the townspeople in *The Golden Ass* prepare for Psyche's "wretched wedding," they think of her as a "living corpse," whom they bring "not to her marriage, but to her final end and burial" (Adlington 197). Dorothea's social circle registers a similar horror: Sir James declares Casaubon "an old bachelor" with "one foot in the grave," while Mrs. Cadwallader calls Dorothea's marriage "as good as going to a nunnery" (Eliot 54). Even those who express their disapproval less strongly, like Mr. Brooke and Celia, think there is something ghastly about Dorothea's choice. Both stories also contain a betrayal on the part of the husband; neither Psyche nor Dorothea know to whom she is married. For Psyche, this is because she could not choose and cannot see the man who comes to her every night. For Dorothea this is because—as she realizes during her honeymoon—she has projected her own quality of feeling onto her husband, rather than actually understood his character. Both Dorothea and Psyche passionately commit themselves to the man who has betrayed them; both are punished for their curiosity about his true identity. Cupid conceives of Psyche's curiosity as a betrayal, for which he casts her back to earth; Casaubon responds to Dorothea's attempt to know him in Rome by recoiling emotionally (recall her refrain of, "but do you care about them?"). The dual nature of Cupid (mercurial/loving) is echoed in the mystery surrounding Psyche's wedding: her family treats it as a funeral, but she is flown to a palace where she becomes queen. There is a similar duality in Dorothea's experience with Casaubon: she imagines that she will "see a wide opening" where she follows Casaubon, only to find that "Mr. Casaubon himself [is] lost among the small closets and winding stairs," both literally and figuratively (Eliot 185). He can no more easily guide her through the wonders of Rome towards a "wide opening" of intellectual, emotional, sensory—and the unspoken term here is erotic—experience than he can finish his own project (185).

If recognizing mythic repetition allows us to read a counter-narrative in the novel, what is the more primary narrative that this reading works against? The novel invites us, through its Prelude, to read allegorically. By offering us the identification between Dorothea and Teresa of Ávila, it sets us up to read this complex novel as being primarily about one thing: Dorothea's struggle to live an "epic life" in an era which is hostile to that project (Eliot 3). Although central to any reading of *Middlemarch*, the allegorical framework offered by the Prelude and the Finale limits the possibilities for interpreting the novel. We must remember that this novel is deeply suspicious of all 'keys' to interpretation that seem to offer absolute certainty; think of Casaubon's "key to all mythologies" (Eliot 58). The mythic structure I have identified in the novel allows us to identify patterns and consider whether such patterns are destined to recur, but it does not guide our interpretation as strictly as the novel's allegorical framework does. Myth, unlike allegory, is not a key, but a structure. When we try to think 'mythically,' rather than 'allegorically' about the text, new readings become possible. Although Casaubon seems to embody the monstrous betrayal that Cupid perpetrates on Psyche, Ladislaw also becomes identified with the figure of Cupid. The mythical structure of Psyche's story—willing sacrifice, violation and betrayal, unjust punishment, final reward—allows for both Casaubon and Ladislaw to play roles. From her first encounter with Ladislaw in Rome, Dorothea conceives of him in terms that draw out his connection to the mythical Cupid: "The first impression on seeing Will was one of sunny brightness.... When he turned his head quickly his hair seemed to shake out light.... Mr. Casaubon, on the contrary, stood rayless" (Eliot 196). Ladislaw, too, quickly realizes that Dorothea's marriage is based on a misunderstanding on her part, constructing this in mythical terms: "she was an angel beguiled" (195). When Psyche is married, her family puts her on a mountain top and waits for a monster to come and carry her away. Ladislaw imagines Dorothea's marriage in similar style; at one point, he compares Casaubon to a "dragon who ha[s] carried her off to his lair with his talons" (196). Various elements of the myth appear again and again throughout the story, but they are not so coherently organized that we can easily interpret them.

There are two subtle references to the myth of Cupid and Psyche that precede Casaubon's direct reference to it. One is the epigraph to chapter 20 (the chapter in which Casaubon's reference to the myth occurs):

A child forsaken, waking suddenly,
Whose gaze afeard on all things round doth rove,
And seeth only that it cannot see
The meeting eyes of love. (Eliot 180)

This epigraph is one of Eliot's own, and it dramatizes the psychological experience of betrayal which both Psyche and Dorothea feel in their marriages; the reference to love—significantly uncapitalized—allows us to read both characters' experiences into the line, for Cupid is often referred to simply as 'Love' in Greek mythology. Not only does the epigraph dramatize Psyche's confusion and terror, but it also ironizes her situation because the loving eyes she looks for are those of Love capitalized: Cupid. Applied to Dorothea, the epigraph metaphorically depicts the moment at which she realizes that her husband's most supreme failure is that he shrinks from connection, for he cannot 'meet' her eyes. Casaubon's reference to Cupid and Psyche a few pages later, however, invites us to consider whether the epigraph refers only to Dorothea's predicament.

Many moments from the early chapters of the book take on new meaning when we consider the implications of the myth. As I have mentioned, Cupid's rape or seduction of Psyche is euphemized by almost all translations of the Latin as he "made her his wife" (Adlington 205). When it first occurs to Dorothea that Casaubon may propose, we read: "It had now entered [her] mind that Mr. Casaubon might wish to make her his wife" (Eliot 26). She is overwhelmed by the idea, and the narrator records her ecstasy: "How good of him—nay, it would be almost as if a winged messenger had suddenly stood beside her path and held out his hand towards her" (26)! The "winged messenger," of course, suggests Cupid. The literal reference the narrator is making is to an earlier description of Casaubon, in which Dorothea imagines him as "Milton's affable archangel" Raphael, who translates the story of the war in heaven into language intelligible to Eve in Milton's *Paradise Lost* (22). When we consider the implications of the Cupid and Psyche myth, however, the moment is retrospectively ironized; for we can also read it as an iteration of Cupid's first visit to Psyche's bed, tinged with the same betrayal as that encounter. Reading backwards from their honeymoon, we see Dorothea's "reverential gratitude" as sadly misguided and doomed to be disappointed (26). Casaubon does not have the mastery over his own content to make it intelligible to Dorothea; he is not a benevolent translator like the Angel Raphael.

(It can hardly be lost on us that the painter of the Cupid and Psyche frescoes in Rome is another Raphael.) Rather, Casaubon is like Cupid before Psyche's curiosity reveals his true identity: he offers her the promise of something, but whether he will turn out to be a God (as Dorothea imagines) or a monster (as Sir James imagines) remains to be seen.

As I have suggested, it seems that Eliot purposely obscures the connection between Dorothea's story and that of Cupid and Psyche. Late in the novel, however, there is a scene in which Ladislaw is quite obviously figured as Cupid. Chapter 55 begins at the moment when Dorothea thinks she has said goodbye to Ladislaw forever, at which point the narrator asks the reader to consider whether it is not a characteristic of youth to believe that "each crisis [is] final, simply because it is new" (Eliot 514). In this way, the narrator proposes the existence of mythic repetition, reminding the reader that though it seems unlikely, "we are told the oldest inhabitants of Peru do not cease to be agitated by earthquakes, but they probably see beyond each shock, and reflect that there are plenty more to come" (514). We then read of Dorothea's unchecked grief over the loss of Ladislaw, which recalls the separation of Cupid and Psyche after her discovery of his identity: "He was going away into the distance of unknown years, and if ever he came back he would be another man" (514). In *The Golden Ass*, Cupid angrily departs from Psyche after he catches her holding a lamp to his face while he sleeps: "he flew away from his woeful wife's kisses and embraces without saying a word" (Rudin 107). Dorothea and Ladislaw's farewell is in itself a kind of repetition of the past, for Ladislaw's grandmother had been banished by his family after marrying a man the family objected to. In Casaubon's house there is an old picture of Ladislaw's grandmother, which Dorothea looks at wistfully after Ladislaw leaves. She takes the picture down from the wall, "liking to blend the woman who had been too hardly judged with the grandson whom her own heart and judgment defended" (514). The narrator then launches into an extended metaphor that positions Dorothea as Psyche and the departing Ladislaw as Cupid:

[Dorothea] did not know then that it was Love who had come to her briefly, as in a dream before awaking, with the hues of morning on his wings—that it was Love to whom she was sobbing her farewell as his image was banished by the blameless rigour of irresistible day. She only felt that there was something irrevocably amiss and lost in her lot…. (Eliot 515)

Here Dorothea is imagined as Psyche in the moment that Cupid abandons her. As Ladislaw leaves, 'Love' flies away from her, leaving her bereft. We recall the epigraph to chapter 20: "a child forsaken, waking suddenly,/ whose gaze afeared on all things round doth rove,/ And seeth only that it cannot see/ The meeting eyes of love" (Eliot 180). At that point, it had been unclear whether the phrase "the meeting eyes of love" metaphorically referred to eyes that might express love or to a figure who personified love. In that moment, the psychological drama was one of existential terror, where the child wakes to find herself in a space of profound absence; in this later moment, the drama is one of particular loss: Dorothea wakes to find herself losing the man she loves. In the epigraph, it is the failure to recognize anything loving, which produces terror; here, it is the recognition of a particular love, which produces the awareness of loss.

Although the novel begins and ends with allegorical references to Saint Teresa, another way to describe the novel's frame would be to say that it begins with a question to which it returns at the end, albeit without an entirely fulfilling answer. The question is: how can a modern woman lead an "epic life" (Eliot 3)? I argue that this question is framed, right from the beginning, in terms of the stories that get told about such lives; such stories are then compared to those of women whose lives contain the same dilemmas, but who never produce any monument. The power of narrative over lives is registered again and again in the novel's Prelude. Saint Teresa, born to greatness, could not be satisfied by the stories that offered models to women of her era; these are the "many volumed romances of chivalry," which suggest that the greatest achievement a woman can hope for is "social conquest" through marriage (3). But Teresa, unlike Dorothea's contemporaries, has an out: she lives in an age with a "coherent social faith," which creates for her an epic realm beyond the arena of marriage (3). She founds a religious order and is remembered for this "long-recognizable deed" (3). Dorothea, on the other hand, lives in an era without a consensus about what counts for knowledge (the diversity of epistemological systems represented in the novel attests to this). This lack of social coherence means that there is no realm where a woman can be recognized for trying to "shape [her] thought and deed in noble agreement" (3). These "later-born Theresas" are trapped between the "common yearning of womanhood"—the desire to participate in erotic and maternal attachments—and their "vague ideal[s]" (3); we see that this crisis between nature and context is the recurring pattern, the mythic or structural element of women's lives that the novel is trying to narrate. It is not trying to replicate the interpretation of womanhood that contemporary representations of women present ("the sameness of women's coiffure and the favorite love-stories in prose and verse"), but to tell a different story (3). Thinking mythically—that is, acknowledging the meaning of the structural repetitions of women's lives—is what allows us to find contact between human life on an epic scale (these "later-born Theresas") and the individual's unique experience (3).

If the Prologue of the novel presents this problem in abstract terms, as one facing women in general, its Finale closes the loop by describing the results of the crisis between temperament and context in Dorothea's own life. We again encounter, in specific terms, the general figures who were described in the Prologue: the "common eyes" to whom the "struggles [of the later-born Theresas] seemed mere inconsistency and formlessness" become those of the chorus of *Middlemarch*, for Dorothea "was spoken of to a younger generation as a fine girl who married a sickly clergyman, old enough to be her father, and [then] gave up her estate to marry his cousin—young enough to have been his son, and not well-born" (Eliot 3; 784). Dorothea's two marriages represent the two kinds of "ardour" that the Prologue claims women are criticized for: she, like the other "later-born Theresas ... alternated between a vague ideal and the common yearning of womanhood; so that one was disapproved as extravagance, and the other condemned as a lapse" (3). This is indeed exactly how Dorothea's community has perceived her two marriages; the first seemed to sacrifice all erotic feeling, and thus was perceived as an expression of Dorothea's excessive disengagement from the world, while the second sacrificed too much in terms of worldliness, and thus was perceived as the result of an overindulgent erotic attachment. The villagers, we read, conclude that Dorothea "could not have been 'a nice woman,' else she would not have married either the one or the other" (784).

I have claimed that the novel's Prelude encourages us to read Dorothea's tale allegorically and thus to limit our possibilities of interpretation. In the final moments of the novel, however, the narrator blends the boundary between the allegorical and the mythic. The narrator references Saint Teresa again but, this time, does so in order to describe a class of women: "new Theresa[s]." Saint Teresa's story is not offered as a 'key' to understanding that of Dorothea, but as a repetition of a recurring structure in its own right:

> A new Theresa will hardly have the opportunity of reforming a conventional life, any more than a new Antigone will spend her heroic piety in daring all for the sake of a brother's burial: the medium in which their ardent deeds took shape is gone. (Eliot 784)

These women will feel as strongly as Saint Teresa and Antigone did, but will experience different outcomes, for "the medium in which [Saint Teresa and Antigone's] ardent deeds took shape is gone." The figure of Psyche shares the plight of the new Teresas and new Antigones. Unlike Saint Teresa and Antigone, Psyche is a figure whose myth actually dramatizes the same crisis that the novel seeks to narrate: the tragedy of being "ill-suited" to one's context (Eliot 4). In the beginning of the story, her "divine beauty" marks her as otherworldly, just as Dorothea's has marked her: "Everyone marveled at her divine beauty, but only as it were at some image well painted and set out" (Apuleius 193). This beauty makes Psyche the subject of great reverence, which angers Venus and begins the chain of events that involves Cupid in her life. She cannot really exist in Cupid's realm either, however, and is cast out of it by him and then punished by Venus. She is tricked and cajoled throughout the story by humans and Gods alike, and her history is much like that of Dorothea: after a series of blunders and punishments, as her "loving heart-beats and sobs … tremble off and are dispersed among hindrances," she ends up nothing more than a wife and mother, without "some long-recognizable deed" to her name (Eliot 4). In fact, if any moral can be read into the tale as it is told in by Apuleius, it is not for Psyche's benefit; rather, Jupiter agrees to make her immortal so that she will forever be married to Cupid, and thus help mend his wanton and mischievous ways. In many ways, she is really the figure whose myth most resembles Dorothea's story, who never gets an opportunity for epic action like Saint Teresa or Antigone, but is volleyed back and forth between her "ideals" and the "common yearning of womanhood" (3).

In a contemporary review of *Middlemarch*, Henry James called the novel "at once one of the strongest and one of the weakest of English novels" ("*Galaxy* Review" 353). He writes that while reading he had hoped that the novel would take the "form … of an organized, moulded, balanced composition, gratifying the reader with a sense of design and construction" ("*Galaxy* Review" 353). He went on to claim that "*Middlemarch* [was] a treasure house of details, but … an indifferent whole ("*Galaxy* Review" 353). Here James critiques the novel for being—to use a term that he had not yet coined—"a loose baggy monster" (*The Tragic Muse* 5). He wants organization, molding, and balance; he wants the story of Dorothea to be formally accentuated rather than crowded among the multiplots within which it exists. I differ from James in contending that this crowding is the form of the novel; rather than being a "mere chain of episodes, broken into accidental lengths and unconscious of the influence of [a] plan," the diffuse, multifarious nature of the novel is its plan. Within that "treasure house of detail" we have myriad iterations of the story of conflict between "inward being" and "what lies outside" that being (785). In the Prologue, we encounter the new Teresas "ill-suited" to their surroundings, and the "cygnet … reared uneasily among the ducklings" (Eliot 4). There is Lydgate, whose engagement with the social world and passion for Rosamond overwhelms the other "story of ... passion" in his life: his "dream of himself as a discoverer" (135–7). There is Ladislaw, who dreams of himself as the rescuer of Dorothea but is bound by his social and legal debt to Casaubon. There are Fred Vincy and Mary Garth, who are never recognized by the villagers of Middlemarch for their contributions: no one believes that Fred might really have written a useful book about farming and Mary might really have written a learned book of children's stories. There is Dorothea, ill-fit for her context in many ways: her beauty and natural vivacity, which make her the focus of erotic interest that she initially has little use for; her money, which makes it socially impossible for her to use her energy in literal work; her "love of extremes," which makes her unfit for the modern world (9). In all these cases, what lies beyond the bounds of the self intrudes on what lies within it until responsibility and causality are almost hopelessly muddled.

Recognizing mythic repetition is, I argue, our way through this muddle. *Middlemarch* is consistently aware of the stories that do get told (like the chivalric romances of the Prologue or the gossip of the Middlemarch residents), but it wants to tell a different story. The story it does tell—of the figure ill-suited for his or her context—is harder to tell because it defies narrative conventions of, as Henry James claimed, "form" and organization ("*Galaxy* Review" 353). We respond to it because we recognize it, and yet it does not have the epic grandeur of the stories of Teresa or Antigone. Its grandeur lies, however, in the linking of the massive and the particular. While describing Dorothea's first moment of insight, during her honeymoon, the narrator tells us that

> The element of tragedy which lies in the very fact of frequency, has not yet wrought itself into the coarse emotion of mankind; and perhaps our frames could hardly bear much of it. If we had a keen vision and feeling of all ordinary human life, it would be like hearing the grass grow and the squirrel's heart beat, and we should die of the roar that lies on the other side of silence. As it is, the quickest of us walk about well wadded with stupidity. (Eliot 182)

Here the narrator suggests that we feel "keen[ly]" what we imagine lies in the "tragic" or epic register, but that we miss the "exceptional" moments that occur all the time (182). This, we are told, is probably for the best, as it would be overwhelming to be truly aware of the multitude and meaning of the events that occur every second of every day. What *Middlemarch* offers us with myth, however, is an inroad into this awareness; the patterns that we notice, that connect us to other humans of our own and other ages, are the places at which we can grasp what is usually too overwhelming to contend with: "the roar that lies on the other side of silence."

Dorothea has one of these moments at the end of the novel, after she wrongly assumes that Rosamond and Ladislaw are having an affair and subsequently acknowledges her own love for Ladislaw. As she sits looking out her window, after a night of sobbing, she sees:

> ...a man with a bundle on his back and a woman carrying her baby; in the field she could see figures moving—perhaps the shepherd with his dog. Far off in the bending sky was the pearly light; and she felt the largeness of the world and the manifold wakings of men to labour and endurance. She was a part of that involuntary, palpitating life, and could neither look out on it from her luxurious shelter as a mere spectator, nor hide her eyes in selfish complaining. (Eliot 741)

She sees the people in her view symbolically bound to the central obligations of their lives, a man "carrying his bundle ... and a woman carrying her baby" (Eliot 741). The symbolic distillation of the scene suggests the broadest mythic repetition in human life: all the "manifold wakings of men to labour and endurance" (741). In this moment, Dorothea realizes that all lives are like hers—"involuntary"—and that this makes her neither a spectator nor a victim, but a participant. Her recognition of the mythic repetition in the scene is the means by which Dorothea relates without projecting; myth, we see, is the way of understanding the world that can maintain an understanding of difference, while still acknowledging connection. Like the aged inhabitants of Peru, who have experienced many earthquakes, the experience of recurrence has widened her perspective.

Recognition of mythic recurrence is not only a route towards this widening of ethical vision; it is also a narrative structure that allows Eliot to connect the two kinds of experience that she wants to put in relation to each other: the world historical and the individual particular. Casaubon's invocation of the myth of Cupid and Psyche calls myth into service at the moment when Dorothea is caught awkwardly between the epic and the particular. Dorothea's disappointment in her marriage is "not unusual" or even noteworthy when one thinks in terms of human history; when one considers Dorothea's personal history, however, it contains an "element of tragedy," which is not rendered meaningless because of its frequency (Eliot 182). Eliot uses recurrence as a way to knit together her narrative and ethical concerns, for it is this experience that allows Dorothea to begin to emerge from her "moral stupidity," the state to which "we are all of us born…, [of] taking the world as udder to feed our supreme selves" (198). Release from "moral stupidity" involves the recognition that others have an "equivalent centre of self whence the lights and shadows must always fall with a certain difference" (198). During his debate with Naumann, Ladislaw wishes for a representational system that is "better for being vague" (Eliot 179). Of all the epistemological systems that the novel entertains, myth—in the sense of recurring structure—is the only one that is vague enough to both allow us to see large patterns and recognize connections as well as maintain our understanding of the "certain difference" with which others experience the world. It connects without determining or asking us to make meaning out of those connections. This is the power of myth in the novel; in linking the epic to the endlessly recurring, myth can transcend the distance between the subjective perspective, which sees individual trouble as tragedy, and the world historical view, which perceives such events *en masse*: "the roar that lies on the other side of silence" (20). Myth in *Middlemarch* is the place at which the epic and the individual meet.

Note

1. While Eliot spells the saint's name "Theresa," the figure is known historically as Teresa of Avila.

Works Cited

Apuleius, Lucius. *The Golden Ass: Being the Metamorphoses of Lucius Apuleius.* 1566. Trans. William Adlington. Cambridge, MA: Harvard UP, 1965.

_____. *The Golden Ass.* Trans. Sarah Rudin. New Haven: Yale UP, 2011.

Beer, Gillian. *Darwin's Plots: Evolutionary Narrative in Darwin, George Eliot, and Nineteenth-Century Fiction.* 3rd ed. Cambridge, UK: Cambridge UP, 2009.

Eliot, George. *Middlemarch: A Study of Provincial Life.* 1872. Ed. David Carroll. Oxford, UK: Oxford UP, 2008.

James, Henry. *The Tragic Muse.* Boston & New York: Houghton Mifflin Company, 1918.

_____. "Unsigned Review, *Galaxy*, March 1873." *George Eliot: The Critical Heritage.* Ed. David Carroll. New York: Routledge, 2000.

Kingsley-Smith, Jane. *Cupid in Early Modern Literature and Culture.* Cambridge, UK: Cambridge UP, 2010.

What Can Be Learned from an Adaptation of *The Mill on the Floss*_____

Abigail Burnham Bloom

George Eliot's 1860 novel, *The Mill on the Floss*, presents difficulties for my college students as it has for many readers since its publication. Students tend to be perplexed by the role of the narrator, who seems both intrusive and boring, the idea of renunciation, and the devastating ending of the novel.[1] In addition, the attitudes and manners of the nineteenth century presented in the novel are far different from those of twenty-first-century students. Showing an adaptation of the novel can help students overcome these difficulties by providing a companion and often a comparison to Eliot's words. There are three readily-available film adaptations of this novel, each of which is intriguing.[2] However, the 1937 adaptation lacks structural coherence, while the TV mini-series of 1978 is just too long. The 1997 BBC television movie, directed by Graham Theakson and starring Emily Watson, is less than two hours long; contains strong performances, especially Emily Watson's portrayal of Maggie Tulliver; and employs original imagery and music to develop its themes.

The 1997 *Mill on the Floss* film belongs to a series of costume dramas made for television during the 1990s and known for being high-quality adaptations of excellent literary sources. The producers specialized in high production values and used exceptional acting talent (de Groot 187). According to Jerome de Groot in *Consuming History*, viewers believe in the authenticity of the historical era represented in the films. Despite being fiction, they convey the flavor of the era and their setting (187). As Sarah Cardwell explains in *Adaptation Revisited*, "Although the audience recognizes the stories as fictitious, it accepts the validity of the programme's representation of the past" (114). Today, we are nostalgic for former times, the beauty of the land, the costumes, and the "simpler" way of life. But the past represented on the screen is nothing like the past as it was lived. We are not seeing the era as it was, but as it has been re-imagined for us. Robert Giddings points out that nineteenth-century literature has been translated "into a synthetic 'historical' realism in which everything must seem authentic and true to period"; whereas even the hygiene, teeth, clothing, and looks of the actors and actresses are not like those of people living during the nineteenth century (x). With a forewarning of these considerations, students watching the film become familiar with some of the puzzling aspects of imagining another era.

The Mill on the Floss takes place in a rural area during the early Victorian era, approximately the 1830s. This is a pre-industrial time that students have difficulty visualizing. The structure of the social classes, the treatment of girls and women, even the clothing and manners differ dramatically from today. Although the film may not be an accurate portrayal of how life actually was lived, it can help students feel more comfortable with imagining life during another era. For example, the film enables viewers to visualize the geography, the function of the mill, and the importance of the river for the Tulliver family, elements that George Eliot, writing thirty years after the setting of her novel, attempted to make comprehensible to her readers through the narrator.

Someone who adapts a novel into a film must find a way to retell a story in a different medium, from the vantage point of a different time, for an audience of a different era. When the original is a dense Victorian novel, the result condenses the work substantially as even a miniseries cannot contain everything in a complex novel like *The Mill on the Floss*. Making use of the high recognition value of the work being adapted, the BBC films of the 1990s stayed close to their source in terms of setting, action, dialogue, and plot. Yet, all adaptations differ from their source, and fidelity to the source does not ensure that an adaptation will be successful as a film. By examining the interstices of the difference between film and novel,[3] components of the novel can be made more comprehensible to students. As Julie Sanders explains in *Adaptation and Appropriation*, "it is usually at the very point of infidelity that the most creative acts of adaptations and appropriation take place" (20). In addition, watching the adaptation can be like reading the novel for a second time, as the film takes the viewer back to the incidents and characters while presenting a critical interpretation of the novel through the changes from the original.

I regularly teach *The Mill on the Floss* in an upper-level undergraduate course entitled "Victorian Women Writers." I choose works for the course written by women that concern the position of women in order to explore issues of Victorian society. The course progresses primarily through discussion; using a film to compare with a work stimulates discussion in order to develop critical literacy around narrative decisions and representations of gender and class. As Imelda Whelehan suggests, "Perhaps encouraging more flexibility in analyses of literary texts through the study of adaptations will enable the audience to be more self-conscious about their role as critics and about the activities of reading/viewing that they bring to bear in an academic environment" (Whelehan 19). Students often react to novels by believing that there is a single meaning that can be teased out of them, whereas films, particularly adaptations, require no choice on the part of the filmmakers as they follow the novel. In the classroom, I attempt to get students to see beyond these viewpoints and to consider aspects of the novel and eventually the Victorian era from a new perspective.

"Outside Dorlcote Mill": The Problem of the Narrator

My students are disoriented at the start of the novel by the stance of the narrator on the bank of the Floss. Who is she or he? Is she dreaming? When is she there? What is her relationship to the story? The narration begins slowly and in a time-tangled manner. Students are wary of such involvement on the part of a narrator and tend to skip over the narrative information to get to the action. Yet the narrator plays an important role within the novel by situating the events at a specific time in the past and by broadening the themes of the work to make the story universal.

The novel begins with an emphasis on the river Floss, "A wide plain, where the broadening Floss hurries on between its green banks to the sea, and the loving tide, rushing to meet it, checks its passage with an impetuous embrace" (Eliot 51). This sentence reveals the relationship of the specific river, the Floss, with all waters, the sea. The sentiment is repeated at the start of Book Fourth as the narrator looks at the Rhone and the Rhine and the place of the Dodsons and Tullivers within a larger history. The specific becomes universal; the river gains a mythic dimension that connects it with other rivers and to the people who live along them. From the start of the novel, the river Floss is interconnected with Maggie and her future, for as the narrator views the water flowing through the wheel of the mill, she sees a little girl watching the water as well. The romantic language of the first sentence, with the "loving" tide and the "impetuous embrace" anticipates how Maggie seeks expressions of love from her brother throughout the novel and finally dies in his arms. Coming back to the first sentence after reading the novel, students can see that Maggie's romances are not the primary relationships of the novel, but rather that Maggie's relationship with her brother takes precedence.

The importance of the river Floss is emphasized further in the novel with Mr. Tulliver's concerns over the depth of the water and his riparian rights, Mrs. Tulliver's worry that her daughter will fall in the river and drown, tales of past floods, and the connection of Maggie with the mythic boatwoman of St. Ogg. The river unites different elements of the plot of the novel and connects Maggie with her brother and Stephen Guest as well. Her earliest memory is of her brother and the river. When Maggie first meets Stephen, Eliot writes, "Maggie's destiny, then, is at present hidden, and we must wait for it to reveal itself like the course of an unmapped river; we only know that the river is full and rapid, and that for all rivers there is the same final home" (409). Maggie and the river are again shown as entwined, and the two major moments of her life will take place on the river, the one leading to the other. The final home for rivers is the sea, and the final home for humans is death, making Maggie's watery death at the end of the novel inevitable.

Margaret Harris attributes the paucity of adaptations of George Eliot's novels (with the exception of *Silas Marner*) to the difficulty of dealing with, "narrative standpoint, focalization, and authorial commentary." She suggests that "George Eliot's narrators pose too great a challenge" (Harris 27), a challenge that cannot be translated successfully onto the screen. Film directors have found different means of accomplishing some of the tasks of the narrator in the novel. At the start of the 1997 film adaptation, the viewer is disoriented by a green screen with fuzzy shapes and forms. This slowly comes to be recognized as a view of the surface of the river from underneath. Distinctive music plays and the credits run. The bottoms of rowboats pass overhead. There are two kinds of boats visible—one like the one Maggie is on with Stephen, and the other is a shorter, broader boat, like the one Maggie takes to rescue Tom during the flood. A view from above shows a woman, the adult Maggie, dreamily drifting alone in a boat while people watch from a riverbank. The scene begins as calm and relaxing but quickly becomes menacing. A rowboat, with a man at the oars, passes by another boat containing Lucy, who turns to look at Maggie with a frozen face. An indistinct voice, which can only be Maggie's, repeats the words, "I'm sorry." People on the riverbank look like cut outs, paper doll versions of themselves. They are not shown as individuals, but as a united force in opposition to Maggie, adding to the dream-like nature of the vision. The sequence ends with Maggie calling, "Tom, Tom, Tom" but sounding as if underwater. My students seek to clarify the confusing images and are consequently brought into the story more quickly than Eliot was able to engage them. The introductory images are not completely repeated later in the film, but they are called to mind in later scenes.

Music composed by John Scott complements this dreamy evocation of the river in the first scene of the 1997 adaptation. The published CD of the music identifies the attempt of the music to capture the mood and depict:

> ... the Floss itself, the river that shapes the character's lives and, ultimately, their tragic fates. This limpid melody evokes the tranquility of the setting in the heart of the English countryside; but, like the best of folk songs, it is also endowed with a reflective quality ... [T]he river and its music dominate from beginning to end. (Editorial Review)

The evocative look at the river and the accompanying music suggest the specific setting of the story on the river Floss and the universal theme of the interconnectedness of all water. The haunting theme is repeated at critical times in the film, bringing the reader back to the opening sequence and to concern for Maggie. When I showed this introduction in the classroom, one student was reminded of the Greek myth of the dead being rowed across the river Styx because of the unreal nature of the figures and the dreamy, melancholic mood of the whole. This comment brought out Eliot's frequent references to myth and the projection of the novel towards the universal.

By watching the start of the 1997 adaptation of *The Mill on the Floss* and then going back to the novel, some of the roles of the narrator become clearer. The opening scene of the film locates the universal within the specific, by showing images of importance to Maggie, and by providing themes and a musical leitmotif that will be revisited elsewhere in the work. The viewer feels that Maggie's fate is linked to the river, and the tone of the scene suggests that her fate is not joyous. In the novel, the narrator brings out similar ideas through the repetition of images and themes.

The initial scene of the film reflects the role of dreaminess in Maggie as she drifts in a boat and the closeness of death, themes developed throughout both the film and the novel. This dreamy state has been present at the start of the novel with the situation of the narrator. In her childhood, Maggie allowed Tom's rabbits to die because she forgot to feed them; her mind has never worked in the same way as her brother's. As an adult, Maggie is induced into a dreamy state by music and falls asleep while with Stephen on the river. The images presented in the opening sequence of the film are not taken directly from the novel; for example, Maggie never drifts by herself in the novel as is shown in the film. However, this view of her emphasizes both her dream state and her isolation when she returns from the river foray with Stephen and how she will be judged by others.

Throughout the novel, the narrator aids the reader in understanding concepts, ideas, and points of view. Maggie, following her river journey with Stephen, is judged by the "world's wife"

(Eliot 489–90), and the narrator explains the thinking involved: Maggie and Stephen's marriage would have been accepted had they returned home together in triumph, but Maggie's solitary return makes it appear that Stephen has seduced and abandoned her. Eliot's use of the expression the "world's wife" derives from a British phrase, "the world and his wife," meaning a great many people (*Cambridge Dictionaries Online*). The townspeople turn against Maggie and she becomes unemployable. Maggie, during the introductory sequence of the film, is in a boat and exposed to the cold stares of the townspeople along the riverbank, an image that suggests her condemnation by everyone in the town, those termed the "world's wife" by Eliot. The series of images at the start of the 1997 adaptation interest my students in Maggie more than the words of the narrator in the initial chapters of the novel, yet looking back at the novel, students come to understand how the narrator introduces the novel's diverse themes.

"Waking": Maggie's Renunciations

Maggie goes through three different renunciations: the first, her renunciation of the world as a young girl; the second, her renunciation of Philip; and the third, her renunciation of Stephen. Renunciation as a way of dealing with the world appeals to Maggie, although she doesn't immediately understand its ramifications. She learns more as she renounces more and her world narrows. My students, for the most part, don't comprehend her thinking and the lure of renunciation. Part of this stems from a lack of knowledge about a woman's place during the Victorian era and part from a more modern emphasis in their own lives on the importance of happiness rather than of duty.

Maggie's renunciation of the world occurs because of her family's changed situation within the community and her own isolation. Following her father's bankruptcy, she attempts to work to help pay off her father's debt, but is defeated by the lack of opportunity and by her brother who wants to take the man's role and control her conduct. In response, she studies Thomas à Kempis's *The Imitation of Christ*, although "[s]he had not perceived—how could she until she had lived longer?—the inmost truth of the old monk's outpourings, that renunciation remains sorrow, though a sorrow borne willingly" (Eliot 311). The suggestion of future renunciations, which will be a "sorrow borne willingly" as she lives longer, develop from her first renunciation and her own involved sense of duty to those she loves. Maggie focuses on not desiring anything so that she cannot be disappointed. Renunciation becomes a choice when she has no other viable choice. Philip Wakem interests her once again in books and the world. For over a year they see each other surreptitiously, and Maggie benefits both from Philip's appreciation of her and from the intellectual stimulation he provides. In a way, he is a more loving substitute for her brother Tom. She is drawn to Philip because of his mind and because she likes to make him happy. When he seems happy, "She had a moment of real happiness then—a moment of belief that, if there were sacrifice in this love, it was all the richer and more satisfying" (Eliot 352). But this cannot be enough for a fulfilling romantic relationship.

When Tom forces Maggie to stop seeing Philip, she feels both saddened and relieved: "And yet, how was it that she was now and then conscious of a certain dim background of relief in the forced separation from Philip? Surely it was only because the sense of a deliverance from concealment was welcome at any cost" (Eliot 362). Maggie justifies her feelings with an easy explanation, but her relief stems from her knowledge that she is not in love with Philip, and she had hoped to keep him as a brother rather than as a lover. Forced to stop seeing Philip because of her father and her brother's irrational hatred of his father, Maggie accepts the loss in her life without a struggle. But Lucy, wanting Maggie to be as happy as she is, contrives first to get Philip and Maggie to see each other again and hopes eventually to help them marry.[4]

When Stephen Guest meets Maggie, she is everything he does not expect. Maggie and Stephen are immediately attracted to each other and aware of their uncomfortable situation as nearly engaged to others. Stephen provides the sex appeal and excitement that her relationship with Philip lacks. One evening he sings from the *Sonnambula*, "The Sleepwalker," a foretaste of the state that will encapsulate Maggie on the river. The tenor tells the heroine musically that though he may forsake her, "I love thee still" (Eliot 424). Stephen uses music to communicate with Maggie, "to deepen the hold he had on her" (463). She enters a trance state as she hears Stephen sing and play, "in spite of her resistance to the spirit of the song and to the singer, [Maggie] was taken hold of and shaken by the invisible influence—was borne along by a wave too strong for her" (425). The imagery prepares the reader for Maggie's dreamy state on the river with Stephen, during which she is borne along by her sexual attraction to him. Maggie has been starved for music, attention, and love.

George Eliot excused Maggie's love for the undeserving Stephen by stating that even the best people can fall in love with someone not worthy of them:

> Maggie's position towards Stephen—is too vital a part of my whole conception and purpose for me to be converted to the condemnation of it.… If the ethics of art do not admit the truthful presentation of a character essentially noble but liable to great error—error that is anguish to its own nobleness—then, it seems to me, the ethics of art are too narrow, and must be widened to correspond with a widening psychology." (Lovesey 39 n6)[5]

Stephen has little to recommend him as a fitting suitor for Maggie other than his admiration for her mind and looks. He is a careless young man, without self-knowledge, who has not been tested. Indeed, he has not worked but has been supported by his father. Stephen has allied himself with Lucy because she is the kind of woman he has been expected to marry. She is an eminently appropriate choice: lovely, an angel in the house, and from a family of his own social class; yet she lacks intellectual depth.

Having unsuccessfully fought her attraction for Stephen, Maggie must then renounce him. After Stephen and Maggie have overstayed their time on the river, Stephen hopes to persuade Maggie to run off with him and marry. She is torn by her desire to be with Stephen and by her ties to Lucy and Philip. American students today have trouble understanding how difficult it was for a Victorian to break an engagement—or even a connection that borders on engagement, such as the relationship between Stephen and Lucy, or Philip and Maggie. They often believe nothing should stand in the way of her personal happiness and do not comprehend Maggie's talk of duty. Maggie refuses to experience her own happiness by means of something that would bring sadness to Lucy and Philip, people she loves. She cannot allow herself to benefit from their sorrow, "If the past is not to bind us, where can duty lie? We should have no law but the inclination of the moment" (Eliot 477), while Stephen acts on the "inclination of the minute." Unfortunately, Maggie's renunciation of Stephen makes the end of the novel inevitable, and guilty or not, Maggie is punished for her behavior.

Since movies cannot show the interiority of a character's mind with the same intensity as a novel, the lack of access to Maggie's inner dilemmas brings out the accomplishment of the novel in revealing her development and thoughts. The films must find alternative means of suggesting characters' feelings, which they accomplish through the use of actors and their facial expressions and body language, images, music, and conversations. The 1997 film presents a forceful and attractive Philip, which makes him a more appropriate mate for Maggie than the Philip depicted in the novel. While with Philip in the Red Deeps in the 1997 adaptation, Maggie declares she has stopped "wishing," another way of suggesting renunciation. Philip counters that this is wrong, and Maggie immediately makes a wish so that her change, her reconciliation with the world occurs rapidly. As a child, Philip sang to Maggie, and as an adult, he sings the same song, created for the film, which begins, "My ship is rigged and ready and I must be sailing," emphasizing boats and water and also the impossibility of their love. Even if Maggie and Philip are together, forces are moving them apart.

In the 1997 film, speaking with Lucy about her desire for renunciation, Maggie declares, "it's a sin to love myself, to seek my own happiness." She continues, "if we desire nothing then we cannot be disappointed." Lucy states that she seeks happiness and that she sees nothing wrong with that. Although this brings Maggie's desire for renunciation out in the open, speaking to Lucy is very different from talking to Philip, as Maggie does in the novel. Lucy, sweet but simple, cannot comprehend the thoughts, while Philip, who could certainly understand renunciation because of his circumstances, is better able to understand Maggie's point of view. The situation is also simplified in that Maggie feels no relief from the renunciation of Philip. My students respond like Lucy, not understanding the pull of renunciation as a choice Maggie can make and believing Maggie should seek personal happiness. To hear Lucy give students' own reasoning makes the difference of opinion easier to understand, even if they do not agree with Maggie's ideas of renunciation. Class discussion brought out the irony in Lucy's short-sightedness: Lucy encourages Maggie to seek her own happiness without knowing that if Maggie pursued her happiness, it would result in the loss of Lucy's happiness. Lucy lacks perception in not seeing Stephen and Maggie's attraction for each other as she formerly did not see Tom Tulliver's love for her.

With much less emphasis on the use of spoken words than in the novel, the relationship between Maggie and Stephen in the film is presented primarily with musical leitmotifs and heaving chests. At the start of the scene where Stephen and Maggie are on the river together, Maggie has been daydreaming and the film repeats the opening imagery of looking at the surface of the river from underneath. The viewer is reminded of the image of Maggie drifting by herself in the opening sequence. Stephen takes an aggressive position to convince Maggie to stay with him, telling her she cannot bear other people's anger, "Tom will condemn you if you marry Philip, Philip will condemn you if you marry me." Stephen, like Lucy, doesn't understand Maggie. She chooses the hardest path for herself; she is not convinced to renounce Stephen by the behavior of others, but by her own set of beliefs. These beliefs are recast in the film in a manner so that a modern audience, such as my students, can understand them. As Maggie and Stephen are taken aboard a larger boat, some of the images from earlier in the film reappear in a fantasy montage that shows the thoughts of Maggie's mind and solidify her decision. As she explains to Stephen why she is going back home, Maggie says, "I let myself drift," indicating her need for action rather than passivity and an end to her dreamy state of existence. "We cannot choose happiness," she says, "we can only listen to our consciences."

By simplifying Maggie's urge for renunciation, the film makes it easier for students to comprehend, even if they think Maggie is wrong to renounce Stephen. They view Maggie as having a choice between Philip and Stephen, which one student compared to Bella Swan's choice between Edward and Jacob in the *Twilight* saga. The film gives students the opportunity to look at renunciation from another angle. Maggie's renunciation of Stephen prepares the reader for the end of novel, as there appears no escape for her from an untenable situation. Maggie's solitary return to St. Ogg leaves her in the difficult position of being thought of as a fallen woman except by a few who know her. For her brother, the fact that she is considered fallen by others makes her fallen. Her life in the future would be severely limited.

"The Last Conflict": Maggie's Death

Throughout *The Mill on the Floss*, Maggie seeks the love and approval of Tom. This is rather surprising, as Tom is seldom nice to Maggie, even as children, yet Maggie always loves him. She tells Philip of her earliest memory, "standing with Tom by the side of the Floss" (Eliot 325). Tom retains a central position in Maggie's emotional life, and she cannot escape his pull on her, despite seeing his flaws. As Tom and Maggie's childhood ends, Eliot writes, "They had entered the thorny wilderness, and the golden gates of their childhood had forever closed behind them" (224). Eliot describes such an idealized union in her 1869 poem "Brother and Sister," which concludes, "But were another childhood-world my share,/ I would be born a little sister there" (546). In the novel, Maggie yearns for this kind of relationship with Tom, but her plans always go astray as she acts in a manner that is unacceptable to him and for which he cannot forgive her. The relationship is unsatisfying for Maggie because she cannot have Tom's unqualified love.[6]

The ending of the novel reestablishes the relationship between Tom and Maggie. Maggie, filled with love for her brother, takes a boat to rescue him:

> there was an undefined sense of reconcilement with her brother: what quarrel, what harshness, what unbelief in each other can subsist in the presence of a great calamity, when all the artificial vesture of our life in gone, and we are all one with each other in primitive mortal needs? (Eliot 514)

She is left with "only the deep, underlying, unshakable memories of early union" (514).

The reconciliation of the siblings at the end is indicated by Tom's reversion of calling Maggie by her childhood name, "Magsie," effective in its simplicity. They see death coming towards them, and they go down, "Living through again in one supreme moment the days when they had clasped their little hands in love, and roamed the daisied fields together" (517). The sentimental ending refers to an ideal time never seen in the novel and suggests the importance of Maggie's relationship with her brother rather than her relationships with Philip and Stephen. As Philip urges Maggie to marry him in the 1997 adaptation Maggie responds, "I will do nothing that will divide me from Tom forever." Running off with Philip would divide her from Tom, and although she might be able to reconcile with Tom if she ran off with Stephen, she cannot accept that behavior herself.

The start of the 1997 adaptation had Maggie's voice saying she was sorry, words she never speaks in the novel. But these words point to her increased sense of guilt and indicate a greater reason for death as a punishment. At the end of the 1997 adaptation, as Maggie attempts to rescue Tom in the flood, the river is calm. Rather than their boat being destroyed by machinery as in the novel, in this film, Tom gets tangled in the rope under the water. Maggie's voice yells, "Tom, Tom, Tom," the cry that was heard at the start of the film. As Maggie goes underwater to help Tom get disentangled, the scene shifts to show brother and sister in the water under the boat, and the green look of the river is similar to images in the introduction and at the start of the scene with Maggie and Stephen on the river. This image then works to unify the film, much like the narrator in the novel. At the start of this film, the viewer is underwater—just as Maggie is at the end—putting the viewer in Maggie's position. When Maggie sees that Tom is dead, she appears to give up the struggle with the rope and with her life. The scene shifts to Tom and Maggie as children sitting in a tree together and then running together towards the mill, a final fantasy. Although there is no overt reconciliation between Tom and Maggie, the tone and imagery imply that they have found peace together in death. The last scene of the film focuses on Maggie and Tom, showing Tom's central place in Maggie's life.

Although readers may be upset by having Maggie die so quickly after spending so long with her, her death is well prepared for through the imagery of the novel. Yet Maggie's death seems a punishment for something that students do not see as a crime. The manner of her death in the film appears to be suicide. Suicide is not suggested by Eliot in the novel; Tom and Maggie perish by chance, by the force of machinery in the river moved from its place by the flood. Suicide, according to the predominate religions of the era, would involve the damnation of Maggie's soul, an even worse fate in the view of most Victorian readers than her untimely death. Yet the suicide in the film helps my students return to the novel and reflect on Victorian society, Maggie's situation, and the limited opportunities available to her due to her gender.

Comparing the start and the end of a novel and a film often provides excellent focal points as "key motifs and images are established early and reaffirmed at the end" (Carroll, Palmer, Thomas, and Waese 234). This is certainly true of the novel and the 1997 adaptation of *The Mill on the Floss*. Studying them together can orient students to the era portrayed and the physical feel of the setting. By seeing the film and then going back to the novel to reconsider the differences between them, the role of the narrator in *The Mill on the Floss* can be better understood, as can Maggie's relationships with Tom, Philip, and Stephen, and the idea of Maggie's renunciations. Ultimately, discussions arising from watching the film in conjunction with the novel can increase understanding of the dynamics of gender and class within Victorian society. As one adaptation scholar has phrased it, comparisons of novels and films "can provide focal points for more general arguments by reframing Victorian fiction and Victorian culture" (Leitch 12). Students can be brought to reflect on Maggie's role in society based on the changed financial circumstances of her family early in the story, Maggie and Tom's educational opportunities, their career prospects, their different beliefs in the concept of duty, as well as Maggie's "fallen" state later in the novel. Such discussions can lead students to a better understanding of *The Mill on the Floss* in general, as well as the difficult position of the Victorian woman.

Notes

1. Rosemary Ashton describes the problems with the novel, which have been noticed since publication, in similar terms: "They concern the structure and balance of the novel as a whole; the morality and probability (not the same thing) of the denouement; and the appropriateness of the tragic ending" (14).

2. Two silent versions were made in 1913 and 1915. The British 1937 film was the first George Eliot "talkie" (Harris). Several later versions have been made, including a short version in 1953, a Mexican version, a BBC television serial in 1965, a TV mini-series in 1978, and a made-for-television version in 1997, the subject of this paper.

3. George Eliot was not positively disposed towards adaptations of her works. She responded to someone seeking permission to adapt *Romola*, "You will no doubt on reflection appreciate as well as imagine the reasons that must prevent a writer who cares much about his writings from willingly allowing them to be modified and in any way 'adapted' by another mind than his own" (Harris 30).

4. *The Mill on the Floss* adaptations of 1937 and 1978 have forgiveness as a major theme. Near the end of both films, Tom regrets his intractability and forgives Maggie and the Wakems. Although this theme is not present in the novel, other than Tom calling Maggie "Magsie," it does keep Tom at the center of the work.

5. According to Rosemary Ashton, "Few critics have been content with Stephen Guest. He makes his appearance too late to be completely

credible as an important element in the drama to come. Moreover, how could George Eliot let Maggie be attracted to such a 'thing' (Swinburne), a 'mere hairdresser's block' (Leslie Stephen), a 'sad lapse' on George Eliot's part (Leavis)?" (15).

6.   George Eliot does not give Maggie the strength and talent that she herself possessed. When she decided to live openly as man and wife with George Lewes, she was thought fallen by many, including her brother Isaac, who would have nothing to do with her. Despite this, George Eliot was able to maintain a close and satisfying relationship with Lewes and to develop an exceptional career as a novelist. There is no possibility for a reconciliation between Maggie and Tom as there was for George Eliot, whose brother reconciled with her during the last year of her life, after the death of George Lewes and when she married John Walter Cross.

Work Cited

Ashton, Rosemary. *The Mill on the Floss: A Natural History*. Boston: Twayne, 1990.

Bloom, Abigail Burnham & Mary Sanders Pollock. *Victorian Literature and Film Adaptation*. Amherst, MA: Cambria, 2011.

Cardwell, Sarah. *Adaptation Revisited: Television and the Classic Novel*. New York: Manchester UP, 2002.

Carroll, David, ed. *George Eliot: The Critical Heritage*. London: Routledge & Kegan Paul, 1971.

Carroll, Laura, Christopher Palmer, Sue Thomas, & Rebecca, Waese. "Austen's and Michell's *Persuasion*." *Victorian Literature and Film Adaptation*. Ed. Abigail Burnham Bloom & Mary Sanders Pollock. Amherst, MA: Cambria, 2011. 225–241.

de Groot, Jerome. *Consuming History: Historians and Heritage in Contemporary Popular Culture*. New York: Routledge, 2009.

"Editorial Review." The original soundtrack album from Jos Records of the John Scott score to *The Mill on the Floss*. Amazon.com, 2002. Web. 23 Jun. 2015.

Eliot, George. *The Mill on the Floss*. Ed. Oliver Lovesey. Peterborough, Ontario: Broadview, 2007.

Giddings, Robert, Keith Selby, & Chris Wensley. *Screening the Novel: The Theory and Practice of Literary Dramatization*. New York: St. Martin's Press, 1990.

Harris, Margaret. "George Eliot on Stage and Screen." *Open Journals Library*. The University of Sydney, n.d. 17–49. Web. 23 Jun. 2015. <http.//openjournals.library.usyd.edu.au/index.php/ART/article/viewFile/5617/6284>.

Leitch, Thomas. "Introduction: Reframing the Victorians." *Victorian Literature and Film Adaptation*. Ed. Abigail Burnham Bloom & Mary Sanders Pollock. Amherst, MA: Cambria, 2011. 1–23.

Lovesey, Oliver. "Introduction." *The Mill on the Floss*. By George Eliot. Peterborough, Ontario: Broadview, 2007. 8–43.

Martin, Graham. "*The Mill on the Floss* and the Unreliable Narrator." *George Eliot: Centenary Essays and an Unpublished Fragment*. Ed. Anne Smith. London: Vision Press, 1980.

The Mill on the Floss. Dir. Graham Theakston. Perf. Emily Watson, Cheryl Campbell, James Frain. Mobil Masterpiece Theatre, 1997. TV movie.

Nugent, Frank S. "Movie Review: *The Mill on the Floss* (1937)." *New York Times*. The New York Times Company, 15 Nov. 1939. Web. 30 Jun. 2015.

Sanders, Julie. *Adaptation and Appropriation*. New York: Routledge, 2006.

Whelehan, Imelda. "Adaptations: The contemporary dilemmas." *Adaptations: From Text to Screen, Screen to Text*. Ed. Deborah Cartmell & Imelda Whelehan. New York: Routledge, 1999. 3–19.

"World's wife." *Cambridge Dictionaries Online*. Cambridge UP, 2016. Web. 19 July 2015.

RESOURCES

Chronology of George Eliot's Life

1819	November 22: Mary Anne Evans born at South Farm, Arbury, Warwickshire. November 29: Evans baptized at Chilvers Coton Church.
1820	Family moves to Griff House, Chilvers Coton.
1824	Evans attends Dame's School, then Miss Lathom's boarding school at Attleborough.
1828	Evans attends Mrs. Wallington's school at Nuneaton, meets teacher Maria Lewis.
1832	Evans attends the Miss Franklin's school in Coventry.
1836	February 3: Evans' mother dies. Evans leaves school.
1837	Evans becomes housekeeper to her father upon the marriage of her sister Chrissey. Changes her first name from Mary Anne to Mary Ann.
1838	Evans visits London with her brother Isaac.
1840	Evans' first publication, a poem, is published in the *Christian Observer*.
1841	Evans and her father move to Bird Grove, Coventry. She meets Charles and Cara Bray at Rosehill in November.
1842	January 2: Evans refuses to attend church with her father. They do not reconcile until she agrees to attend church again in May. She meets Sara Hennell in the summer.

1844	January: Evans begins her translation of Strauss' *Das Leben Jesu*.
1845	Evans is proposed to by an unnamed picture-restorer.
1846	Publication of *The Life of Jesus, Critically Examined*. Her essays, "Poetry and Prose from the Notebook of an Eccentric" are published in the *Coventry Herald*.
1849	May 31: Evans' father dies. June 12: Evans goes to Europe with the Brays but remains at Geneva on her own. Changes her name to Marianne and then Marian.
1851	Evans lodges with John Chapman in London, returns to Rosehill after unrest with Chapman's wife and mistress. Returns to London as the assistant editor of the *Westminster Review*. In October, she meets G. H. Lewes.
1852	June: Bessie Rayner Parkes introduces Evans to Barbara Leigh Smith. Friendship with Herbert Spencer ends in August.
1853	Evans begins translation of Feuerbach's *Das Wesen des Christenthums*.
1854	Publication of *The Essence of Christianity*. July 20: Evans leaves for Germany with Lewes. She continues to write for the *Westminster Review* and begins to translate Spinoza's *Ethics*.
1855	Evans and Lewes return to England and live together.
1857	Evans adopts the pseudonym George Eliot. When she tells her brother Isaac of her union with Lewes, he breaks off all family relations.

1858	Publication of *Scenes of Clerical Life*. Evans and Lewes visit Germany.
1859	Publication of *Adam Bede* and *The Lifted Veil*. March: Evans' sister Chrissey dies.
1860	Publication of *The Mill on the Floss*. Evans and Lewes visit Rome, Naples, Florence, and Switzerland.
1861	Publication of *Silas Marner*.
1863	Publication of *Romola*. Evans and Lewes purchase The Priory, North Bank, Regent's Park.
1866	Publication of *Felix Holt*. Evans and Lewes visit Spain.
1868	Publication of *The Spanish Gypsy*. Evans and Lewes visit Germany and Switzerland.
1869	Lewes' son Thornton lives with them and dies in October.
1870	Evans and Lewes visit Germany, Prague, and Austria.
1871-2	Publication of *Middlemarch*.
1874	Publication of *The Legend of Jubal*.
1875	Lewes' son Herbert dies of tubercular fever.
1876	Publication of *Daniel Deronda*. Evans and Lewes purchase The Heights in Surrey.
1878	November 30: Lewes dies.
1879	Publication of *Impressions of Theophrastus Such*. Evans founds a Lewes Studentship at Cambridge.

| 1880 | May 6: Evans marries John Cross. Her brother Isaac sends his congratulations. December 22: Evans dies at age sixty-one. December 29: Evans is buried in Highgate Cemetery, next to Lewes. |

Works by George Eliot

Novels

Adam Bede (1859)

The Mill on the Floss (1860)

Silas Marner (1861)

Romola (1863)

Felix Holt, the Radical (1866)

Middlemarch (1871–2)

Daniel Deronda (1876)

Poetry

The Spanish Gypsy (1868)

Brother and Sister (1869)

The Legend of Jubal (1874)

Other

Translation of *Das Leben Jesu, kritisch bearbeitet,* by David Strauss (1846)

Translation of *Das Wesen des Christentums*, by Ludwig Feuerbach (1854)

"Silly Novels by Lady Novelists" (1856)

"The Natural History of German Life" (1856)

Scenes of Clerical Life (1857)

The Lifted Veil (1859)

Brother Jacob (1864)

Impressions of Theophrastus Such (1879)

Bibliography

Ashton, Rosemary. *George Eliot: A Life*. London: Hamish Hamilton, 1996.

Beer, Gillian. *Darwin's Plots: Evolutionary Narrative in Darwin, George Eliot and Nineteenth-Century Fiction*. Cambridge, UK: Cambridge UP, 2000.

Bell, Michael. *The Cambridge Companion to European Novelists*. Cambridge, UK: Cambridge UP, 2012.

Bellringer, Alan. *George Eliot*. New York: St. Martin's Press, 1993. Modern Novelists Ser.

Brady, Kristin. *George Eliot*. New York: St. Martin's Press, 1990. Women Writers Ser.

Calder, Simon. "The Art of Conduct and Mixed Science of Eliot's Ethics." *George Eliot Review* 41 (2010): 60–74.

Carpenter, Mary W. *Imperial Bibles, Domestic Bodies: Women, Sexuality, and Religion in the Victorian Market*. Athens, OH: Ohio UP, 2003.

Carroll, Alicia. *Dark Smiles: Race and Desire in George Eliot*. Athens, OH: Ohio UP, 2003.

Coleman, Dermont. *George Eliot and Money: Economics, Ethics, and Literature*. Cambridge, UK: Cambridge UP, 2015.

Eagleton, Mary & David Pierce. "Aspects of Class in George Eliot's Fiction." *Attitudes to Class in the English Novel: From Walter Scott to David Storey*. London: Thames & Hudson: 1985.

Easley, Alexis. *First-Person Anonymous: Women Writers and Victorian Print Media, 1830–70*. Aldershot, UK: Ashgate, 2004.

Eliot, George. *The Essays of "George Eliot."* New York: Funk & Wagnalls, 1883.

Engels, Friedrich & Karl Marx. *Ludwig Feuerbach and the End of Classical German Philosophy*. Moscow: Progress Publishers, 1969.

Feuerbach, Ludwig, Karl Marx, Friedrich Engels, & Wolfgang Schirmacher. *German Socialist Philosophy*. New York: Continuum, 1997.

Fleishman, Avrom. *George Eliot's Intellectual Life*. Cambridge, UK: Cambridge UP, 2010.

Franklin, Jeffrey. "The Victorian Discourse of Gambling: Speculations on *Middlemarch* and *The Duke's Children*." *English Literary History* 61.4 (Winter 1994): 899–921.

Furst, Lilian. "Struggling for Medical Reform in *Middlemarch*." *Nineteenth-Century Literature* 48.3 (Dec. 1993): 341–46.

Gilbert, Sandra & Susan Gubar. *The Madwoman in the Attic: The Woman Writer and the Nineteenth-Century Literary Imagination*. New Haven, CT: Yale UP, 2000.

Hardy, Barbara. *George Eliot: A Critic's Biography*. London: Continuum, 2006.

Harris, Margaret, ed. *George Eliot in Context*. Cambridge, UK: Cambridge UP, 2013.

Henry, Nancy. *The Life of George Eliot*. Oxford: Wiley-Blackwell, 2012.

Himmelfarb, Gertrude. *The Jewish Odyssey of George Eliot*. New York: Encounter, 2009.

Hirsch, Pam. "Women and Jews in *Daniel Deronda*." *George Eliot Review* 25 (1994): 45–50.

Hoffman, Daniel & Samuel Hynes. *English Literary Criticism: Romantic and Victorian*. New York: Appleton-Century-Crofts, 1963.

Homans, Margaret. "Dinah's Blush and Maggie's Arm: Class, Gender, and Sexuality in Eliot's Early Novels." *Victorian Studies* 36 (1993): 155–79.

Houston, Natalie. "George Eliot's Material History: Clothing and Realistic Narrative." *Studies in Literary Imagination* 29 (1996): 23–33.

Hughes, Kathryn. *George Eliot: The Last Victorian*. London: Fourth Estate, 1998.

Kaufmann, David. *George Eliot and Judaism: An Attempt to Appreciate "Daniel Deronda."* New York: Haskell House, 1970.

Krockel, Carl. *D.H. Lawrence and Germany: The Politics of Influence*. Amsterdam: Rodopi, 2007.

Lallier, Andrew. "'The Generations of Ants and Beavers': Classical Economics and Animals in *The Mill on the Floss*." *George Eliot Review* 43 (2011): 47–55.

Levine, Caroline & Mark Turner. "Introduction: Gender, Genre, and George Eliot." *Women's Writing* 3.22 (1996): 95–6.

Levine, George, ed. *The Cambridge Companion to George Eliot.* Cambridge, UK: Cambridge UP, 2001.

_____. *An Annotated Critical Biography of George Eliot.* New York: St. Martin's Press, 1988.

Linehan, Katharine Bailey. "Mixed Politics: The Critique of Imperialism in *Daniel Deronda.*" *Texas Studies in Literature and Language* 34 (1992): 323–46.

Maddox, Brenda. *George Eliot: Novelist, Lover, Wife.* London: Harper, 2009.

Mahawatte, Royce. *George Eliot and the Gothic Novel: Genres, Gender, and Feeling.* Cardiff, UK: U of Wales P, 2013.

Marx, Karl & John C. Raines. *Marx on Religion.* Philadelphia: Temple UP, 2002.

McCormack, Kathleen. *George Eliot and Intoxication.* New York: St Martin's Press, 2000.

Meyer, Susan. "Safely to Their Own Borders: Proto-Zionism, Feminism, and Nationalism in *Daniel Deronda.*" *English Literary History* 60 (1993): 733–58.

Mooney, Bel. "George Eliot the Journalist." *The George Eliot Fellowship Review* 14 (1983): 74–84.

Mugglestone, Lynda. "'Grammatical Fair Ones': Women, Men, and Attitudes to Language in the Novels of George Eliot." *The Review of English Studies* 46 (Feb. 1995): 11–25.

Nestor, Pauline. *George Eliot.* New York: Palgrave, 2002.

Newton, K. M. "George Eliot and Jacques Derrida: An Elective Affinity." *Textual Practice* 23 (2009): 1–26.

Pangallo, Karen, ed. *The Critical Response to George Eliot.* New York: Greenwood, 1994.

Raines, Melissa. "Awakening the 'Mere Pulsation of Desire' in *Silas Marner.*" *George Eliot Review* 38 (2007): 24–31.

Ranjini, Philip. "Maggie, Tom, and Oedipus." *Victorian Newsletter* 82 (1993): 35–40.

Rignall, John. "George Eliot and the Furniture of the House of Fiction." *George Eliot Review* 27 (1996): 23–30.

Ruth, Katrina. "The Imaginary Vision in *Adam Bede.*" *George Eliot Review* 27 (1996): 49–55.

Scholl, Lesa. *Translation, Authorship and the Victorian Professional Woman: Charlotte Brontë, Harriet Martineau, and George Eliot.* Surrey, UK: Ashgate, 2011.

Slaugh-Sanford, Kathleen. "The Other Woman: Lydia Glasher and the Disruption of English Racial Identity in George Eliot's *Daniel Deronda.*" *Studies in the Novel* 41 (2010): 407–17.

Tush, Susan R. *George Eliot and the Conventions of Popular Women's Fiction.* New York: Peter Lang, 1993.

Wernick, Andrew. *Auguste Comte and the Religion of Humanity: The Post-Theistic Program of French Social Theory.* Cambridge, UK: Cambridge UP, 2001.

Williams, Wendy S. *George Eliot, Poetess.* Surrey, UK: Ashgate, 2014.

About the Editor

Katie R. Peel is an associate professor of English at the University of North Carolina, Wilmington. Her research and teaching areas include Victorian, young adult, children's, and queer literatures, as well as women's and gender studies. She edited the *Critical Insights: Jane Eyre* collection and has published articles on Charlotte Brontë's *Villette* as well as *Jane Eyre*. Most recently, she has served as the director of her campus' Women's Studies and Resource Center.

Contributors

Abigail Burnham Bloom teaches Victorian literature at Hunter College, CUNY and is managing editor of *Victorian Literature and Culture*. She recently published *The Literary Monster on Film*, coedited *Victorian Literature and Film Adaptation*, and edited *Personal Moments in the Lives of Victorian Women*. She has published articles on Robert Louis Stevenson, Jane Carlyle, Geraldine Jewsbury, and the Brontë family.

Mark Edelman Boren is a professor of literature at the University of North Carolina, Wilmington. He has published extensively on nineteenth-century British and American writers and culture.

Janis Chakars is an assistant professor in the Division of Language, Literature and Fine Arts at Gwynedd Mercy University. His research has appeared in *Journalism History*, *American Journalism*, the *Central European Journal of Communication*, *International Research in Children's Literature*, and elsewhere.

Joanne Cordón is an adjunct professor at the University of Connecticut and at Eastern Connecticut State University. Her research interests include the novel, the eighteenth-century theatre, and women's studies. She has published in *Frontiers: A Journal of Women's Studies*.

Constance M. Fulmer is a professor of Victorian literature at Seaver College, Pepperdine University, in Malibu, California. She holds the Blanche E. Seaver Chair of English Literature and serves as associate dean of teaching and assessment. She is working on a biography of Edith J. Simcox and a study of George Eliot's morality. In addition to editing Edith Simcox's journal the *Autobiography of a Shirtmaker* (Garland, 1998) with Margaret E. Barfield, she has published several articles on Simcox and her work and, at numerous conferences, has presented papers related to Simcox and George Eliot. Her advanced degrees in English are from Vanderbilt University in Nashville, Tennessee.

Gareth Hadyk-DeLodder is currently pursuing his doctorate at the University of Florida. He works primarily in nineteenth-century studies, and his interests include cultural forms of memory, translation, and gender studies. His dissertation traces some of the ways in which German romanticism, different typologies of nostalgia, and the retrospective gaze were taken up and repurposed by prominent Victorian authors.

Emilia Halton-Hernandez is a graduate student in English at the University of British Columbia. She has published papers and presented research at conferences on Victorian and modernist literature, life-writing, and psychoanalytic theory. She is currently writing her thesis on the way that language and the image intersect in the telling of the self in modernist and contemporary life-writing.

Jeffrey E. Jackson is assistant professor of nineteenth-century British literature at Monmouth University. His interests include book history, print culture, and film adaptation.

Katherine Montwieler teaches in the English Department and Women's Studies program at the University of North Carolina, Wilmington. She's recently published essays on Edgar Allan Poe's *The Narrative of Arthur Gordon Pym of Nantucket*, Elizabeth Strout's *Olive Kitteridge*, and Charlotte Brontë's *Jane Eyre*.

Magdalena Nerio teaches literature and women's studies in the English department at the University of Texas at San Antonio. Her research interests include late eighteenth- and nineteenth-century Anglo-American literature, with a focus on women's writing, epistolarity, and the transatlantic literary public sphere. She is developing a book project linking Victorian women's letter writing to Mary Wollstonecraft's correspondence and political thought.

Heidi L. Pennington received her PhD from Washington University in St. Louis and is visiting assistant professor of English at James Madison University in Harrisonburg, Virginia. With a background in English and comparative literature, her teaching and research endeavors to explore the intersections of identity, fictionality, emotion, and ethics in texts ranging from the Victorian novel to film adaptations of classic literature to contemporary graphic novels. Narrative theory and genre history are among the favored implements in her methodological tool box. Her current book project considers the structural traits, historical context, and cultural function of the Victorian fictional autobiography, proposing that this curious subgenre—of which Eliot's *The Lifted Veil* is an example—reveals a latent Victorian commitment to the idea of personal identity as a collaborative, fictional construct. She has previously published articles in *a/b: Auto/Biography Studies*, *Victorians Institute Journal*, and *Journal of Philosophy: A Cross-Disciplinary Inquiry*.

Carroll Clayton Savant is finishing a PhD in literature at the University of Texas at Dallas, where he has taught rhetoric and literary studies. He has also taught composition and literature at various Dallas/Fort Worth-area colleges. His research interests investigate the interdisciplinary relationship between music and Victorian literature, in particular, in the novels of George Eliot, Thomas Hardy, and George Gissing. He is currently working on a project that examines the reciprocal relationship between music and feelings and the sounds of location that influence identity.

Danny Sexton is an assistant professor of English and a deputy chair of the English department at Queensborough Community College/City University of New York. His fields of study and research are Victorian literature and culture, gender and sexuality, masculinity, postcolonial literature, and race. He has presented at numerous conferences and published articles on race, gender, Victorian, and postcolonial literature. He is currently working on study of the Indian Mutiny of 1857 and the passing of the Matrimonial Causes Act in terms of gender and authority.

Erin A. Spampinato is a PhD candidate at the Graduate Center, CUNY and a teaching fellow at Queens College. Her current research focuses on representations of rape in the nineteenth-century British novel.

Shandi Stevenson is a teacher, tutor, and freelance writer living in Travelers Rest, South Carolina. Shandi teaches world and British literature at the Upstate Homeschool Co-op and has contributed to several previous publications, including *The Mirror Crack'd: Fear and Horror in J.R.R.*

Tolkien's Major Works, edited by Lynn Forest-Hill; *Doors in the Air: C. S. Lewis and the Imaginary World*, edited by Anna Slack; and *Baptism of Fire: The Birth of British Fantasy in World War I*, edited by Janet Croft.

Wendy S. Williams is visiting assistant professor in the John V. Roach Honors College at Texas Christian University, where she was named "Honors Professor of the Year" in 2014. Her book, *George Eliot, Poetess* (Ashgate, 2014), represents the first full-length study of the poetry of George Eliot and explores Eliot's reliance on a poetess tradition that was deeply invested in religion and feminine sympathy.

Index

Thackeray, William Makepeace
67, 73
Theakson, Graham 244
Thiel, Elizabeth 5
Thomas, Jeanie 75
Trollope, Anthony 27, 68
Tucker, Herbert F. 167
Tulliver, Maggie 89, 173, 174,
188, 193, 195, 196, 225, 244
Tulliver, Tom 254
Tush, Susan Rowland 52

Uglow, Jenny 85
Underwood, Doug 128

Van den Broek, Antonie Gerard
167, 168
Victorian periodical press 81
Victorian women 91, 276
Vincy, Fred 240
Vincy, Rosamund 89, 90
Violante, Doña 41

Wakem, Philip 251
Watson, Emily 244, 260

Watt, Ian 65, 69, 101
Waxman, Barbara 19
Whelehan, Imelda 246, 260
Williams, Gary 84
Williams, Raymond 50
Wilson, A. N. 186
Wilt, Judith 113
Winthrop, Dolly 207
Wollstonecraft, Mary x, 78, 79,
80, 81, 83, 85, 87, 88, 89,
90, 91, 93, 95, 276
Wood, Jane 213
Woolf, Virginia 3, 48, 67, 78, 96
World War I 184, 278
Wright, Richard 6

Yonge, Charlotte 66
Young, Edward 156
Young, Percy 132

Zenzinger, Ted 223
Zimmerman, Philip 3, 19